OECD Sovereign Borrowing Outlook 2014

OECD
BETTER POLICIES FOR BETTER LIVES

Please cite this publication as:
OECD (2014), *OECD Sovereign Borrowing Outlook 2014*, OECD Publishing.
http://dx.doi.org/10.1787/sov_b_outlk-2014-en

ISBN 978-92-64-20416-4 (print)
ISBN 978-92-64-20755-4 (PDF)

Series: OECD Sovereign Borrowing Outlook
ISSN 2306-0468 (print)
ISSN 2306-0476 (online)

Photo credits: Cover © Inmagine/Designpics.

Corrigenda to OECD publications may be found on line at: *www.oecd.org/about/publishing/corrigenda.htm*.

Foreword

Each year, the OECD's Bond Market and Public Debt Management Unit circulates a survey on the borrowing needs of member governments. The responses are incorporated into the OECD Sovereign Borrowing Outlook *to provide regular updates of trends and developments associated with sovereign borrowing requirements, funding strategies, market infrastructure and debt levels from the perspective of public debt managers. The Outlook makes a policy distinction between funding strategy and borrowing requirements. The central government marketable gross borrowing needs for the OECD area are calculated based on budget deficits and redemptions using a standard methodology. The funding strategy entails decisions on how these borrowing needs are financed using different instruments (e.g. long-term, short-term, nominal, indexed) and on which distribution channels (e.g. auctions, tap, syndication) are being used.*

*Accordingly, this sixth Borrowing Outlook (*OECD Sovereign Borrowing Outlook 2014*) provides data, information and a background on sovereign borrowing needs, and discusses funding strategies and debt management policies for the OECD area and country groupings, by addressing the following issues:*

- *Gross borrowing requirements.*
- *Net borrowing requirements.*
- *The evolution of long-term rates.*
- *Central government marketable debt.*
- *Sovereign stress and the supply of safe public assets.*
- *Challenges of the exit from central bank asset purchase programmes for sovereign issuers.*
- *Funding strategies and instruments.*
- *Distribution channels.*
- *Liquidity in secondary markets.*

The OECD Sovereign Borrowing Outlook 2014 *is published this year for the third time as a stand-alone publication. This edition reports for the first time on the gross borrowing needs of individual countries. Shorter assessments of sovereign borrowing needs were published in* OECD Journal: Financial Market Trends, *Volumes 2009/1, 2009/2, 2010/2 and 2011/2. (See www.oecd.org/daf/publicdebtmanagement).*

This Borrowing Outlook *was prepared by a drafting group from OECD's Bond Market and Public Debt Management Unit, composed of Hans J. Blommestein (Team Leader), Hakan Bingol (Public Debt Analyst) and Perla Ibarlucea Flores (Research Assistant). Comments and suggestions may be sent to Dr Hans J. Blommestein, Head of Bond Market and Public Debt Management Unit, OECD, Paris, France, hans.blommestein@oecd.org.*

Table of contents

Tables

Figures

Follow OECD Publications on:

http://twitter.com/OECD_Pubs

http://www.facebook.com/OECDPublications

http://www.linkedin.com/groups/OECD-Publications-4645871

http://www.youtube.com/oecdilibrary

http://www.oecd.org/oecddirect/

This book has...

StatLinks

A service that delivers Excel® files from the printed page!

Look for the *StatLinks* at the bottom of the tables or graphs in this book. To download the matching Excel® spreadsheet, just type the link into your Internet browser, starting with the *http://dx.doi.org* prefix, or click on the link from the e-book edition.

Acronyms and abbreviations

AFT	Agence France Trésor
AKK	Hungarian Debt Management Agency
AOFM	Australian Office of Financial Management
APF	Asset Purchase Facility Operations
APP	Asset Purchase Programme
BOE	Bank of England
BOJ	Bank of Japan
BTP	Buono del Tesoro Poliennale
BOT	Buoni Ordinari del Tesoro
CAC	Collective Active Clause
CAPM	Capital Asset Pricing Model
CB	Central Bank
CDS	Credit Default Swap
CGFS	Committee on the Global Financial System
CPI	Consumer Price Index
CRA	Credit Rating Agency
CRD	Capital Requirements Directive
CRR	Cash Reserve Ratio
CTZ	Certificato del Tesoro Zero Coupon
CY	Calendar Year
DDA	Dutch Direct Auction
DMO	Debt Management Office
DSL	Dutch State Loan
DTC	Dutch Treasury Certificates
ECB	European Central Bank
EFSF	European Financial Stability Facility
EFSM	European Financial Stabilisation Mechanism
EIB	European Investment Bank
EM	Emerging Markets
EMTN	Euro Medium-Term Note
ERIE	Economic Research Institute of Erie
ESA	The European system of national and regional accounts
ESM	European Stability Mechanism
ESMA	European Securities and Markets Authority
EU	European Union
FAS	Fiscal Authorities
FED	Federal Reserve
FFT	Financial Transaction Tax
FOMC	Federal Open Market Committee

FRA	Forward Rate Agreement
FRBNY	Federal Reserve Bank of New York
FRN	Floating Rate Note
GBR	Gross Borrowing Requirement
GDP	Gross Domestic Product
GEMM	Gilt-edged Market Maker
HQA	High Quality Assets
ICMA	International Capital Market Association
IGCP	Portuguese Treasury and Debt Management Agency
ILB	Index Linked Bond
IMF	International Monetary Fund
IRC	Incremental Risk Charge
JGB	Japanese Government Bond
KTB	Korea Treasury Bond
LHS	Left-Hand Side
LSAP	Large-Scale Asset Purchase
LT	Long-term
LTRO	Longer-Term Refinancing Operation
MEP	Maturity Extension Programme
MiFID	Markets in Financial Instruments Directive
NBR	Net Borrowing Requirement
NCB	National Central Bank
NTMA	National Treasury Management Agency
NZDMO	New Zealand Debt Management Office
OECD	Organisation for Economic Co-operation and Development
OLO	Obligation Linéaire Ordinaire
OMT	Outright Monetary Transaction
ONS	Office for National Statistics
OSI	Official Sector Involvement
PDM	Public Debt Management
PDs	Primary Dealers
PSI	Private Sector Involvement
QE	Quantitative Easing
QQE	Quantitative and Qualitative Monetary Easing
RBNZ	Reserve Bank of New Zealand
RHS	Right-Hand Side
RWA	Risk-Weighted Asset
SCCL	Single Counterparty Credit Limit
SGB	Sweden Government Bond
SMP	Securities Market Programme
SNA	System of National Accounts
SOMA	System Open-Market Account
SPFA	Slovenian Public Finance Act
ST	Short-term
TIPS	Treasury Inflation-Protected Securities
UMP	Unconventional Monetary Policy
WB	World Bank
WPDM	Working Party on Public Debt Management

Editorial

Government borrowing needs have peaked, but redemption profiles are challenging while government debt ratios continue to rise

The *OECD Sovereign Borrowing Outlook 2014* indicates that the combined gross borrowing needs of OECD governments seem to have peaked in 2012. Nonetheless, although overall sovereign market stress in the OECD area seems to have subsided somewhat, the borrowing environment for governments continues to be shaped by fairly high gross borrowing needs in conjunction with, at times, complex market dynamics during periods of higher sovereign debt stress in some countries.

The *Borrowing Outlook* also shows that many issuers are facing a challenging redemption profile of outstanding medium- and long-term central government debt for the next three years. This prospect highlights the importance of managing debt maturities in order to address rollover risk.

Government debt ratios are expected to further increase and remain at elevated levels in the near future. In fact, general government debt as a percentage of GDP for a group of selected major OECD countries is projected to surpass the World War II peak of around 116%.

Issuers, especially in emerging markets, are facing rising global volatility and higher rates

Government issuers worldwide had to deal with rising global volatility and higher long-term rates associated with uncertainty about the timing of the Quantitative Easing (QE) exit and tapering by the US Federal Reserve. Market dynamics (as opposed to significant changes in policy fundamentals) drove much of the change in US long-term nominal and real rates in May through June of 2013, as well as the international spill-over into other markets.

Risk premiums in emerging markets rose, reflecting in part the increased sensitivity of emerging-market yields to changes in external financing conditions, notably reduced liquidity. The steep decline in emerging market currencies in January of this year has unsettled global markets with mounting pressure to increase rates. These developments confirm market expectations that government borrowing costs in emerging markets are likely to rise further.

Responses to a continued challenging issuance environment

In order to cope with periods of considerable volatility, relatively high borrowing volumes and fairly uncertain issuance conditions, many debt management offices (DMOs) at times adjusted their issuance strategies, sales procedures and offering of debt instruments. OECD sovereign issuers are also attaching greater importance to transparency, and have improved their investor relations policy and related communication strategies.

The *Borrowing Outlook* argues that it is important to carefully assess the possible implications of the various monetary exit strategies for sovereign issuance strategies and procedures. A smooth exit from unconventional monetary policy (UMP) programmes is of great significance for issuers. To that end, effective communications with markets about the unwinding strategy of UMP programmes, although a novel challenge, are crucial. With proper planning, effective exit tools, good communications by both DMOs and CBs – as well as a transparent borrowing strategy with an issuance calendar – tapering and asset sales by CBs will not necessarily disrupt the functioning of government bond markets in the OECD area.

Structural shortage in the supply of safe sovereign assets?

The demand for safe sovereign assets has increased owing to regulatory changes, the use of UMP, the greater use of high-grade collateral and other structural factors. At the same time, some analysts believe that the supply of "safe" sovereign assets has fallen (after credit rating agencies began to downgrade OECD governments). This in turn seems to have created some concern that there is a growing structural shortage of safe (sovereign) assets.

If true, this would be problematic. An adequate supply of safe sovereign assets (functioning as "information-insensitive" instruments that can serve as secure stores of value) is crucial for the proper functioning of the financial system. Nevertheless, the *Borrowing Outlook* argues that there is no decisive evidence for supporting the belief that there is a lasting or structural shortage in the aggregate supply of safe sovereign assets. While local and temporary supply-demand imbalances are possible, they are likely to trigger endogenous policy and market responses.

Carolyn Ervin

Director, OECD Directorate for Financial
and Enterprise Affairs

Executive summary

OECD sovereign issuers continue to face major challenges in a complex environment

Government securities issuers are grappling with concerns about increased market and liquidity risks, higher long-term interest rates and obstacles to global economic growth. There are questions about when, how fast and how central banks will begin to exit from unconventional monetary policy (UMP) programmes. Issuance is complicated in countries where large public deficits and very high debt ratios have not begun to decline, since the huge legacy of public debt continues to expose governments to potential shifts in confidence when credible medium-term fiscal consolidation plans are not in place. There are concerns over legacy risks from incomplete financial sector reforms and the possible adverse impact on market liquidity of (pending) new regulations. In response, many debt management offices (DMOs) have had to adjust their issuance strategies and sales procedures. Some have also introduced new debt instruments, or are planning to do so.

Borrowing peaked in 2012 and will drop in 2014, but debt ratios remain high and growing

Although the combined gross borrowing needs of OECD governments appear to have peaked in 2012 at USD 11 trillion, OECD debt managers continue to face considerable funding challenges while government debt ratios are still rising. Total OECD gross borrowing requirements are expected to have fallen slightly in 2013, to USD 10.8 trillion. They are projected to drop further in 2014, to around USD 10.6 trillion, but with a relatively high level of redemptions. Net borrowing is estimated to fall to USD 1.5 trillion in 2014, while government debt ratios for the OECD as a whole are expected to grow.

In this context, raising considerable volumes of funds at the lowest cost, with acceptable rollover risk from maturing debt that has to be refinanced, remains a challenge. Many OECD debt managers continue to rebalance their portfolios by issuing more long-term instruments and moderating bill issuance.

Key findings

- Borrowing should drop in 2014, but debt ratios will remain high. For a group of selected major OECD countries, general government debt in 2014 is expected to reach the highest level since World War II.
- For 2013 and 2014, the share of short-term bonds issued is expected to remain in the range 45-46%, well below the pre-crisis share of almost 49%.

- The share of long-term debt in government portfolios is estimated at around 87% in 2013 and is expected to reach 88.1% in 2014.
- Long-term government bond yields across advanced major economies are highly correlated historically.
- Sovereign refinancing needs for the OECD as a whole pose a significant challenge and will reach about 29% of its outstanding long-term debt in the next 3 years.
- There is no shortage in the aggregate supply of safe sovereign assets, particularly if a broader measurement for sovereign risk is used. Rather than applying the "triple-A standard", government debt rated AAA, AA or A should also be considered safe.
- DMOs have expressed concerns about the pressure on existing primary dealer systems and the impact of (forthcoming) regulations on liquidity in primary and secondary government securities markets.
- Changes in central banks' UMP stance may lead to highly volatile government bond markets. Exit measures (including the pace of tapering) must be carried out with great prudence, clear communication to the market and proper two-way communications between central bankers and government issuers.

Chapter 1

Sovereign borrowing overview

Total OECD gross borrowing requirements are expected to have fallen slightly from USD 11 trillion in 2012 to USD 10.8 trillion in 2013 and are projected to drop to around USD 10.6 trillion in 2014. Net borrowing is estimated to fall to USD 1.5 trillion in 2014. However, debt ratios for the OECD area as a whole are expected to grow and general government debt for a group of OECD countries is even projected to surpass the World War II peak.

Raising the required funds remains a challenge. Most OECD debt managers continue to rebalance debt portfolios by issuing more long-term instruments, and seeking to moderate bill issuance. Enhancing fiscal resilience encourages maintaining diverse nominal and variable rate instruments along the maturity spectrum.

Long-term real and nominal rates, as well as volatility of benchmark yields, were very low as of early May 2013, but then US yields rose sharply after the Federal Reserve signalled possible tapering of bond purchases.

The statistical data for Israel are supplied by and under the responsibility of the relevant Israeli authorities. The use of such data by the OECD is without prejudice to the status of the Golan Heights, East Jerusalem and Israeli settlements in the West Bank under the terms of international law.

1.1. The combined gross borrowing needs of OECD governments seem to have peaked but government debt ratios continue to rise

Although the borrowing needs of OECD governments seem to have peaked in 2012, OECD debt managers continue to face considerable funding challenges, with relatively high levels of redemptions in several countries. The sixth OECD Sovereign Borrowing Outlook[1] shows that the combined gross borrowing needs of OECD governments are expected to fall slightly from USD 11 trillion in 2012 to USD 10.8 trillion in 2013. For 2014, they are projected to drop further to around USD 10.6 trillion (Figure 1.1 and Table 1.1). Longer-term redemptions for the OECD area are estimated to decrease from 8.1% (of GDP) in 2012 to 7.7% in 2013, although they are projected to rise to 8.2% in 2014 (Figure 1.8 in Section 1.9).

Against the backdrop of continued uncertainty about economic prospects,[2] the OECD Economic Outlook projections show an improvement in general government balances. In 2012 general government deficits for the OECD area stood at 5.9% of GDP, while they are estimated to fall to 4.8% in 2013 and further to 4.0% in 2014. Real GDP growth in the OECD area[3] is estimated to be 1.2% in 2013 and 2.3% for 2014.[4]

Although overall sovereign market stress in the OECD area seems to have subsided somewhat, the issuance climate remains influenced by important policy challenges (Chapter 2). The borrowing environment for governments continues to be shaped by fairly high gross borrowing needs in conjunction with, at times, multifaceted market dynamics during periods of higher sovereign debt stress in some countries.[5] Government debt ratios are expected to further increase and remain at elevated levels in the near future. In fact, general government debt as a percentage of GDP is projected to surpass the World War II peak (Figure 1.13 in Section 1.11).

The Outlook makes a policy distinction between funding strategy and borrowing needs. Central government marketable gross borrowing needs are calculated based on budget deficits and redemptions, using the OECD standardised method for calculating gross short-term borrowing needs. (Failure to use a sensible methodology results in highly inflated estimates for gross short-term borrowing needs.)[6]

The funding strategy entails decisions on how borrowing needs are going to be financed using different instruments (e.g. long-term, short-term, nominal, indexed, etc.) and distribution channels.[7]

Information on methods and sources of the OECD Sovereign Borrowing Outlook can be found in annex B.

The general government deficit for the OECD area as a whole is estimated to reach 4.8% of GDP in 2013 (the equivalent of approximately USD 2.3 trillion), with a projected decrease to nearly 4.0% of GDP in 2014 (the equivalent of around USD 2.1 trillion) – see Figure 1.1 and Table 1.1.

Central government marketable net borrowing requirements are estimated to fall from nearly USD 2.0 trillion in 2013 to around USD 1.5 trillion in 2014 (Figure 1.1). This amounts to a significant decrease from around 4.1% of GDP in 2013 to 2.8% in 2014.

Figure 1.1. **Fiscal and borrowing outlook in OECD countries for the period 2007-14**

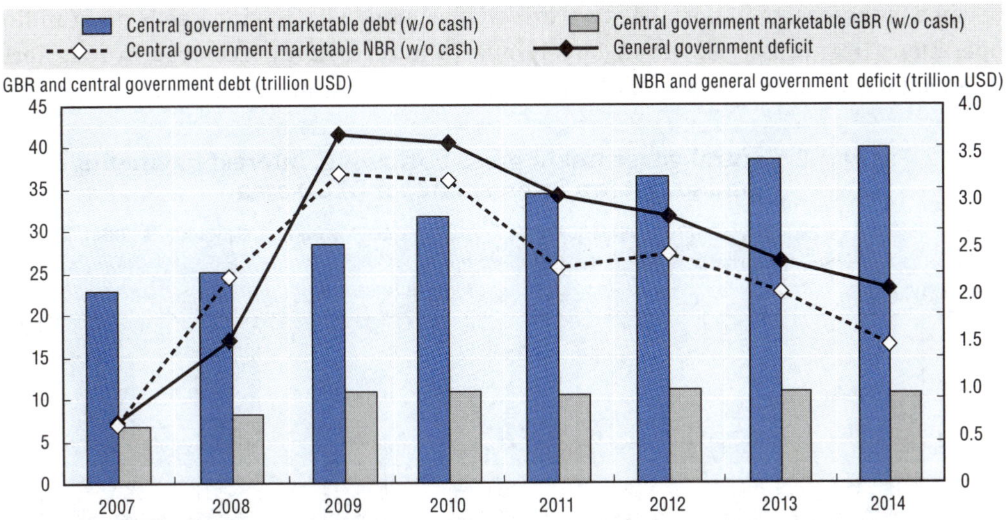

Note: GBR = gross borrowing requirement; NBR = net borrowing requirement. General government deficit is on SNA basis.
Source: 2013 Survey on central government marketable debt and borrowing by OECD Working Party on Debt Management; *OECD Economic Outlook 94 Database*; and OECD staff estimates.

StatLink http://dx.doi.org/10.1787/888932993389

Table 1.1. **Central government marketable gross borrowing and marketable debt in the OECD area**

Trillion USD

	2007	2008	2009	2010	2011	2012	2013	2014
Central government marketable GBR (with cash)	7.1	8.7	11.2	11.3	10.8	11.5	11.2	11.1
Central government marketable GBR (w/o cash)	6.7	8.2	10.7	10.9	10.4	11.0	10.8	10.6
Central government marketable debt (w/o cash)	22.9	25.2	28.4	31.7	34.3	36.4	38.4	39.8
Central government marketable NBR (w/o cash)	0.6	2.2	3.3	3.2	2.3	2.4	2.0	1.5
General government deficit	0.6	1.5	3.7	3.6	3.0	2.8	2.3	2.1

Note: Figures are calculated using the exchange rates as of 1st December 2009.
Source: 2013 Survey on central government marketable debt and borrowing by OECD Working Party on Debt Management, *OECD Economic Outlook 94 Database*, and OECD staff estimates.

StatLink http://dx.doi.org/10.1787/888932994149

Government liabilities were initially driven largely by the recessionary impact of the unprecedented 2007-8 global liquidity and credit crisis, including government expenditures due to fiscal stimulus programmes and later by the influence of recession-induced negative growth dynamics. Because of this, and despite falling interest rates during 2008-12, the general government gross debt-to-GDP ratio for the OECD area as a whole is expected to grow from around 110.3% in 2013 to 111.8% in 2014 (Figure 1.14 in Section 1.11).

For the OECD area as a whole, the outstanding central government marketable debt is expected to increase from USD 38.4 trillion in 2013, to around USD 39.8 trillion at the end of 2014. As a percentage of GDP, central government marketable debt is projected to be slightly higher than 77% in 2014. However, a closer look at groups of countries gives a more differentiated picture (see Figure 1.16 in Section 1.12).

Although short- and long rates dropped since the peak of the global financial crisis in 2008 (Section 1.5), interest payments increased in the period 2007-12 and, as a result, became of increasing importance as a driver of sovereign borrowing needs and funding operations (Figure 1.2). However, largely due to a very strong decrease in long term interest rates over the period 2011-13, net interest payments are estimated to fall in 2013.

Figure 1.2. **Central government gross borrowing, interest payments and long-term interest rate for OECD area**

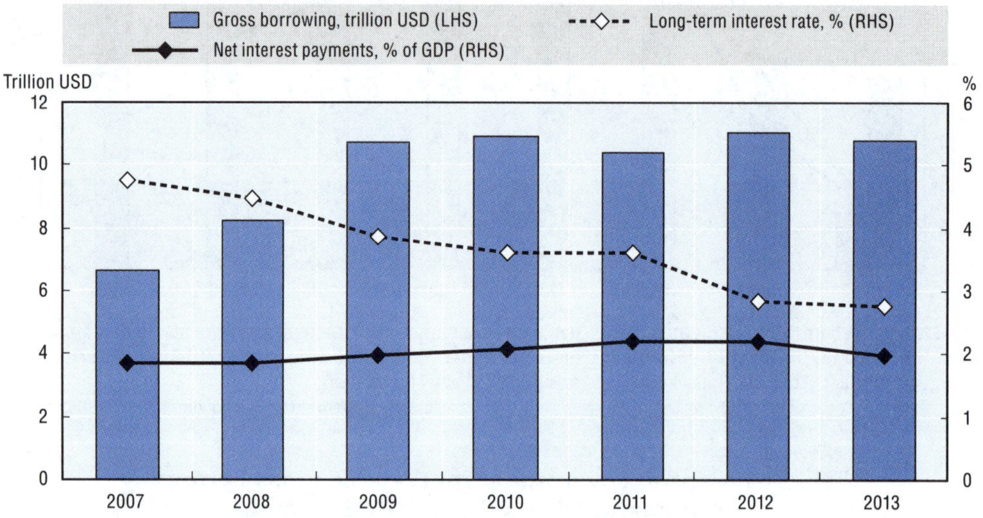

Note: GDP–weighted average long-term interest rate.

Source: 2013 Survey on central government marketable debt and borrowing by OECD Working Party on Debt Management; *OECD Economic Outlook 94 Database*, and OECD staff estimates.

StatLink http://dx.doi.org/10.1787/888932993408

1.2. Higher levels of confidence but mixed signals on volatility

In the period from the autumn of 2012 to the spring of 2013, issuers were facing relatively calm financial markets, with market concerns about previously prominent tail risks decreasing. Despite significant uncertainty and complex market dynamics, market volatility remained at relatively low levels since central banks continue to be on standby to deal with tail risk. By using unconventional monetary policy (UMP) tools, central banks in major OECD markets were considered to play a key role in setting the level of risk appetite. Accordingly, over the same period, and against the backdrop of a low interest environment, risk taking increased.[8]

Long-term real and nominal rates were very low as of early May 2013. Following Chairman Bernanke's May 22 testimony and after the June 18-19 Federal Open Market Committee (FOMC) meeting, US yields rose sharply. Government issuers had to deal with rising global volatility and higher long-term rates associated with confusions about the timing of the exit and tapering by the US Federal Reserve (Chapter 3).

Risk premiums in emerging markets rose, reflecting in part the increased sensitivity of emerging market yields to changes in external conditions.

Market dynamics is quite complex with the market impact of new information sometimes hard to assess. This includes hard-to-predict shifts in term premiums as a source of significant volatility in interest rates.[9] Moreover, speculations about the anticipation of tapering by the US Federal Reserve had a major knock-on effect on long rates elsewhere (see Section 1.5 below on long-term rates). Initially, asset price correlation increased, while liquidity deteriorated across markets.

In sum, OECD debt managers continue to face continued sizeable borrowing operations amid a still fairly challenging environment with headwinds to global economic growth, heightened concerns about market and liquidity risk, higher long-term borrowing rates, the high uncertainty of the exact timing of the exit and tapering plans regarding asset purchase programmes by central banks, legacy risks related to incomplete financial sector reforms, the possible adverse impact on market liquidity of new regulations, reducing leverage and increasing capital cushions of banks in particular in the euro area, and downside risks with a build-up of imbalances in a wide range of emerging markets.

1.3. Outlook for central government marketable gross borrowing needs for OECD groupings

The unprecedented global liquidity and credit crisis that started in August 2007 was at first associated with dysfunctional and collapsing financial institutions and markets. The response to this crisis set the stage for the second phase: the surge in government deficits and government (contingent) liabilities, further amplified by the fiscal response to concerns about the threat of a depression-size economic impact of the global financial crisis.[10] For the OECD area as a whole (Figure 1.1 and Table 1.1), and for all OECD country groupings considered here (Figure 1.3), general government financial balances improved, while for most groupings deficits peaked in 2009. In comparison with "Total OECD", "G7" and the OECD countries of the "Euro area", the performance of "Other OECD" and "Emerging OECD" was (and is expected to remain) relatively good.[11]

Gross marketable borrowing needs in the OECD area continue to decline but remain at elevated levels. However, the decrease in estimated net marketable borrowing in 2014 is striking (Figure 1.1), reflecting relatively high redemptions. Figure 1.4 shows estimates

Figure 1.3. **General government financial balance-to-GDP ratios in OECD country groupings**

Percentage of GDP

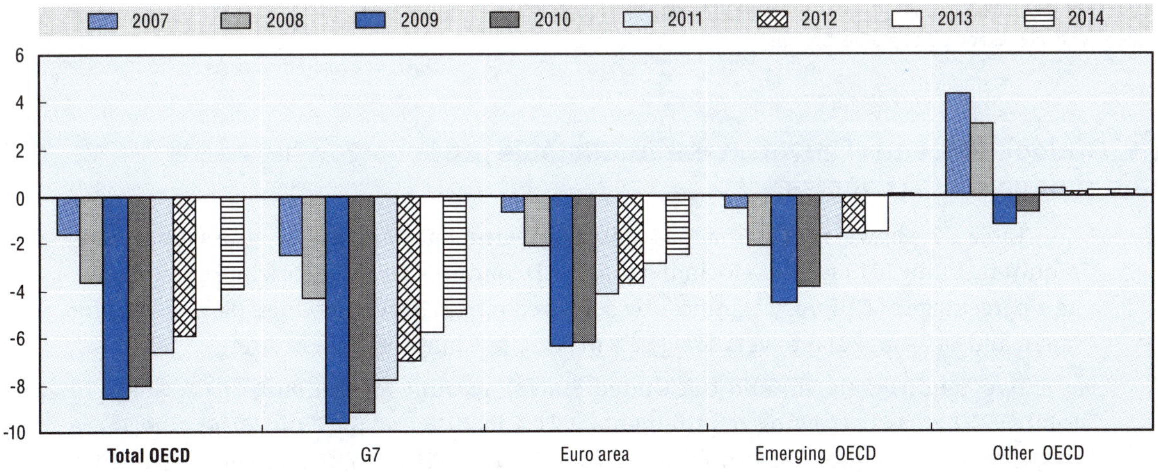

Note: General government financial balances are on SNA basis.
Source: *OECD Economic Outlook 94 Database*; and OECD staff calculations.

StatLink http://dx.doi.org/10.1787/888932993427

and projections of central government marketable gross borrowing requirements as a percentage of GDP for the various country groupings.

After having peaked in 2009, gross borrowing needs are projected to fall in all country groupings. For example, "G7" gross borrowing requirements of the central government as a percentage of GDP are expected to continue to decline (by a projected 1.2% in 2014). Of particular interest is also that the average gross borrowing ratio to GDP of the OECD countries in the "Euro area", after having peaked in 2009 (reaching 18.4 as a percentage of the GDP), strongly declined since then (by an estimated 4%), and is projected to fall to around 15.7% in 2013 and to decline further to approximately 14.4% in 2014 (being equal to a decrease of around 1.3% of GDP in 2014).

However, for all country groupings (except "Emerging OECD") borrowing needs remain at elevated levels in comparison to pre-crisis levels (Figure 1.4).

Figure 1.4. **Central government marketable gross borrowing by OECD country grouping**

Percentage of GDP

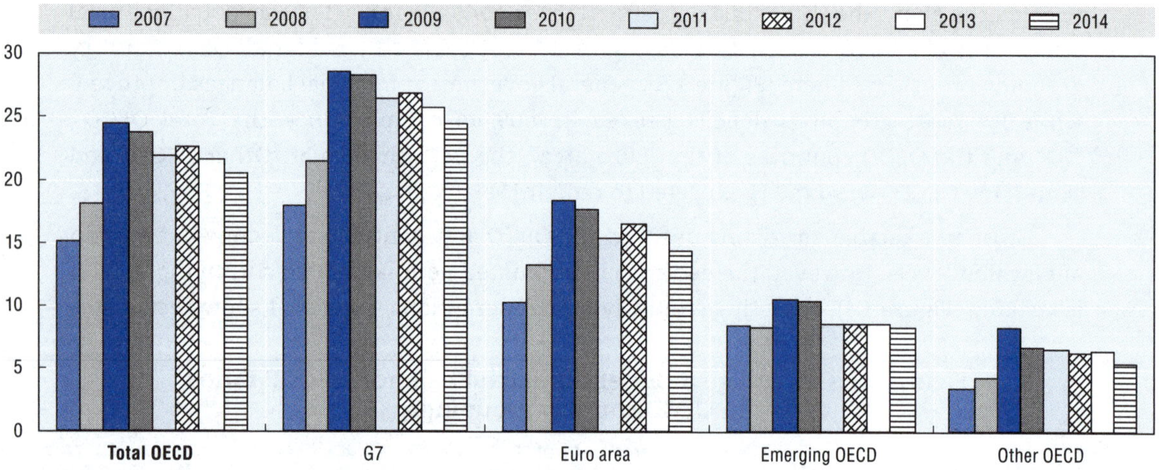

Source: 2013 Survey on central government marketable debt and borrowing by OECD Working Party on Debt Management; *OECD Economic Outlook 94 Database;* and OECD staff estimates.

StatLink http://dx.doi.org/10.1787/888932993446

1.4. Outlook for central government marketable gross borrowing needs of individual OECD countries

Table 1.2 shows the estimated central government marketable gross borrowing requirements in 2013 and 2014 for individual OECD countries. Gross borrowing requirements as a percentage of GDP vary significantly across countries, from very high (66% in 2013 for Japan and 64.7% in 2014) to very low (1.9% in 2013 for Chile and 2.1% in 2014).

Two countries (Japan and the United States) account for the bulk of the share in total OECD gross borrowing requirements (67.4% in 2013 and 68.3% in 2014). The share of G7 countries is projected to increase from 86.9% in 2013 to 87.4% in 2014. The Euro area share is projected to continue to fall from a peak of 22.9% in 2009 to 21% in 2013 and 20% in 2014.

Table 1.2. **Central government marketable gross borrowing by country**

Million USD

	2013			2014		
	Total gross borrowing requirement (GBR)	Country share in total GBR, %	GBR as % of GDP	Total gross borrowing requirement (GBR)	Country share in total GBR, %	GBR as % of GDP
Australia	76 572	0.7	5.4	72 371	0.7	4.9
Austria	39 679	0.4	8.4	44 206	0.4	9.1
Belgium	108 698	1.0	18.8	96 839	0.9	16.3
Canada	254 344	2.4	14.2	255 120	2.4	13.8
Chile	5 135	0.0	1.9	6 282	0.1	2.1
Czech Republic	14 095	0.1	6.3	22 433	0.2	9.8
Denmark	23 654	0.2	6.3	23 585	0.2	6.1
Finland	30 581	0.3	10.5	29 353	0.3	9.8
France	518 401	4.8	16.6	525 943	5.0	16.6
Germany	350 586	3.3	8.5	310 754	2.9	7.3
Greece	22 500	0.2	8.2	22 556	0.2	8.4
Hungary	31 493	0.3	19.3	28 113	0.3	16.5
Iceland	747	0.0	5.1	328	0.0	2.1
Ireland	49 086	0.5	19.8	13 277	0.1	5.2
Israel	30 869	0.3	11.0	24 774	0.2	8.4
Italy	607 100	5.6	25.8	542 396	5.1	22.7
Japan	3 666 486	34.1	66.0	3 693 610	34.9	64.7
Korea	72 738	0.7	6.4	72 738	0.7	6.1
Luxembourg	4 600	0.0	6.8	1 508	0.0	2.2
Mexico	103 008	1.0	8.3	107 342	1.0	8.0
Netherlands	147 200	1.4	16.2	141 300	1.3	15.4
New Zealand	14 213	0.1	8.9	9 960	0.1	5.9
Norway	40 793	0.4	7.6	25 323	0.2	4.5
Poland	42 899	0.4	7.2	43 101	0.4	6.9
Portugal	39 347	0.4	15.8	46 981	0.4	18.7
Slovak Republic	11 312	0.1	10.3	11 161	0.1	9.8
Slovenia	7 688	0.1	14.7	6 255	0.1	12.0
Spain	321 645	3.0	20.8	323 823	3.1	20.8
Sweden	46 474	0.4	8.9	41 777	0.4	7.7
Switzerland	19 034	0.2	3.2	16 115	0.2	2.6
Turkey	102 848	1.0	9.9	106 284	1.0	9.3
United Kingdom	373 514	3.5	13.9	382 741	3.6	13.7
United States	3 587 973	33.3	21.4	3 544 303	33.5	20.2
Total OECD	10 765 312	100.0	21.6	10 592 650	100.0	20.5

Notes:

1. Figures are calculated using the exchange rates as of 1st December 2009.
2. All figures refer to calendar years.
3. Estimates (projections) are based on country responses to the OECD Survey and comments by OECD Debt Management Offices (DMOs) on preliminary calculations by the Secretariat.
4. The Secretariat uses the following general conventions in calculating central government marketable gross borrowing requirements (GBRs): deficit projections (publicly available information from official national sources) plus redemptions (publicly available information from official national sources and Bloomberg). GBRs exclude cash management instruments (i.e., only T-bills and long-term instruments are being used). Short-term (ST) GBRs are calculated using the standardised OECD method: ST debt stock at the end of the previous year plus ST net borrowing over the calendar year. (See annex B for more details on methods and sources of the OECD Sovereign Borrowing Outlook.)
5. Some estimates (based on OECD methodology) may differ from those calculated by governments as different concepts are applied (e.g. fiscal year-calendar year conversions and net financing requirement concept) and/or a different basis is used for official projections.
6. Cut-off date for information (projections) used in the estimates is 5 December 2013.
7. GBR as a percentage of GDP is calculated using nominal GDP data from the OECD Economic Outlook 94/Vol 2, 19 November 2013.

Source: 2013 OECD (Working Party on Debt Management) Survey on central government marketable gross debt and GBRs; National Debt Management Offices; National authorities' sources; OECD Economic Outlook 94 database; Bloomberg; DataStream and OECD staff estimates.

StatLink http://dx.doi.org/10.1787/888932994168

1.5. The behaviour of long-term government borrowing rates in OECD government securities markets

Long-term interest rates are at historically low levels in many OECD countries.[12] Figure 1.5 shows the 10-year government bond yields in six major OECD countries: United States, Japan, United Kingdom, Germany, France and Canada. The debt managers from these countries were facing quite similar (movements in) borrowing rates. Indeed, there are remarkable linkages or correlations between the movements of these longer-term yields. Moreover, with the notable exception of Japan, the levels are very similar as well.

Figure 1.5 also shows the sharply upward move of US long-term government bond rates since May 2013. Over the same period, long term bond yields in Canada, the euro area and the United Kingdom posted a broadly similar increase.

Figure 1.5. **Historical 10-year government bond yields in major OECD economies**

Percentage

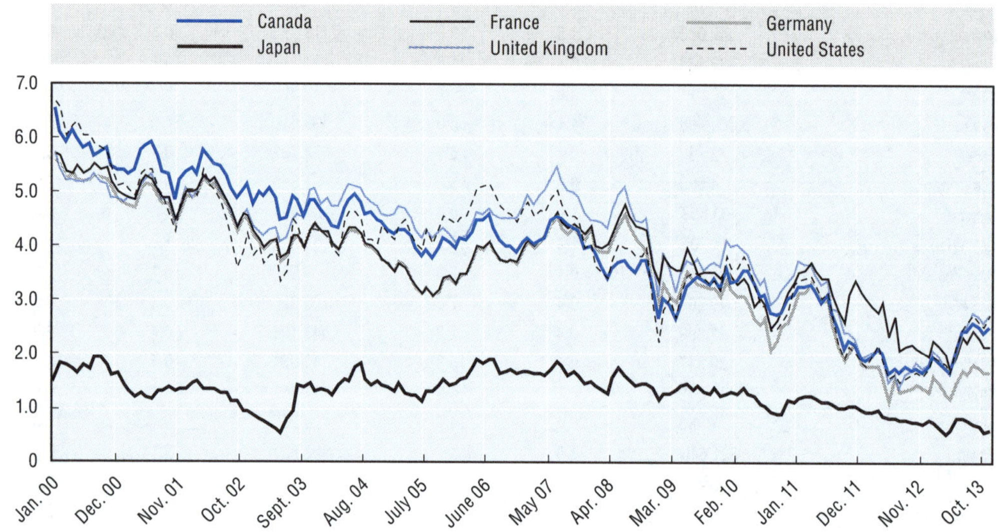

Note: Cut-off date is 29 November 2013.
Source: Datastream.

StatLink http://dx.doi.org/10.1787/888932993465

1.6. Why are long-term borrowing rates strongly correlated?

Figure 1.5 shows that long-term interest rates across advanced major economies have been highly correlated historically. What are the drivers of this outcome? Federal Reserve (FED) Chairman Bernanke gives the following answer: "The similar behaviour of these yields attests to the global nature of the economic and financial developments of recent years, as well as to the broad similarity in how the monetary policymakers in the advanced economies have responded to these developments."[13] To make this answer more precise, it is useful to decompose the long-term rate LR(t) into three components:

$$LR(t) = E\ (\text{inflation}) + E\ (\text{real rates}) + \text{Term Premium}$$

Trends and co-movements in LR(t) may be driven by all three channels: (i) expected long-term inflation, (ii) the expected path of short-term real interest rates, and (iii) the term premium. For example, all three channels contributed to the decline in the US LR(t) since 2007. The expected US inflation component showed a downward trend for many years and has become fairly stable. The US Federal Reserve contributes much of the longer-run decline in yield since 2010 to a sharp fall in the term premium, and to a lesser extent by a moving down of short-term real rates.[14]

The term premium is determined by the degree investors are willing to assume duration risk. This risk appetite is determined by a range of (in part overlapping) factors including perceived creditworthiness of the sovereign, volatility, bond correlations with equity, safe haven considerations, demand for international reserves and unconventional monetary policy.[15]

As noted, correlations in long-term rates across countries are driven by correlations in its components. Correlations in the expected path of short rates reflect monetary policy inter-linkages across countries. These correlations in monetary policy, in turn, are driven by common global shocks and/or the transmission of changes in policy rates in country X to the monetary policy stance in other countries (see for details section 1.7 below on the direction of the transmission of monetary policy shocks).

The strong co-movement or correlations of long term bond yields shown in Figure 1.5 can be quantified via a statistical principal components analysis. Our analysis[16] shows that 99% of the variance in co-movements of long-term yields can be explained by the first principal component. These longer-term correlations are largely driven by co-movements in short-term rates. The first principal component[17] explains 91% of the variance in the co-movements of short-term rates (see Figure 1.6 on the evolution of one year yields in government bills).

Figure 1.6. **Evolution of 1-year yields on government bills in major OECD economies**

Percentage

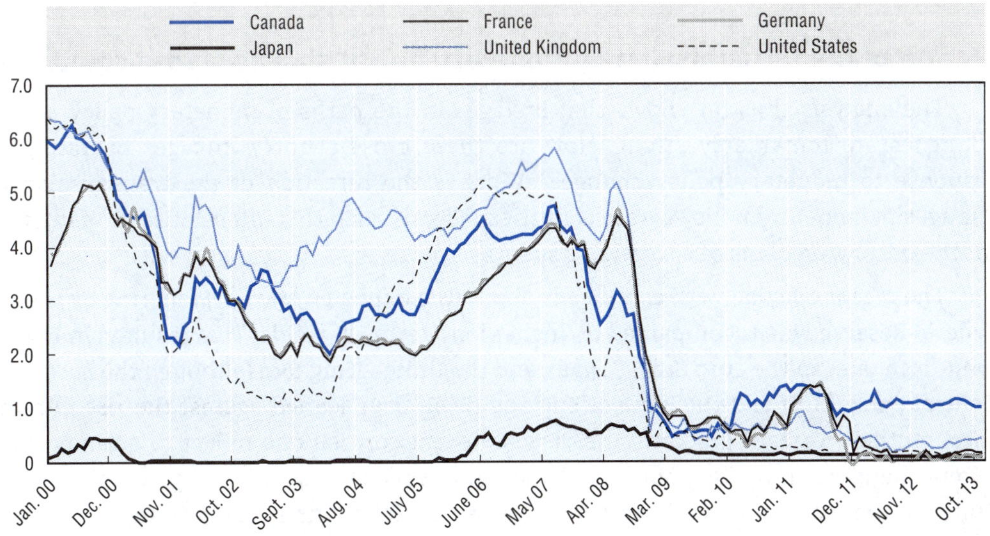

Note: Cut-off date is 29 November 2013.

Source: Bloomberg, Board of Governors of the Federal Reserve System; and Datastream.

StatLink http://dx.doi.org/10.1787/888932993484

The anchoring of long-term inflation expectations at low levels is to an important degree determined by the credibility of monetary policy in achieving low inflation goals. The expected path of short-term real interest rates is importantly driven by the present stance of monetary policy and expectations about future policy. Expected real yields over the longer term (as measured by the yields on inflation-indexed, long-term government bonds) are (i) very low for the five major OECD countries[18] mentioned in Figure 1.7 (in fact, they turned negative) and (ii) also very similar across these economies. In addition, this strong similarity suggests the importance of common global factors or shocks.[19]

Figure 1.7. **Inflation-indexed government bonds yields**

Percentage

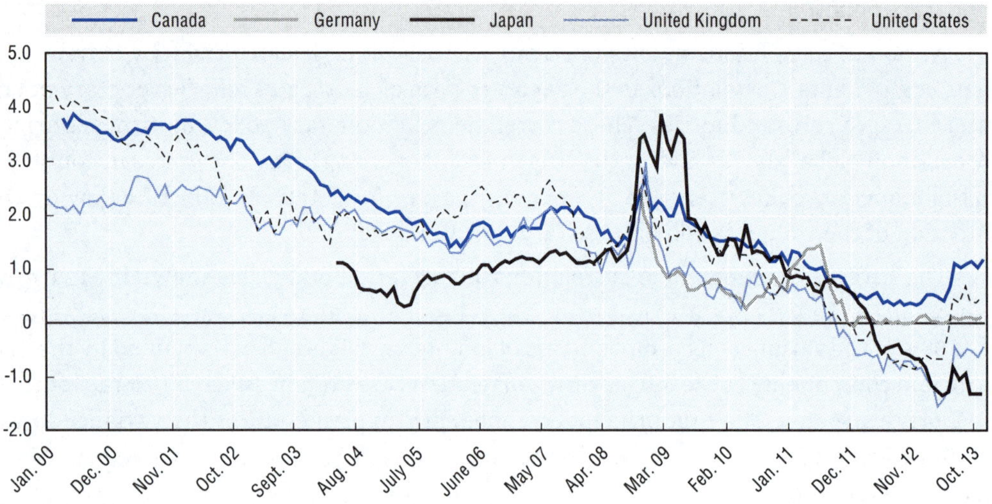

Notes: Cut-off date is 29 November 2013.
The maturity for the US, UK, and German bonds is 10 years. The current maturity for the Japanese bond is five years. For Canada, the data refers to the Government of Canada Real Return Bond (RRB) long-term yield, current maturity is eight years.
Source: Bloomberg; and Bank of Canada.

StatLink http://dx.doi.org/10.1787/888932993503

1.7. Direction of the transmission of monetary policy shocks across countries

The analysis thus far shows that linkages in the paths of monetary policy across countries are remarkably strong. How are these cross-country linkages operating in response to monetary policy changes? What is the direction of the transmission of changes in monetary policy across countries? Clearly, also this information is of interest for the borrowing plans of sovereign issuers.

The recent episode with confusions about (the expected start of) tapering by the US Federal Reserve was accompanied by higher long-term US yields. This resulted in higher long-term rates in the euro area, Canada and the United Kingdom (although the European Central Bank (ECB) and the Bank of England (BOE) have leaned against the rise in rates through their forward guidance messages). Recent correlations reflect to an important extent changes in monetary policy with monetary policy linkages flowing from the United States to the rest of the world (but not vice versa). Calculations using Granger causality tests[20] support this pattern for a longer period using 1-year yields on sovereign bills.[21] Clearly, this finding is also important for assessing the potential international spill-over effects of the exit from UMP (see Chapter 3).

1.8. The interest rate effects of government debt and its maturity

When portfolio balance effects are effective and significant they can be used to explain why both the size and the maturity of sovereign debt matter for the determination of long-term interest rates. In this analytical framework changes in the relative supplies of government debt have a significant role in shaping the yield curve.[22] This theory implies that increasing the maturity of public debt should raise long-term interest rates (relative to the path of future short-term rates).[23]

Recent empirical research shows that changes in public debt and its maturity are significant factors for explaining movements in long-term interest rates. Chadha et al (2013) find that a one percentage point rise in the debt-to-GDP ratio is associated with about a two basis points increase in long-term rates. They also estimated that lengthening the maturity of government debt held by the public by one month is associated with an increase of around 12-13 basis points.[24]

1.9. The challenge of raising large volumes of funds with acceptable rollover risk

For countries that were facing relatively high spreads in 2012 (in particular in the euro area), issuance conditions began to improve significantly in the second half of 2012 with further progress in 2013. However, debt managers are well advised to keep in mind how capricious markets can behave. As noted in OECD Sovereign Borrowing Outlook 2012 and 2013, very rapid increases in (perceived) sovereign risk can occur without (important) changes in fundamentals. Financial markets often react in a non-linear fashion to delayed or postponed fiscal adjustments as well as to sudden mood swings, thereby creating the risk of cliff effects where markets suddenly lose confidence in yesterday's safe sovereign assets.[25]

The mood swings of financial markets between periods of "euphoria" and "depression" are amplified at times by the actions of credit rating agencies (CRAs). Clearly, mood swings associated with changes in perceptions of sovereign risk can be a major complicating factor for sovereign issuers as bond market pressures have the potential to trigger ultra-high funding costs by demanding compensation for (perceptions of) higher sovereign risks.[26]

The European Securities and Markets Authority (ESMA) published recently a report identifying a number of deficiencies that pose a risk to "the quality, independence and integrity" of sovereign ratings produced and issued at the three largest CRAs.[27]

Clearly, these considerations and findings are in particular of importance for countries that are facing high borrowing needs and challenging redemption profiles. Indeed, the redemption profile of medium- and long-term central government debt in the OECD area is fairly challenging with large projected payment flows for the G7 and euro area governments for 2013 and 2014 (Figure 1.8).

Higher rollover risk is in particular reflected in the challenging redemption profiles for the coming three years (Figure 1.9). For the OECD area as a whole, governments will need to refinance close to 29% of its outstanding long-term debt in the next three years. Of particular interest is that emerging OECD countries have the highest long-term refinancing requirements (almost 32.3% of its outstanding long-term debt) in the next three years (Figure 1.9).

Challenging redemption profiles combined with high deficits imply greater refinancing risk. During episodes with high sovereign stress, some sovereigns may be vulnerable to

Figure 1.8. **Medium-and long term redemptions of central government marketable debt in OECD country groupings**

Percentage of GDP

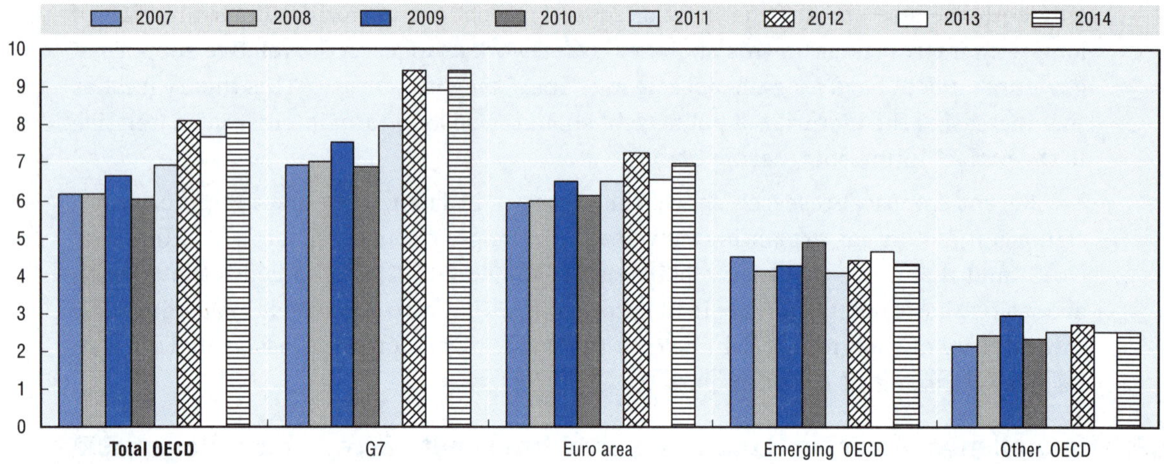

Source: 2013 Survey on central government marketable debt and borrowing by OECD Working Party on Debt Management; *OECD Economic Outlook 94 Database*; and OECD staff estimates.

StatLink http://dx.doi.org/10.1787/888932993522

Figure 1.9. **Percentage of debt maturing in next 12, 24 and 36 months**

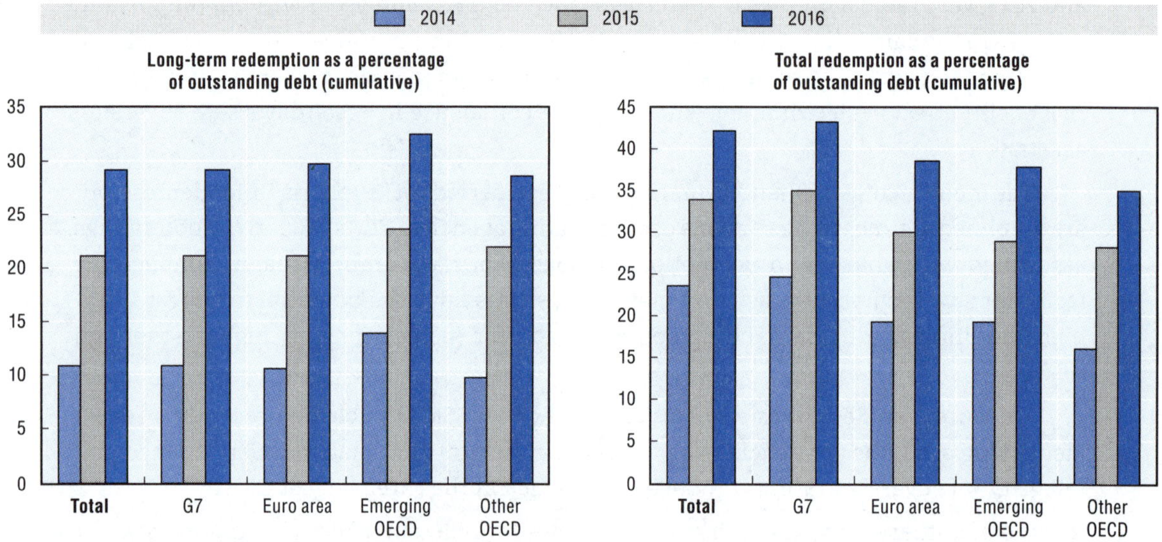

Source: 2013 Survey on central government marketable debt and borrowing by OECD Working Party on Debt Management; national authorities' data; Bloomberg; and OECD staff estimates.

StatLink http://dx.doi.org/10.1787/888932993541

spikes in borrowing rates, while others, "flight to safety" countries, may face the opposite borrowing situation characterised by ultra-low (sometimes negative) yields.

Episodes with serious financial market turmoil since 2008 have highlighted the importance of managing debt maturities in order to address rollover risk. The results of an OECD questionnaire on debt portfolio management confirmed that financial crises did render the funding task of most debt managers more difficult.[28] Overall, about a third of countries confirmed that the crisis impact on funding activities did affect their ability to achieve their various risk metric targets.

Average maturity is the most common indicator to assess rollover risk. A country with a higher average maturity is expected to be less vulnerable for a strong rise in interest rates.

Accordingly, most sovereigns seek to keep their average maturity at (better than) pre-crisis levels (Figure 1.10) in order to mitigate rollover risk. Several sovereigns have a higher average maturity than before the crisis. The United Kingdom, Chile and Ireland have the highest average term to maturity (Figure 1.10).

Figure 1.10. **Average term to maturity of outstanding marketable bonds**

Years

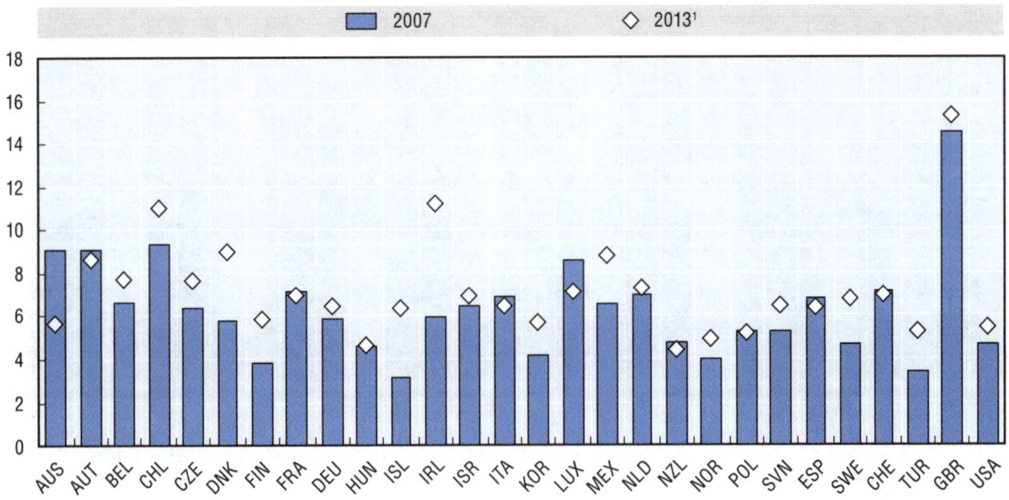

1. The figures are based on the latest, publicly available information from national sources on 15 November 2013.

Source: OECD Central Government Debt Statistical Yearbook Database; National authorities' data; and OECD staff calculations.

StatLink http://dx.doi.org/10.1787/888932993560

For the United Kingdom and Chile this risk measure reflects to an important degree the importance of their private pension sectors. Pension funds have long-term liabilities, which they seek to match with long term assets by buying long-term government bonds.

The weighted-average maturity of Ireland's long-term marketable government debt was 7.3 years at the end of 2012. The weighted-average maturity at the end of May 2013 was 11.2 years. The increase in the average term to maturity since end 2012 largely reflects the issuance in February 2013 of eight new floating rate Treasury Bonds with maturities from 25 up to 40 years (see also Chapter 2).

Some sovereigns, with better than average fiscal fundamentals, have shortened maturities in order to take advantage of very low short term rates.

Against this backdrop, most OECD debt managers continue to rebalance the profile of their debt portfolios by issuing more long-term instruments and moderating bill issuance. These debt management considerations are in many markets taken against the backdrop of elevated debt-to-GDP ratios and fiscal consolidation. Many governments aim to enhance fiscal resilience (see Section 1.10) by seeking to mitigate refinancing and rollover risk (by spreading out the redemption profile along the maturity spectrum).[29] Buybacks and switches have been used as successful and important liability tools for reducing rollover peaks, thereby lowering refinancing risk.[30]

For the OECD area as whole, the share of short-term issuance to total gross issuance by governments jumped from almost 49% in 2007 to 55.5% during the height of the financial crisis in 2008 (Figure 1.11). The following year, the share of short-term instruments dropped to below the 2007 share, i.e. to around 45%. For 2013 and 2014, the share of short-term issuance is expected to remain in the range 45-46%, well below the pre-crisis share.

Figure 1.11. **Maturity structure of gross issuance operations in the OECD area**

Percentage

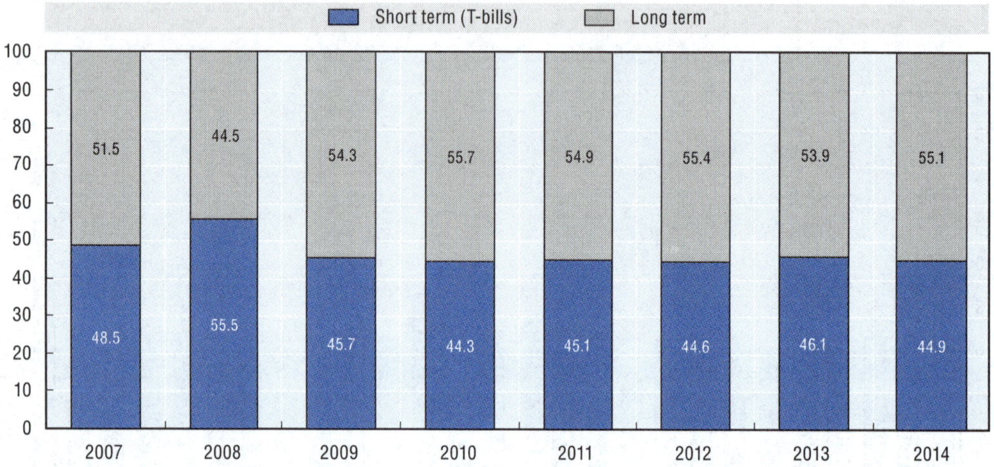

Source: 2013 Survey on central government marketable debt and borrowing by OECD Working Party on Debt Management; and OECD staff estimates.

StatLink http://dx.doi.org/10.1787/888932993579

1.10. Funding strategy

The funding strategy is informed principally by cost versus risk considerations.[31] In this context, also the government's preference to enhance fiscal resilience plays an important role. This policy perspective encourages the maintenance of a diversity of nominal and price-indexed instruments along the maturity spectrum. The emphasis on fiscal resilience is reflected in debt management considerations during periods of fiscal consolidation in response to a situation of fiscal dominance in many OECD countries. Fiscal dominance is a situation shaped by serious fiscal vulnerabilities, worsening perceptions of sovereign risk and considerable uncertainty about future interest rates, which are likely to last for a considerable amount of time.[32] Serious fiscal vulnerabilities arising from many years of high government debt has created new and more complex interactions between the funding strategy and monetary policy, in particular the use of unconventional monetary policy measures.[33] Although their formal mandates have not changed, recent balance sheet policies of many Central Banks (CBs) have tended to blur the separation of their policies from fiscal policy.[34] The mandates of debt management offices (DMOs) have usually had a microeconomic focus (viz, keeping government debt markets liquid, limiting refunding risks, etc.). Such mandates have usually eschewed any macroeconomic policy dimension.[35] For these reasons, all clashes in policy mandate between CBs and DMOs have been latent and not overt.

Table 1.3 reflects the funding structure in terms of types of instruments and maturity.[36] Issuance of long-term marketable instruments is dominated by fixed rate, local currency bonds. It is estimated that the issuance of long-term, fixed-rate instruments will decrease slightly in 2013-14, while the issuance of price-indexed bonds[37] is projected to increase to above pre-crisis levels in 2014. It is also of interest that in 2009 (the period with record borrowing needs) somewhat more foreign currency debt was issued, while this funding pattern returned to lower levels in 2010 and beyond.

The core purposes of T-bills in debt management (that is, excluding their use for cash management purposes) are cost effectiveness, relative ease of access (as compared to other segments), investor diversification, the smoothing of the financing needs (including redemptions), their use as an in-year buffer role and the use and the management of portfolio risks.[38]

The use of variable rate instruments (like Floating Rate Notes – FRNs) as debt management tool is not widespread. The main motive seems to be portfolio/instrument diversification. The use of FRNs has not (yet) returned to pre-crisis levels but an increase is projected for 2013-14 (Table 1.3 and Figure 1.12). In this context, it is of importance to note that the United States is planning to start a programme (with 2-year maturity) in January 2014. During the recent meeting of the US Treasury Borrowing Advisory Committee held on the 6th of November 2013, it was observed that this new programme would be a replacement for Treasury bill issuance[39] (see Chapter 4 for details).

Table 1.3. **Funding strategy based on marketable gross borrowing needs in OECD area**

Percentage

	2007	2008	2009	2010	2011	2012	2013	2014
Short Term (T-bills)	48.5	55.5	45.7	44.3	45.1	44.6	46.1	44.9
Long Term	51.5	44.5	54.3	55.7	54.9	55.4	53.9	55.1
Fixed rate	42.9	40.0	50.4	51.9	50.2	51.2	49.2	49.7
Index linked	3.2	2.6	1.8	2.4	2.9	3.2	3.3	3.4
Variable rate	1.7	1.0	1.0	0.8	0.7	0.4	0.9	1.4
Other	3.6	0.9	1.1	0.6	1.1	0.6	0.6	0.5
Of which:								
Local currency	51.2	44.0	53.6	55.2	54.5	54.9	53.4	54.6
Foreign currency	0.3	0.5	0.7	0.5	0.4	0.5	0.5	0.5

Source: 2013 Survey on central government marketable debt and borrowing by OECD Working Party Debt Management; and OECD staff estimates.

StatLink http://dx.doi.org/10.1787/888932994187

1.11. Government debt at a glance: General government debt as a percentage of GDP is projected to surpass the World War II peak

Fiscal accounts deteriorated sharply in the wake of the global financial crisis. In fact, the direct fallout of this crisis explains roughly two-thirds of the rise in the debt ratio among the advanced economies markets.[40] As a result, government debt levels in many OECD countries increased to close to the historical peak in the 1940s. Figure 1.13 gives the development of gross public debt since 1880 for selected OECD economies. The peak of general government debt as a percentage of GDP for these countries is linked to World War II (1941–45), the latter event taking the GDP PPP-weighted average debt ratio to

Figure 1.12. **Issuance of linkers and variable rate instruments in the OECD area**

Billion USD

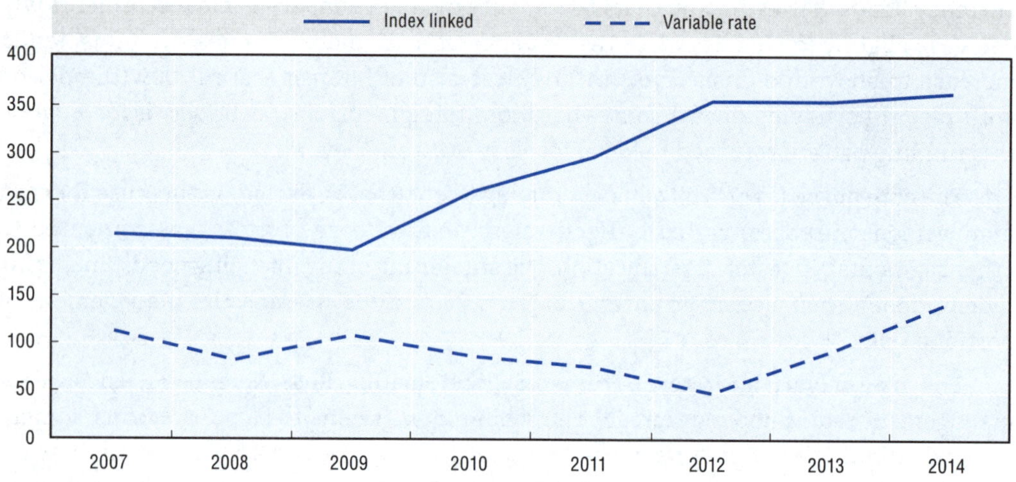

Source: 2013 Survey on central government marketable debt and borrowing by OECD Working Party on Debt Management; and OECD staff estimates.

StatLink http://dx.doi.org/10.1787/888932993598

around 116% of GDP.[41] The fall-out of the 2007-9 global financial crisis (the most serious financial crisis on record) has put such pressure on the increase in government debt ratios in the OECD area that with an estimated ratio of 115.6% of GDP for 2013 the World War II peak is being nearly scaled. In fact, general government debt, as a percentage of GDP, is projected to surpass the World War II peak in 2014 (Figure 1.13).

The 2007-09 global financial crisis as the most serious crisis on record set the stage for a surge in government debt and contingent liabilities caused by the decisive actions of governments to avert a total collapse of the private financial intermediary system.

Figure 1.13. **Gross public debt of selected[1] advanced economies: 1880-2014**

Percentage of GDP

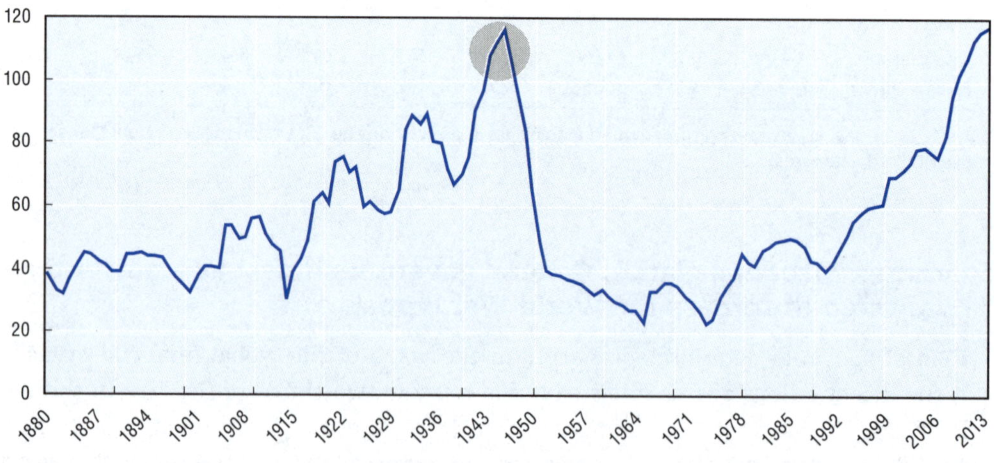

Notes: Historical debt levels, GDP-weighted average.

1. Includes Australia, Canada, France, Germany, Italy, Japan, Korea, Spain, United Kingdom and United States.

Source: IMF Historical Public Debt Database; OECD Economic Outlook 94 Database; and OECD staff calculations.

StatLink http://dx.doi.org/10.1787/888932993617

"A near-seizure of the international financial system after the collapse of Lehman Brothers administered a particularly large adverse shock to animal spirits."[42] This shock initiated a period of weak activity, although a much more serious collapse in demand was avoided by governments supporting the financial sector. In addition, the rapid acceleration in sovereign debt was further boosted by the massive fiscal response to concerns about the possibility of a severe economic slump. However, a prolonged period of subdued activity in the wake of a financial crisis is difficult to avoid, because the process of balance sheet repair by financial institutions, businesses and households inevitably takes considerable time.[43] Moreover, the mutation from an imminent Great Crash of the private financial intermediary system into market concerns about imminent or actual local sovereign debt crises, added to a further decline in confidence among investors, financial intermediaries and households thereby putting downward pressure on economic growth.

Weak economic activity, in turn, is putting pressure on government balances and a further increase in government debt. Ratios of general government gross debt-to-GDP for different OECD country groupings are expected to increase further in 2013 and 2014 (Figure 1.14).

The gross general debt-to-GDP ratio of G-20 governments is estimated to grow from 77.3% in 2007 to 110.6% in 2013 and to increase further to a projected 112.2% in 2014 (Figure 1.14).

Figure 1.14. **General government gross debt for different country groupings**

Percentage of GDP

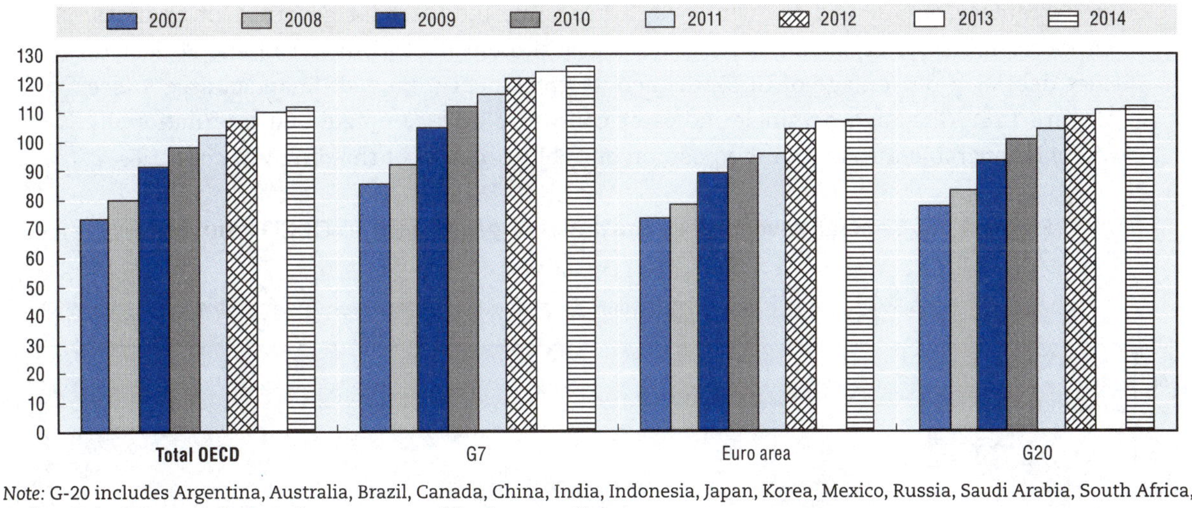

Note: G-20 includes Argentina, Australia, Brazil, Canada, China, India, Indonesia, Japan, Korea, Mexico, Russia, Saudi Arabia, South Africa, Turkey, United States and selected governments of the European Union.

Source: *OECD Economic Outlook 94; Database; IMF World Economic Outlook Database* and OECD staff calculations.

StatLink http://dx.doi.org/10.1787/888932993636

1.12. Gross central debt versus gross and net financial general government debt

Various definitions of gross central government debt are playing a key role in sovereign debt management. The simplest measure is gross nominal marketable central government debt (calculated as the sum of the amounts that the government is legally obliged to pay when a debt instrument matures). It may also be necessary to add accrued

Figure 1.15. **General government net debt in OECD countries**

Percentage of GDP

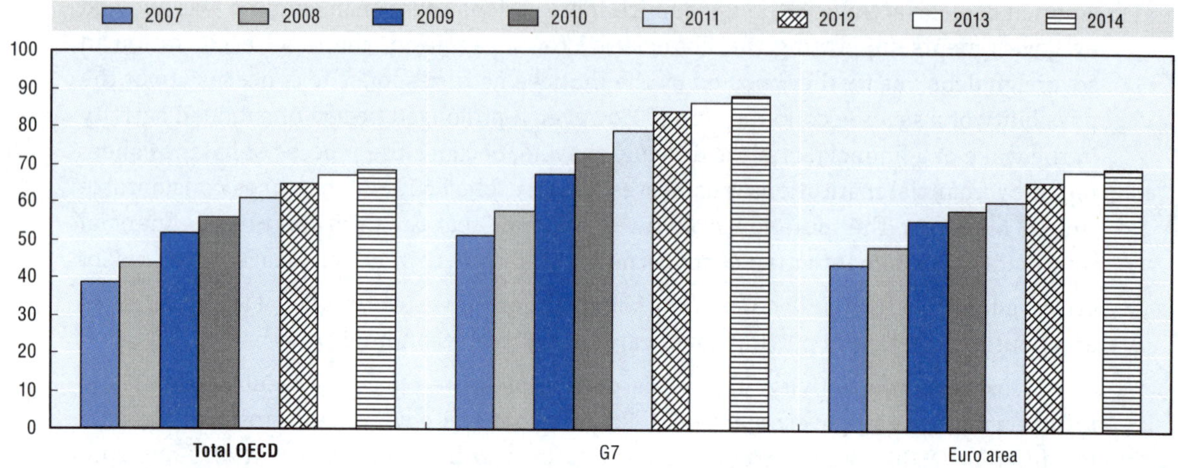

Note: General government net debt figures are calculated on a SNA basis.
Source: OECD *Economic Outlook 94;* and OECD staff calculations.

StatLink http://dx.doi.org/10.1787/888932993655

inflation compensation for inflation-linked bonds. When financial assets are taken into account (such as money market assets and on-lending to the central bank), net central government debt measures, as a policy indicator for public debt management, can be calculated.[44]

Gross general government debt (System of National Accounts (SNA) gross debt) as a percentage of GDP is a frequently used head line indicator for government finances. Another indicator is net financial general government debt (SNA net financial debt or net debt as a percentage of GDP), defined as gross debt minus all financial assets (see Figure 1.15). Although no single indicator can serve as a complete and internationally fully comparable measure of the position of public finances of the different countries, it

Figure 1.16. **Central government marketable gross debt in OECD countries**

Percentage of GDP

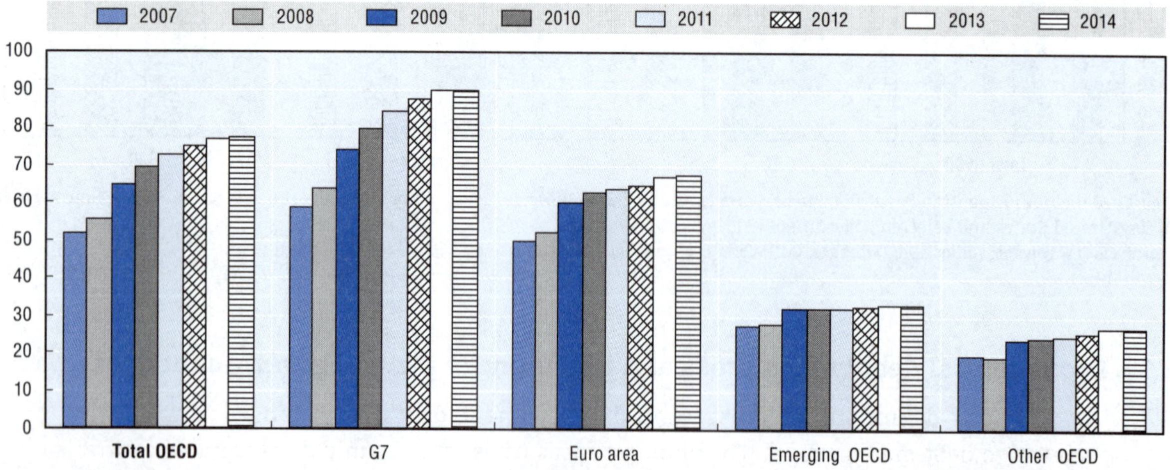

Source: 2013 Survey on central government marketable debt and borrowing by OECD Working Party on Debt Management; OECD *Economic Outlook 94;* and OECD staff estimates.

StatLink http://dx.doi.org/10.1787/888932993674

can be argued that net debt (as a percentage of GDP) provides a better indication of the (relative) fiscal position than gross debt.[45]

Figure 1.16 shows that the ratios of central government marketable debt-to-GDP of all country groupings have increased since 2007. The G7 central government marketable debt-to-GDP ratio is projected to reach nearly 89.6% in 2014. By comparison, the debt ratio of total OECD is expected to reach 77.1% in 2014. For the Euro area, this ratio is estimated to reach 67.4% in 2014. For Other OECD (which includes a number of OECD countries[46] with a fiscal surplus), this ratio is expected to be slightly higher than 27% in 2014, while for Emerging OECD this debt ratio is projected to reach 33.3% in 2014.

Figure 1.17 provides information about the maturity structure of the outstanding stock of central government marketable debt. At the height of the financial crisis in 2008, there was a sharp drop of almost 4% in the share of long-term liabilities in total marketable central government debt. The share of long-term debt is estimated to reach around 87% in 2013. For 2014, the long-term share is projected to reach nearly 88.1%.

Figure 1.17. **Maturity structure of central government marketable debt for OECD area**

Percentage

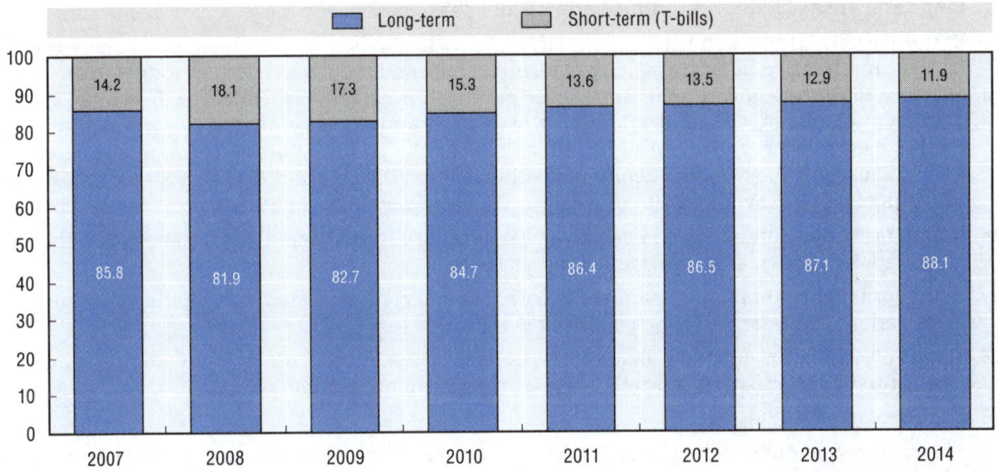

Source: 2013 Survey on central government marketable debt and borrowing by OECD Working Party on Debt Management; and OECD staff estimates.

StatLink http://dx.doi.org/10.1787/888932993693

Notes

1. Figures are calculated using the exchange rates as of 1st December 2009 to make GBR estimates comparable with previous editions of the OECD Sovereign Borrowing Outlook.
2. OECD Economic Outlook 94, November 2013.
3. See Annex A for the definitions of "Total OECD", "G7", "OECD euro area", "Emerging OECD" and "Other OECD" used in this outlook.
4. OECD Economic Outlook 94, November 2013.
5. See Chapter 2 on Outlook for Sovereign Stress.
6. Using an economically meaningful methodology is important because of complications in providing meaningful estimates of gross short-term borrowing requirements that may yield quite different (usually inflated) outcomes that cannot easily be compared across different OECD markets. This means that daily cash management operations need to be excluded. Failure to use OECD's standard

methodology results in highly inflated and misleading estimates for gross short-term borrowing needs. For example, it is estimated that the OECD short-term gross borrowing needs for 2013, using the OECD standardised method, is around USD 5.0 trillion. However, by using a so-called non-standardised methodology this estimate increases to around USD 15.5 trillion. See for details Annex B.

7. See Chapter 4 on Challenges in Primary and Secondary Markets.
8. The hunt for yield, especially down the credit spectrum, intensified [Paul Fisher (2013), Financial markets, monetary policy and credit supply, Speech to Richmond University, London, 2 October].
9. B. S. Bernanke (2013b), Communication and monetary policy, Speech at the National Economists Club Annual Dinner, Herbert Stein Memorial Lecture, Washington DC, 19 November.
10. See for details Hans J. Blommestein (2010) Public Debt Management and Sovereign Risk during the Worst Financial Crisis on Record: Experiences and Lessons from the OECD Area In: Carlos A. Primo Braga and Gallina A. Vincelette (eds.) Sovereign Debt and the Financial Crisis Will This Time Be Different?, World Bank.
11. See Annex B for the definitions of "Total OECD", "G7", "OECD euro area", "Emerging OECD" and "Other OECD" used in this outlook.
12. Ben Bernanke (2013a), Long-Term Interest Rates, Remarks at the Annual Monetary/Macroeconomics Conference: The Past and Future of Monetary Policy, sponsored by the Federal Reserve Bank of San Francisco, March 1.
13. Ben Bernanke (2013a), ibid.
14. Ben Bernanke (2013a),ibid. However, research at the Federal Reserve Bank of San Francisco comes to a different conclusion. Bauer and Rudebusch (2013) find that the secular decline in the US term premium is less pronounced when they use a new statistical methodology. Indeed, they estimate that the decline in US long rates is importantly driven by the other two components: E (inflation) and E (real rates) [M. D. Bauer and G.D. Rudebusch (2013), What caused the decline in long-term yields? FRBSF Economic Letter, 8 July 2013].
15. Bernanke (2013a) notes in this context that "a growing body of research supports the view that LSAPs are effective at bringing down term premiums and thus reducing longer-term rates." See also Chapter 3 on the exit from asset purchase programmes. However, Bernanke (2013b) also opines that …."economists do not have as good an understanding as we would like of the factors determining term premiums.."[Ben S. Bernanke (2013b), Communication and Monetary Policy, Speech at the National Economists Club Annual Dinner, Herbert Stein Memorial Lecture, Washington, D.C. November 19.]
16. Using principal components analysis with ordinary (uncentered) correlations of monthly observations of 10-year government bond yields.
17. Using principal components analysis with ordinary (uncentered) correlations of monthly observations of 1-year yields on government bills.
18. Since 2009, inflation-indexed yields have declined steadily. Currently, they stand below zero (see Figure 1.7 on inflation-indexed, long-term government bonds).
19. Ben Bernanke (2013a), ibid.
20. We have used in our estimates a VAR model for n-vector time series where it is not known a priori whether the variables are integrated, co-integrated or (trend) stationary [H. Y. Toda, T. Yamamoto (1995), Statistical inference in vector autoregressions with possibly integrated processes, Journal of Econometrics].
21. 1-year yields on government bills are strongly correlated with central bank policy rates.
22. This analytical framework is supported by the pioneering research of J.M. Keynes, J. Tobin and M. Friedman. However, from the 1980s to the onset of the global crisis, portfolio balance effects were considered in main stream models (such as the New Keynesian framework) as theoretically irrelevant or empirically very small [Chadha, Turner and Zampoli (2013); Blommestein and Turner, eds., (2012); OECD (2013) and Chapter 3].
23. The existence of these effects implies the failure of Ricardian equivalence [Blommestein and Turner, eds., (2012)].
24. See Chadha, Turner and Zampoli (2013). They use in their calculations the 5-year forward 10-year yields as long-term interest measure as this interest rate is less influenced by the business cycle and monetary policy than the contemporary 10-year yield.
25. See for details Chapter 2 on the Outlook for Sovereign Stress in OECD Sovereign Borrowing Outlook 2012 and 2013.
26. See for details Chapter 2 on the Outlook for Sovereign Stress in OECD Sovereign Borrowing Outlook 2012 and 2013.

27. ESMA identifies deficiencies in CRAs sovereign ratings processes, Press Release, 2 December 2013.
28. This OECD questionnaire on debt-portfolio management was discussed at the annual meeting of the OECD Working Party on Public Debt Management held on 4-5 October 2010.
29. See Annex A, Principles and Trade-offs When Making Issuance Choices in the UK in OECD Sovereign Borrowing Outlook 2012.
30. See Chapter 6 on Buybacks and Exchanges in OECD Sovereign Borrowing Outlook 2013.
31. See Annex A, Principles and Trade-offs When Making Issuance Choices in the UK in OECD Sovereign Borrowing Outlook 2012.
32. Hans J. Blommestein and Philip Turner (2011), Interactions between sovereign debt management and monetary policy under fiscal dominance and financial instability. Paper presented at the ECB's Public Finance Workshop on "Challenges for Sovereign Debt Management in the EU", held on 7 October 2011 in Frankfurt, Germany. *www.ecb.europa.eu/events/conferences/html/ws_pubfinance4.en.html* and at the BIS/OECD Workshop on Policy Interactions between Fiscal Policy, Monetary policy and Government Debt Management after the Financial Crisis, held on 2 December 2011 in Basel, Switzerland. A revised version of this paper was published in Hans J. Blommestein and Philip Turner (2012), eds., Threat of Fiscal Dominance?, BIS Papers No 65, BIS-OECD Publishing.
33. See for details Chapter 3 on "Debt Management in the Macro Spotlight" (in OECD Sovereign Borrowing Outlook 2013) and Chapter 3 on "What are the Challenges for Public Debt Management of the Use of, and Exit from, Central Bank Asset Purchase Programmes?" (in this Borrowing Outlook).
34. See Chapter 3 in OECD Sovereign Borrowing Outlook 2013.
35. The formal mandates of some DMOs include a reference to macroeconomic policy in their debt management objective. For example, the objective of UK's DMO requires consistency with the aims of monetary policy. Other debt managers do not include macroeconomic objectives. The US Treasury Borrowing Advisory Committee has argued that debt maturity decisions should be taken "regardless of monetary policy".
36. As noted, the funding strategy entails decisions on how gross-borrowing needs are going to be financed using different instruments (e.g. long-term, short-term, nominal, indexed, etc.).
37. See Chapter 4 on Challenges in Primary and Secondary Markets.
38. These reasons were mentioned during the meeting of the OECD Working Party on Public Debt Management, held on 30-31 October 2013 at OECD Headquarters.
39. See "Report to the Secretary of the Treasury from the Treasury Borrowing Advisory Committee of the Securities Industry and Financial Markets Association", 6 November 2013.
40. Christine Lagarde, Banque de France Financial Stability Review on Public Debt – Special Address to Panel Discussion, IMF, Washington D.C., 21 April 2012.
41. S. Ali Abbas and others (2010), "Strategies for Fiscal Consolidation in the Post-crisis world", IMF Fiscal Affairs working paper 10/04.
42. Charles Bean (2012), Central banking in boom and slump, JSG Wilson Lecture in Economics, University of Hull, Hull, 31 October 2012.
43. Charles Bean (2012), Central banking in boom and slump, JSG Wilson Lecture in Economics, University of Hull, Hull, 31 October 2012.
44. See the forthcoming report by the OECD Task Force on the Transparency of Debt Statistics, Operations and Policies for more details.
45. The use of net debt, instead of gross debt, may affect the ranking of governments in terms of the size of indebtedness. OECD (2013), Government Finance Indicators: Truth and Myth, Working Party on Financial Statistics, COM/STD/DAF(2013)16.
46. OECD Economic Outlook November 2013 projections show a positive fiscal balance in 2013 for Germany, Korea, Mexico, Norway, and Switzerland. Moreover, Germany, Korea, Mexico, Norway, and Poland are expected to run a surplus in 2014.

References

Abbas S. Ali., et al. (2010), "Strategies for Fiscal Consolidation in the Post-crisis world", IMF Fiscal Affairs working paper, No. 10/04.

Abbas S. Ali, B. Nazim, E. Asmaa and M. Horton, (2010), "A historical public debt database", IMF working paper, No. 10/245.

Bauer, M. D. and G.D. Rudebusch (2013), "What caused the decline in long-term yields?", FRBSF Economic Letter, July 2013.

Bean, C. (2012), "Central banking in boom and slump", JSG Wilson Lecture in Economics, University of Hull, October 2012.

Bernanke, B. (2013a), "Long-Term Interest Rates", remarks at the Annual Monetary/Macroeconomics Conference: The Past and Future of Monetary Policy, sponsored by the Federal Reserve Bank of San Francisco, 1 March.

Bernanke, B. (2013b), "Communication and monetary policy", speech at the National Economists Club Annual Dinner, Herbert Stein Memorial Lecture, Washington DC, 19 November.

Blommestein, H.J. (2010), "Public Debt Management and Sovereign Risk during the Worst Financial Crisis on Record: Experiences and Lessons from the OECD Area", in Carlos A. Primo Braga and A. Vincelette Gallina (eds.), Sovereign Debt and the Financial Crisis Will This Time Be Different?, World Bank.

Blommestein H.J. and P. Turner (2012), "Interactions between sovereign debt management and monetary policy under fiscal dominance and financial instability", in H.J. Blommestein and P. Turner (2012) (eds.), Threat of Fiscal Dominance?, BIS Papers No 65, BIS-OECD Publishing.

Blommestein H.J., O.S. Jensen and T. Olofsson (2010), "A New Method for Measuring Short-term Gross Borrowing Needs", OECD Journal: Financial Market Trends, Vol. 2010/1.

Blommestein, H.J. and A. Gok (2009), "OECD Sovereign Borrowing Outlook 2009", OECD Journal: Financial Market Trends, Vol. 2009/1.

Chada, J., P. Turner and F. Zampolli (2013), "The interest rate effects of government debt maturity", BIS Working Papers, No 415.

European Central Bank (2012), ECB Monthly Bulletin, November, 2012.

European Central Bank (2012), ECB Monthly Bulletin, October, 2012.

European Securities and Markets Authority (2013), "ESMA identifies deficiencies in CRAs sovereign ratings processes", ESMA Press Release, 2 December.

Fisher, P. (2013), "Financial markets, monetary policy and credit supply", speech to Richmond University, London, 2 October.

Keynes J.M., The General Theory of Employment, Interest and Money, London: Macmillan, 1936.

Lagarde, C. (2012), "Banque de France Financial Stability Review on Public Debt", special address to panel discussion, IMF, Washington D.C.,21 April.

OECD (2010), Central Government Debt Statistical: Yearbook 2010, OECD Publishing.

OECD (2010), Economic Outlook, November 2010, OECD Publishing.

OECD (2012), OECD Sovereign Borrowing Outlook 2012, OECD Publishing.

OECD (2013), Economic Outlook, June 2013, OECD Publishing.

OECD (2013), Economic Outlook, November 2013, OECD Publishing.

OECD (2013), Government Finance Indicators: Truth and Myth, Working Party on Financial Statistics, 2013, OECD, Paris, document COM/STD/DAF 16.

OECD (2013), OECD Sovereign Borrowing Outlook 2013, OECD Publishing.

Toda, H. Y. and T. Yamamoto (1995), "Statistical inference in vector autoregressions with possibly integrated processes", Journal of Econometrics, Vol. 66.

US Department of Treasury (2013), "Report to the Secretary of the Treasury from the Treasury Borrowing Advisory Committee of the Securities Industry and Financial Markets Association", press release, 6 November.

Chapter 2

Outlook for sovereign stress

The borrowing environment for governments continues to be shaped by market dynamics punctuated by sudden shifts in investor sentiment and perceptions of risk associated with certain sovereigns. Complications for issuers are generated by the pressures of (perceived) increases in sovereign stress. In extreme cases, this can result in a loss of market access. In several countries, the toxic links between banks and (perceptions about) sovereign creditworthiness also played a role.

Interactions between public debt management and monetary policy can be an important channel for changes in long-term rates in government securities markets. Moreover, the political stress surrounding the extension of the US debt ceiling increased uncertainty and created more challenging borrowing conditions.

Lack of consensus on how to measure and price "sovereign risk" is a serious obstacle in assessing sovereign asset safety. This complicates assessing alleged structural shortages in the aggregate supply of safe public assets. There is no decisive evidence of a lasting, structural shortage in the aggregate supply of safe sovereign assets.

The statistical data for Israel are supplied by and under the responsibility of the relevant Israeli authorities. The use of such data by the OECD is without prejudice to the status of the Golan Heights, East Jerusalem and Israeli settlements in the West Bank under the terms of international law.

2.1. Overall sovereign market stress in the OECD area seems to have subsided somewhat...

This chapter deals with the complications for issuers generated by the pressures of (perceived) increases in sovereign stress. In comparison with the previous borrowing outlook, acute stress in several government securities markets seems to have subsided somewhat. Short-term interest rates were low and stable at the short end (Figure 1.6) while long rates fell due to the asset purchase programmes of major central banks (see Chapters 1 and 3 for details). Ultra-high yields dropped to a significant extent while ultra-low yields increased. Accordingly, the spreads between them (as indicators of sovereign stress) narrowed (Figure 2.6).

Europe continued to make progress in key areas of reform, including, quite crucially, in taking steps for weakening or loosening the bank-sovereign nexus. The latter issue involves discussions by European governments on a new bank resolution mechanism as part of the envisaged European banking union. This proposed mechanism includes quite crucially suggestions for so-called bail-in rules encompassing all bank liabilities (apart from those explicitly excluded such as customer deposits).[1] Tangible progress would importantly contribute to less potential pressure on sovereigns, thereby contributing to a further decrease in stress in European government debt markets.[2] Spreads over German Bunds for public debt of key euro area governments considered more vulnerable had narrowed significantly (Figure 2.9). Moreover, money market activity, a key barometer of investor sentiment, recovered in the second quarter in the Euro area.

2.2. But the issuance climate remains influenced by important policy challenges

However, some of the characteristics of recent money market activity in the Euro area (predominantly secured lending with very short durations[3]) continue to reflect concerns about key (remaining) weaknesses such as persisting financial fragmentation and the (potential) adverse feedback loops between weak banks and sovereign balance sheets as well as those between banks and highly indebted corporates with debt servicing problems.[4]

Several OECD sovereigns are addressing the difficult challenges associated with a return to markets (see Section 2.4 below).

Moreover, the political stress surrounding the extension of the US debt ceiling in September-October 2013 resulted in higher uncertainty and more challenging borrowing conditions. A senior US Treasury official noted in this context that the recent debt limit impasse "led to significant disruptions in the secondary market for short-dated Treasury securities and a measurable increase in borrowing costs for newly issued Treasury bills."[5] Market volatility increased with some one-month T-bill rates jumping briefly to above 0.70% before falling back to 0.02 to 0.03%. However, T-bills maturing in February 2014 still showed elevated yields[6] (Figure 2.1).

Figure 2.1. **US Treasury-bills secondary market yields**

Percentages

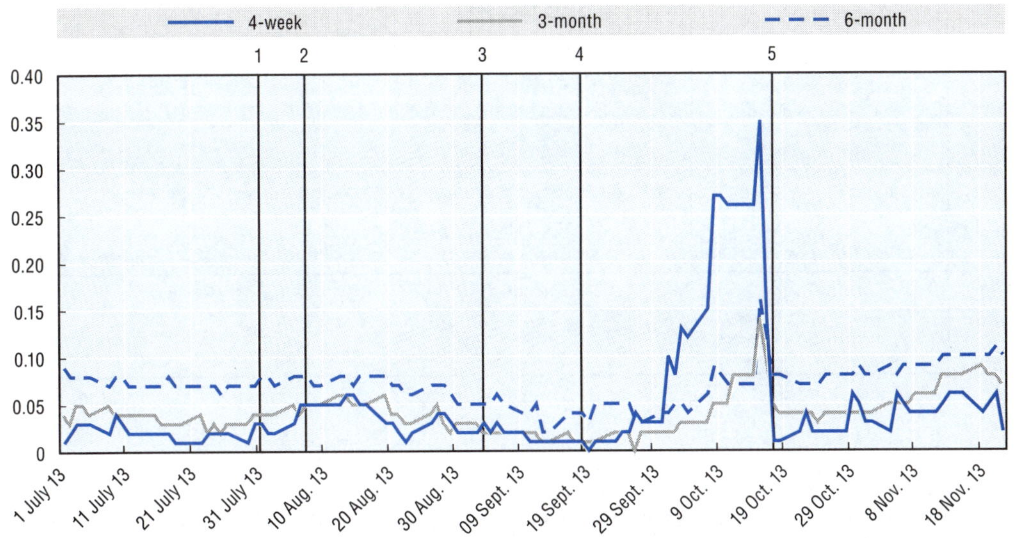

Notes: Cut-off date is 30 November 2013. 1) FOMC statement (31 July 2013); 2) ECB and BOE forward guidance announcement (7 August 2013); 3) ISM manufacturing index data (3 September 2013); 4) FOMC statement (18 September 2013); 5) US Government reopens (17 October 2013).

Source: Datastream.

StatLink http://dx.doi.org/10.1787/888932993712

All in all, sovereign issuers are operating in a borrowing environment shaped by at times quite complex market dynamics punctuated by sudden shifts in sentiment and perceptions of market, credit and liquidity risk, which includes the so-called swings in the "risk-on" and "risk-off" trades. The recent experience with (un)expected changes in the stance of unconventional monetary policy (UMP) shows that interactions between public debt management and monetary policy can be an important channel of changes in long-term rates in government securities markets (see Chapter 3). The analysis in this outlook also shows that linkages in the paths of monetary policy across countries and associated borrowing rates are remarkably strong (see Chapter 1).

2.3. The evolution of fiscal balances and sovereign debt and the threat of fiscal dominance

Since 2010, markets and rating agencies pay more attention to relatively high government deficit and debt situations.[7] As a result, the (sudden) increase in sovereign stress led at times to ultra-high borrowing rates.[8] Rollover risk emerged as a key policy concern for debt managers, in particular in countries with (perceived) debt sustainability problems.

As a result, during the past two years, significant progress has been made in strengthening OECD fiscal balances. For the OECD area as a whole, deficits fell by around 1% of GDP in 2012 and 2013 (standing at 5.9% in 2012 and estimated to reach 4.8% in 2013; compare Figures 2.2 and 2.3), and are projected to fall by almost 0.8% of GDP in 2014 (and projected to reach 4% of GDP).

However, deficits and gross borrowing needs are in many countries not declining enough to stop the rise in public debt (including in relation to GDP). As a result, general government gross debt increased by 2.9% of GDP in 2013 (in 2012 the debt-to GDP ratio

Figure 2.2. **OECD general government gross debt and government deficits, 2012**

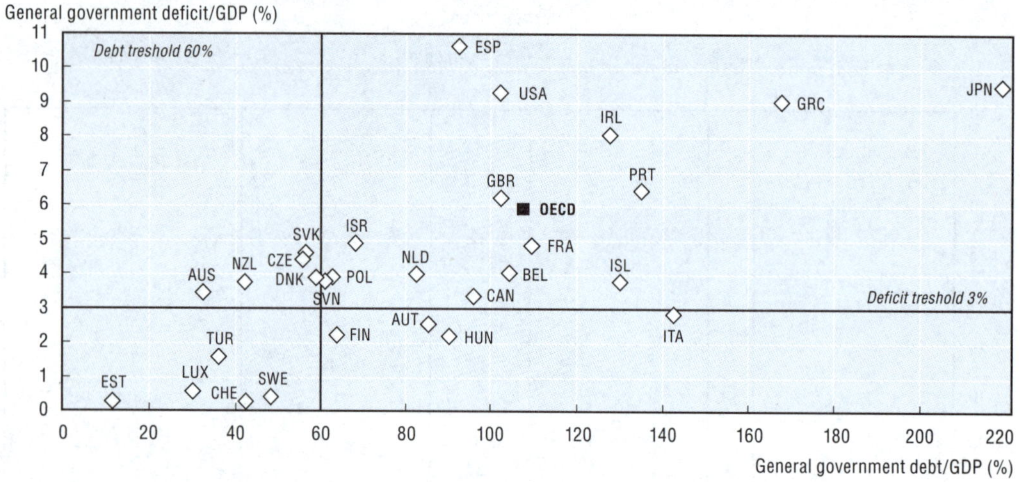

Notes: Chile, Germany, Korea, Mexico and Norway are not included because they show a positive fiscal balance. General government gross debt and deficits are on SNA basis.

Gross debt measures are not always comparable across countries due to a different definition or treatment of debt components. For euro area countries with unsustainable fiscal positions that have asked for assistance from the European Union and the IMF (Greece, Ireland and Portugal), the change in 2010 and 2011 in government financial liabilities has been approximated by the change in government liabilities recorded for the Maastricht definition of general government debt.

Financial balances (deficits) include one-off factors such as those resulting from the sale of mobile telephone licences. As data are on a national account's basis (SNA93/ESA95) for the OECD countries, government financial balances may differ from the numbers reported to the European Commission under the Excessive Deficit Procedure for some European Union (EU) countries. For more details see OECD Economic Outlook Sources and Methods (*www.oecd.org/eco/outlook/sources-and-methods.htm*).

Source: OECD Economic Outlook 94 Database; Chile, Mexico and Turkey national data sources; and OECD staff estimates.

StatLink http://dx.doi.org/10.1787/888932993731

was 107.4% and is estimated to reach 110.3% in 2013; compare Figures 2.2 and 2.3). In 2014, general government debt as a percentage of GDP is projected to reach 111.8%, from 110.3% in 2013.

The good news is that debt ratios are increasing at a significantly slower pace than in the past, declining from an increase of 11.3% in 2008-9 to a projected 1.5% in 2013-14.

2.4. Fiscal consolidation and public debt management policy

However, these averages of fiscal and sovereign debt indicators for the OECD area as a whole conceal important details linked with the relative progress made by individual countries in terms of deficits, gross borrowing requirements, government debt and average maturity of the outstanding debt. Additional insights in the progress made by individual countries can be obtained by dividing the set of countries into three groups. Group 1 includes those countries with stable or declining debt-to-GDP ratios.[9] Group 2 consists of countries where the debt ratio has not yet started to decrease (but is about to do so), while deficits and gross borrowing needs are falling. In Group 3 the fiscal imbalances are larger than in the other two groups.

The relative progress made by the countries in the three groups since 2007 in terms of deficits, gross borrowing requirements, government debt and average maturity of the outstanding sovereign debt, is shown in the Figures below. Figure 2.4 panel A shows the evolution of the average level of the deficit since 2007 (on the vertical axis) and the cumulative increase in the gross debt ratio since 2007 (on the horizontal axis) for the

Figure 2.3. **OECD general government gross debt and government deficits, 2013**

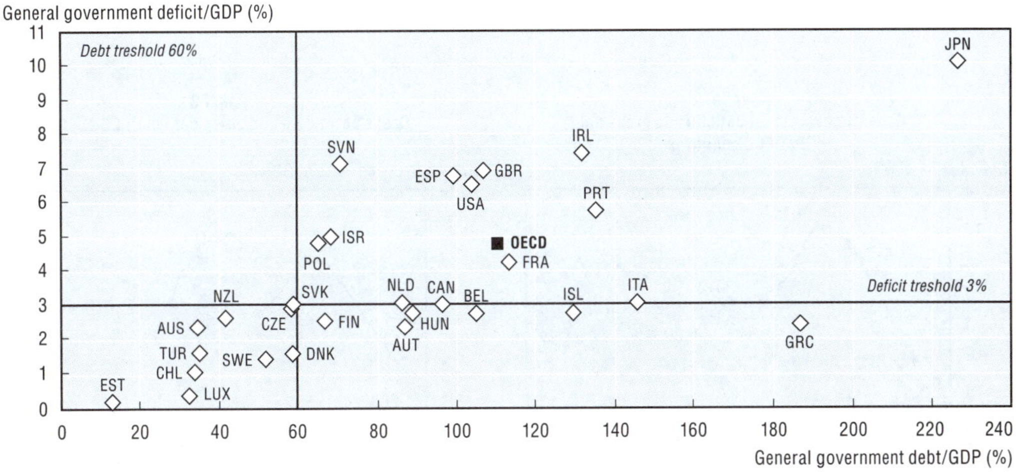

Notes: Germany, Korea, Mexico, Norway and Switzerland are not included because they show a positive fiscal balance. General government gross debt and deficits are on SNA basis.

Gross debt measures are not always comparable across countries due to a different definition or treatment of debt components. For euro area countries with unsustainable fiscal positions that have asked for assistance from the European Union and the IMF (Greece, Ireland and Portugal), the change in 2010 and 2011 in government financial liabilities has been approximated by the change in government liabilities recorded for the Maastricht definition of general government debt.

Financial balances (deficits) include one-off factors such as those resulting from the sale of mobile telephone licences. As data are on a national account's basis (SNA93/ESA95) for the OECD countries, government financial balances may differ from the numbers reported to the European Commission under the Excessive Deficit Procedure for some EU countries. For more details see OECD Economic Outlook Sources and Methods (*www.oecd.org/eco/outlook/sources-and-methods.htm*).

Source: OECD Economic Outlook 94 Database; Chile, Mexico and Turkey national data sources; and OECD staff estimates.

StatLink http://dx.doi.org/10.1787/888932993750

three groups. Figure 2.4 panel B shows the evolution of the average gross borrowing needs (on the vertical axis) and the cumulative increase in the gross debt ratio.

The average deficit of Group 1 countries initially increased (peaking in 2009), while the debt ratio continued to climb. Also gross borrowing needs as a percentage of GDP peaked in 2009. Later, in 2012, the debt ratio of Group 1 starts to catch-up with the falling deficit and borrowing needs.

The average deficit of Group 2 countries began to fall in 2011. Gross borrowing needs initially began to decrease in 2010, but showed a temporary increase in 2012, before dropping further in 2013-14. Over time, the cumulative increase in the debt ratio of Group 2 is slowing down and finally coming to a (near) stand-still.

The average deficit of most Group 3 countries has started to decline (peaking in 2010). Initially, the average gross borrowing needs fell, but since 2011 they showed again an increase. However, they are projected to fall in 2013-14. Moreover, the debt ratios of many countries from this group are still rising and/or standing at a very high level.

All three groups of countries made progress in increasing the maturity of their debt. Figure 2.5 (panels A and B) shows for Group 3 countries that after an initial decrease, the average maturity of their sovereign debt increased steadily, while remaining at a relatively high level. The average maturity of Group 2 countries dropped significantly in the period 2007-9, before rebounding (but remaining at a lower level than at the start of the global crisis). The average maturity of Group 1 countries increased steadily in the

Figure 2.4. **Evolution of deficits, gross borrowing and debt in OECD country groupings**

Percentage of GDP

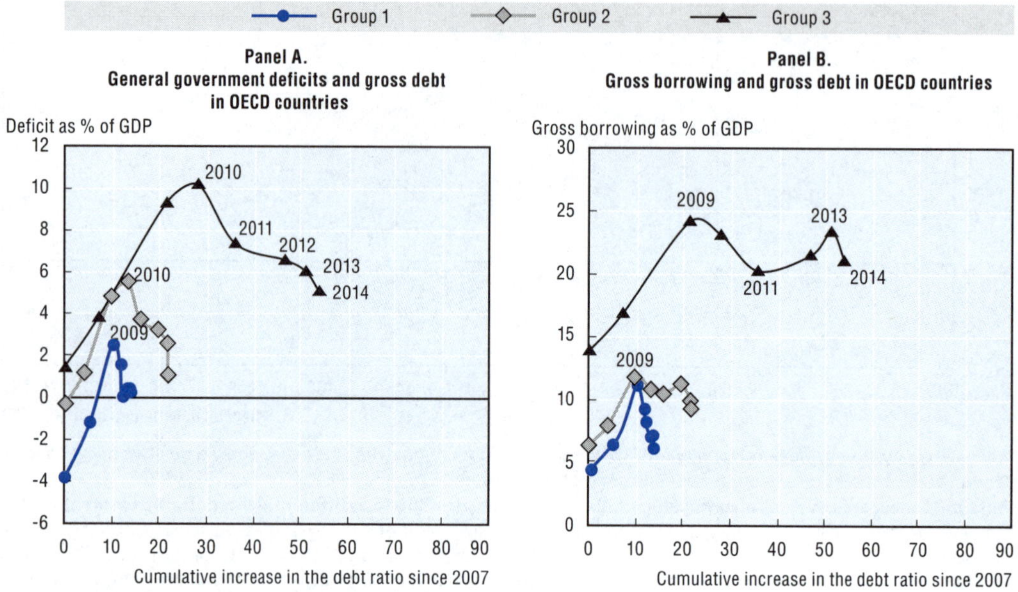

Notes: The vertical axis represents the level of the deficit starting in 2007, and the horizontal axis shows the cumulative increase in the gross debt ratio since 2007.

Group 1 includes: Czech Republic, Denmark, Finland, Germany, Iceland, Korea, Sweden, Switzerland, Chile, Estonia, Israel, Luxembourg, Norway and Turkey. Group 2 includes: Australia, Austria, Canada, Netherlands, New Zealand, Slovak Republic, Mexico and Poland. Group 3 includes: Belgium, France, Ireland, Italy, Japan, Portugal, Slovenia, Spain, United Kingdom and United States.

General government gross debt and deficits are on SNA basis. Gross Borrowing refers to central government. Gross debt measures are not always comparable across countries due to a different definition or treatment of debt components. For euro area countries with unsustainable fiscal positions that have asked for assistance from the European Union and the IMF (Greece, Ireland and Portugal), the change in 2010 and 2011 in government financial liabilities has been approximated by the change in government liabilities recorded for the Maastricht definition of general government debt.

Financial balances include one-off factors such as those resulting from the sale of mobile telephone licences. As data are on a national account's basis (SNA93/ESA95) for the OECD countries, government financial balances may differ from the numbers reported to the European Commission under the Excessive Deficit Procedure for some EU countries. For more details see OECD Economic Outlook Sources and Methods (*www.oecd.org/eco/outlook/sources-and-methods.htm*).

Source: 2013 Survey on central government marketable debt and borrowing by OECD Working Party on Debt Management; *OECD Economic Outlook 94 Database*; Chile, Mexico and Turkey national data sources; and OECD staff estimates.

StatLink http://dx.doi.org/10.1787/888932993769

period 2007-10 (although starting from a relatively low level), dropping slightly in 2011, before rebounding strongly.

The progress shown above in Figures 2.4 and 2.5 reflects to an important degree the progress with the implementation of fiscal consolidation programmes as well as public debt management policies. Additional information is given in Figure 2.6 showing the changes in general government (primary) balances for Japan, the United Kingdom, the United States and the euro area. To an important degree the fiscal policy stance and the associated public debt management strategy is driven by the threat of fiscal dominance.[10]

Figure 2.6 shows that the euro area has relatively good fiscal fundamentals, although this situation is not fully reflected in the relative levels of long-term yields. Nonetheless, the ultra-high yields in the euro area have dropped to a significant extent (Figure 2.9), while ultra-low yields in the United States and the United Kingdom

Figure 2.5. **Average term to maturity in OECD country groupings**

Years

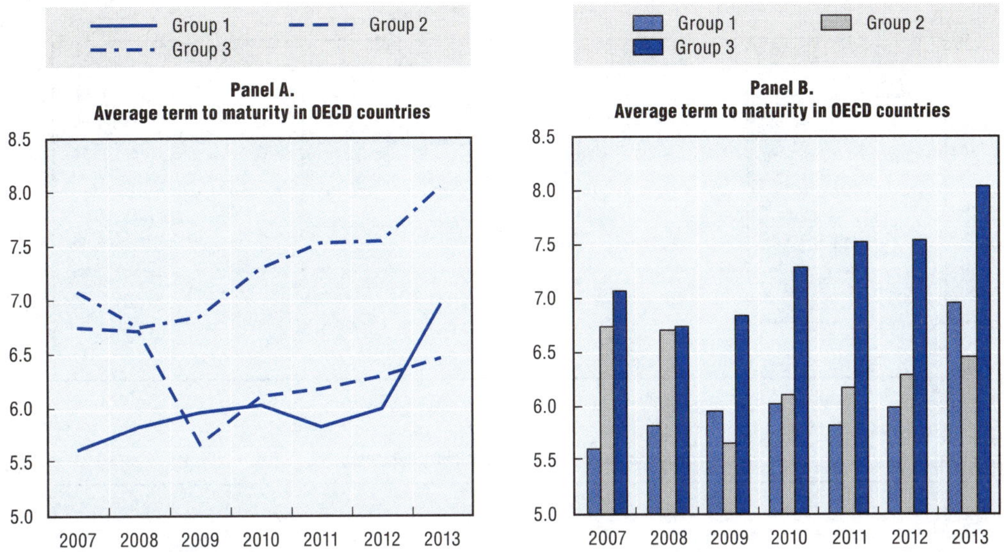

Notes: Data refers to average term to maturity on central government marketable debt.

Group 1 includes: Czech Republic, Denmark, Finland, Germany, Iceland, Korea, Sweden, Switzerland, Chile, Estonia, Israel, Luxembourg, Norway and Turkey. Group 2 includes: Australia, Austria, Canada, Netherlands, New Zealand, Slovak Republic, Mexico and Poland. Group 3 includes: Belgium, France, Ireland, Italy, Japan, Portugal, Slovenia, Spain, United Kingdom and United States.

Source: OECD, *Central Government Debt Statistical Yearbook Database;* countries' national data sources and OECD staff calculations.

StatLink http://dx.doi.org/10.1787/888932993788

increased somewhat. As a result, the long-term yields in the United States, United Kingdom and the euro area converged significantly. Accordingly, the spreads between the (weighted) euro area yield and the UK and US yields (as indicators of sovereign stress in the euro area) narrowed.

The challenging fiscal situation in several countries informs both the content and timing of fiscal consolidation programmes and the associated consequences for public debt management, notably the borrowing and funding strategy. In this context, the preferences of governments to enhance fiscal resilience play an important role in informing the sovereign borrowing and debt strategy (see OECD Sovereign Borrowing Outlook 2013).

Clearly, the relatively slow recovery in many OECD countries is making fiscal adjustment harder. This in turn means that the government borrowing needs of many OECD countries will decrease more slowly than anticipated. As noted in Chapter 1, in 2014, the borrowing needs of OECD sovereigns are projected to decrease only slightly to around USD 10.6 trillion, while general and central government debt ratios for the OECD as a whole are expected to grow or remain at high levels. Accordingly, in many OECD countries, DMOs continue to face a borrowing environment characterised by the prospect whereby the fiscal authorities will need to persist for many years with consolidation efforts if debt ratios are to be brought down to significantly lower levels.

Figure 2.6. **General government balances, sovereign debt and 10-year yields**

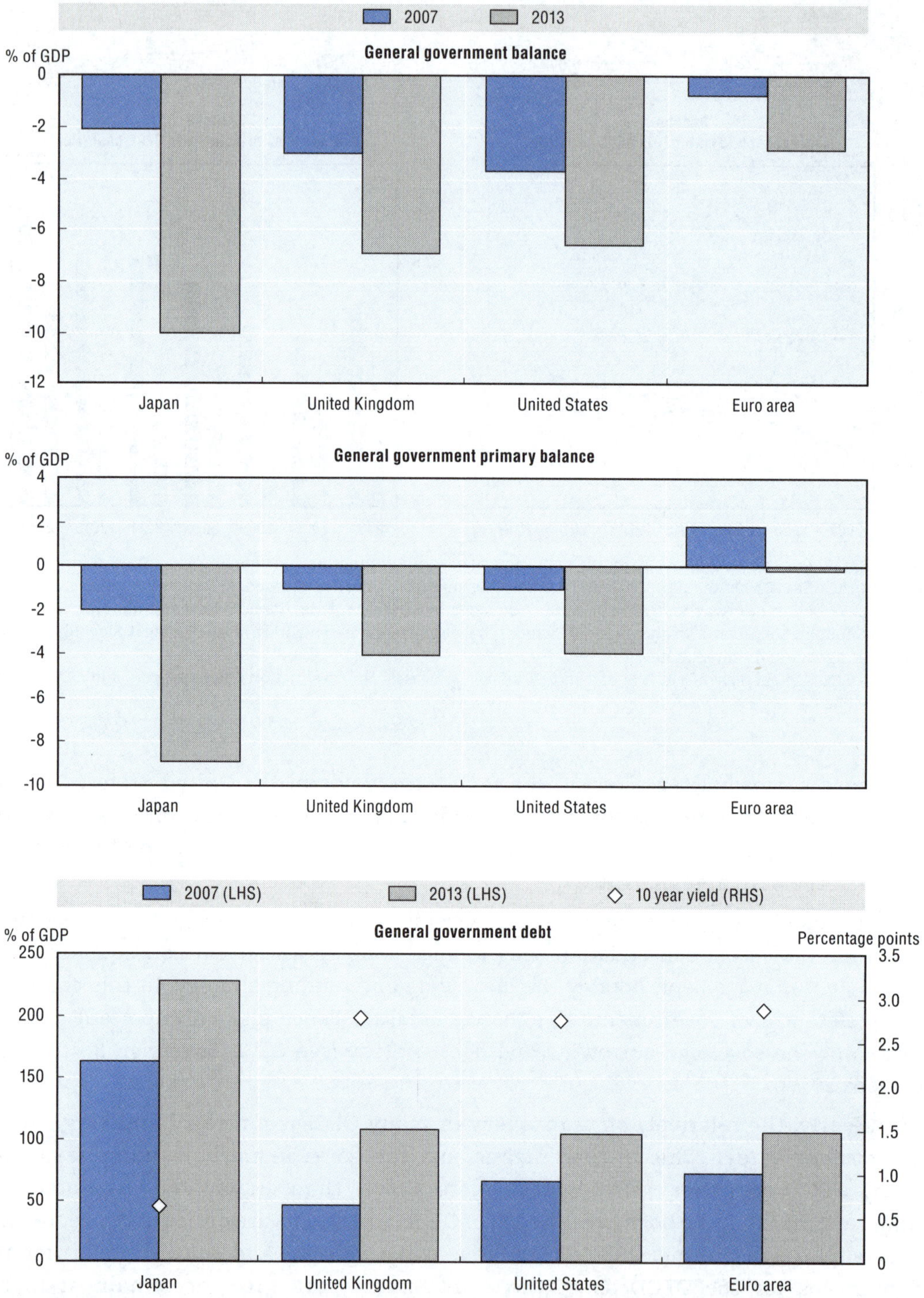

Notes: Cut-off date for GDP-weighted average 10 year government bond yield for euro area: 30 November 2013.
General government gross debt and fiscal balances are on SNA basis. Gross Borrowing refers to central government. Gross debt measures are not always comparable across countries due to a different definition or treatment of debt components. For euro area countries with unsustainable fiscal positions that have asked for assistance from the European Union and the IMF (Greece, Ireland and Portugal), the change in 2010 and 2011 in government financial liabilities has been approximated by the change in government liabilities recorded for the Maastricht definition of general government debt.
Financial balances include one-off factors such as those resulting from the sale of mobile telephone licences. As data are on a national account's basis (SNA93/ESA95) for the OECD countries, government financial balances may differ from the numbers reported to the European Commission under the Excessive Deficit Procedure for some EU countries. For more details see OECD Economic Outlook Sources and Methods (*www.oecd.org/eco/outlook/sources-and-methods.htm*).
Source: Datastream, *OECD Economic Outlook 94 Database*; and OECD staff calculations.

StatLink http://dx.doi.org/10.1787/888932993807

2.5. Overcoming extreme sovereign stress: The return to (international) longer-term markets

OECD countries that lost access to markets had no choice but to embark as soon as possible on drastic fiscal consolidation plans as part of multilateral financial support programmes.

Since November 2006, four OECD countries have lost (over time) access to the longer-term (international or domestic) funding market. Three of them (Iceland in June 2011, Ireland in August 2012 and Portugal in January 2013) have regained (partial) access (Figure 2.7). However, even when these sovereigns lost access to longer-term markets, they kept (for most of the time at least) partial access to short-term funding markets (e.g. for cash management purposes).

Figure 2.7. **Loss of access and return to the long-term funding market (international/domestic)**

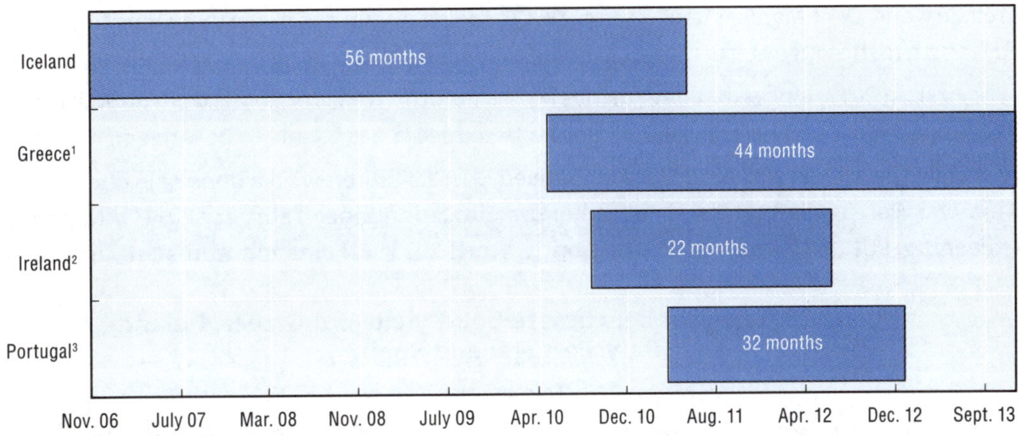

Note: Cut-off date is 30 November 2013.

1. At the cut-off date, Greece has still no access to long-term funding markets.
2. The issuance of amortising bonds by Ireland's debt management agency (EUR 1 billion of bonds via tap sale with maturities of 15, 20, 25, 30 and 35 years) in August 2012 is considered as Ireland's return to the long-term market.
3. Many analysts consider Portugal's issuance of EUR 2.5 billion bonds in January 2013 (with bonds syndicated due in 2017) as the beginning of Portugal's return to the long-term market.

Source: OECD staff calculations.

StatLink http://dx.doi.org/10.1787/888932993826

The re-entry of Iceland in the international capital markets was in June 2011 (after approximately 56 months of absence). Rating agencies graded Icelandic sovereign debt as AAA (just before the crash of its banking sector and economy in October 2008).

Moody's and Fitch confirmed their long-term ratings at Baa3 and BBB with a stable outlook as indicated in February 2013 and October 2013, respectively (see Annex B on "Methods and Sources).

However, in July 2013, Standard & Poor's (S&P) cut the outlook on Iceland's BBB- credit rating, citing concerns that the nation's plans to forgive household debt could put pressure on public finances. Accordingly, S&P affirmed its BBB- rating but revised its outlook from stable to negative.

Thus far, Iceland's Debt Management Office has issued nine long-term government debt instruments amounting to a total of approximately USD 400 million with maturities of nine and 18 years.

Greece has been frozen out of the longer term funding market since May 2010. Thus far, two economic adjustment programmes and a buyback operation have been implemented to create the conditions for a sustainable debt profile and to prepare the return to the longer term funding market (see OECD Sovereign Borrowing Outlook 2013 for details). The programme review of July 2013 noted that "The staff expects the authorities to avoid large issuances, and to avail themselves of official financing that Euro area member states have committed to provide (so long as Greece adheres to program policies), on terms that would enable this financing to play an important catalytic role in securing market re-access."[11]

Nonetheless, an important market signal was given on 4 November 2013, when the yield on 10-year Greek government bonds fell for the first time since May 2010 to below 8% (see Figure 2.8).

Portugal, which has lost access to the longer-term funding market in 2011, is the third euro area country that had to apply for EU–IMF financial assistance. In 2012, the Portuguese Treasury and Debt Management Agency (IGCP) took a number of important steps to prepare the return to the longer-term market (see OECD Sovereign Borrowing Outlook 2013 for details).

First, in 2012, longer dated securities (i.e. 18 months Treasury notes) were issued and an exchange operation was conducted in order to reduce the amounts to be redeemed in 2013.

Later, on 23 January 2013, Portugal raised EUR 2.5 billion with a bond sale due in 2017. This was Portugal's first fixed-rated bond syndication since February 2011 with orders exceeding EUR 12 billion. Moreover, on 12 April 2013, EU finance ministers agreed to

Figure 2.8. **Ten-year benchmark bond yields for Greece, Ireland, Italy, Portugal and Spain**

Percentages

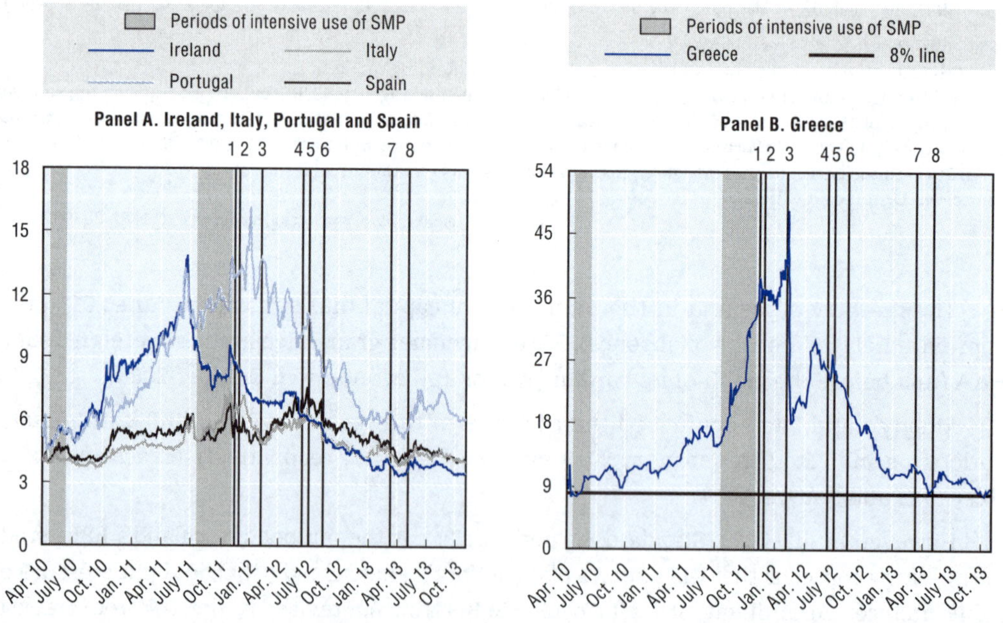

Note: Cut-off date is 30 November 2013.

1) ECB's LTRO announcement (8 December 2011). 2) First LTRO (21 December 2011). 3) Second LTRO (29 February 2012). 4) ECB set the interest rate on the deposit facility to zero % (5 July 2012). 5) Draghi's pledge to do "whatever it takes to preserve the euro..." (26 July 2012). 6) ECB's OMT announcement (6 September 2012). 7) New stage Japanese QE Programme (4 April 2013). 8) Bernanke's statement on tapering (22 May 2013).

Source: Datastream.

StatLink http://dx.doi.org/10.1787/888932993845

extend the repayment of the bailout loans to Ireland and Portugal for a further seven years, thereby decreasing the future redemption pressure on both countries (see Figures 2.10 and 2.12). These operations were regarded as crucial steps toward exiting the bailout programme and a return to longer-term funding markets.

After these successful debt management operations, IGCP raised in the beginning of May 2013 EUR 3 billion through the sale of a new 10 year benchmark government bond (with over EUR 10 billion in orders and where 86% of those orders came from non-domestic investors).

Although the international organisations involved in the Reviews of the Economic Adjustment Programme expect Portugal to regain in the near term full and regular market access, they consider this process as a "...narrow path to full market access."[12]

Despite two successful bond syndications earlier in 2013, the Portuguese spreads against Germany still remain at higher levels compared to Ireland, Italy and Spain (see Figure 2.9).

Figure 2.9. **Ten-year benchmark bond spreads[1] (Ireland, Italy, Portugal and Spain)**

Percentages

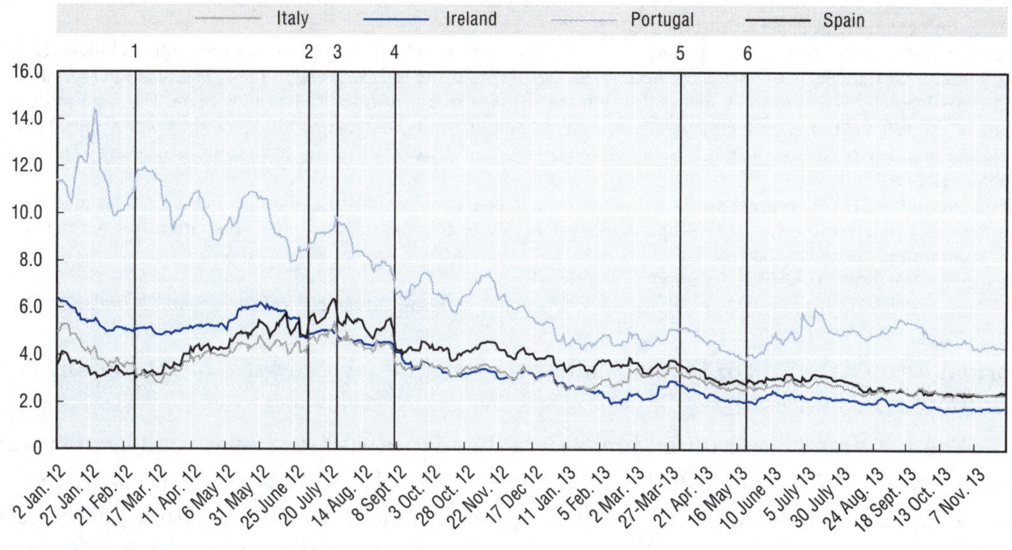

Notes: Cut-off date is 30 November 2013.
1) Second LTRO (29 February 2012). 2) ECB set the interest rate on the deposit facility to zero % (5 July 2012). 3) Draghi's pledge to do "whatever it takes to preserve the euro..." (26 July 2012). 4) ECB's OMT announcement (6 September 2012). 5) New Japanese QE Programme (4 April 2013). 6) Bernanke's statement on tapering (22 May 2013).
1. Vis-a-vis the German 10 year benchmark bond.
Source: Datastream and OECD staff calculations.

StatLink http://dx.doi.org/10.1787/888932993864

Redemptions in the next three years (2014-16) will amount to almost EUR 42 billion (see Figure 2.10). Considering this challenging redemption schedule, an official credit line may be an important financing instrument for Portugal in 2014.

Ireland regained access to borrowing in longer-term instruments in July 2012 (after approximately 22 months of absence; see Figure 2.7). Earlier this year (8 January 2013) the Irish government issued EUR 2.5 and 5 billion of long-term (with maturities of five years and 10 years respectively) bonds. The government regained full market access when it

Figure 2.10. **Changes in the Portuguese redemption profile**

Billion EUR

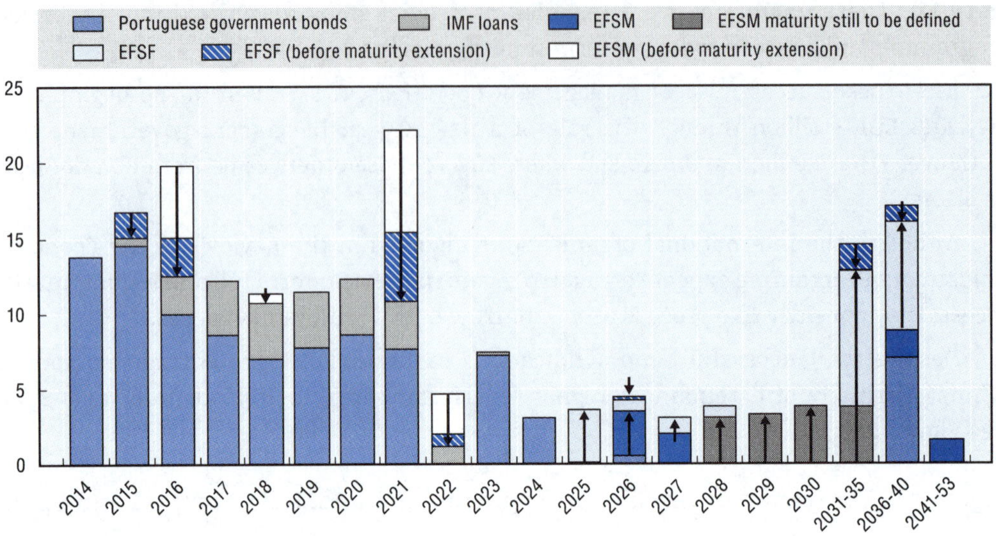

Notes: The chart is a snapshot and does not incorporate expected future borrowing operations. It does not include T-bills and commercial papers. Cut-off date is 30 November 2013.
End Oct 2013. European Financial Stability Facility (EFSF) loans reflect the maturity extensions agreed in June 2013.
On June 21 2013, ECOFIN has decided to extend the average maturity of European Financial Stabilisation Mechanism (EFSM)[13] loans by seven years, which will bring the average maturity from 12.5 to 19.5 years. The final maturity date of the EFSM loans in dark grey bars is still not defined (maturity extension will be defined when approaching original maturity of the loans), but it is therefore not expected that Portugal will have to refinance any of its EFSM loans before 2026.
On 3 December 2013,[14] Portugal performed an exchange operation amounting to around EUR 6 billion in order to reduce debt repayments due in 2014 and 2015. The impact of this debt management operation has not yet been incorporated in the above chart.
Source: IGCP and OECD staff calculations.

StatLink http://dx.doi.org/10.1787/888932993883

formally exited the EUR 67.5 billion bail-out programme (agreed with the EU, IMF and ECB in 2010) in December 2013.

The last time Ireland raised funds from the market with a regular bond auction was in September 2010, two months before the country was forced to seek a bail-out. With the worsening of the financial crisis at the end of 2010, Ireland was cut off from (full) access to Treasury bills and bonds markets and had to ask the EU-IMF for financial assistance in November 2010.

The Irish DMO (the National Treasury Management Agency or NTMA) began to implement a well-designed strategy to regain full market access during 2012. Full access to the T-bills market was regained, first, through its Treasury Bill programme. Furthermore, the Agency conducted two switching operations in January and July 2012, resulting in a reduction in funding requirements for 2013 and 2014 (see OECD Sovereign Borrowing Outlook 2013 for details). The latter liability management operations marked the beginning of Ireland's successful return to the long-term funding market.

In August 2012, the NTMA launched the first sovereign issue of amortising bonds in order to meet the needs of the local pension industry as well as to diversify the government's funding sources.

In January 2013 the NTMA raised EUR 2.5 billion of T-bonds by syndicated tap, maturing in 2017 (at a yield of 3.32%), with strong demand from Europe and the United States.

Figure 2.11. **Irish 10-year and 2-year benchmark bond yields**

Percentages

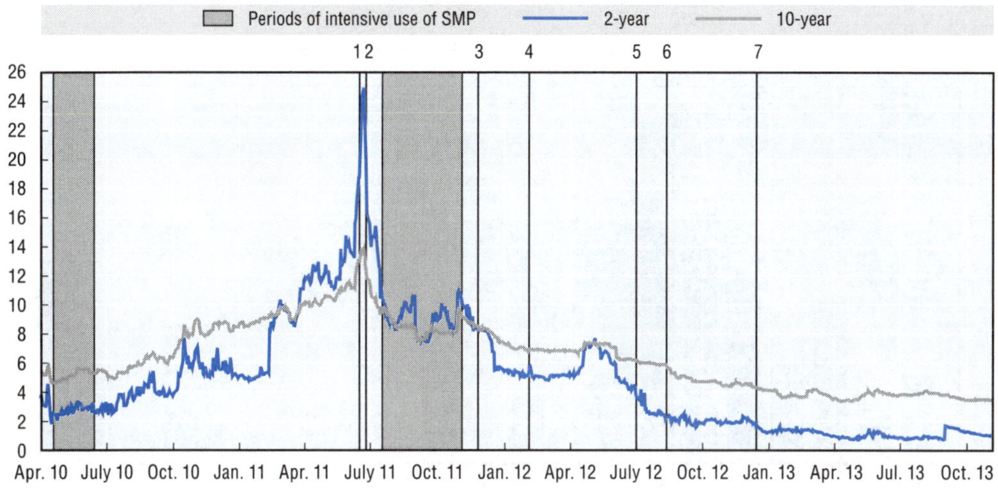

Notes: Cut-off date is 30 November 2013.

1) Moody's downgraded Ireland's foreign- and local-currency government bond ratings to Ba1 from Baa3 (12 July 2011). 2) EU/IMF loan rate reduction (21 July 2011) 3) First LTRO (21 December 2011). 4) Second LTRO (29 February 2012). 5) Draghi's pledge to do "whatever it takes to preserve the euro..." (26 July 2012). 6) ECB's OMT announcement (6 September 2012). 7) NTMA returns to the market with syndicated bond deals (8 January 2013).

Source: Datastream, NTMA.

StatLink http://dx.doi.org/10.1787/888932993902

In February 2013, Ireland and the ECB agreed on the replacement of high-interest promissory notes (amounting to EUR 28 billion) with new long-term government bonds. To this end, eight new floating rate Treasury Bonds for a total amount of EUR 25 billion were issued to the Central Bank with maturities from 25 up to 40 years. The interest rate was around 3% on average as opposed to rates above 8% on the old promissory notes. As a result, the medium-term funding needs for Ireland improved significantly when compared to earlier redemption profiles (not shown here). According to NTMA estimates, Ireland will have to borrow EUR 1 billion annually, instead of EUR 3 billion annually. As a result, near-term funding requirements are expected to fall by EUR 20 billion, while the government deficit will decrease significantly in 2014 and 2015. Furthermore, the weighted-average maturity of 34–35 years for the new floating-rate bonds implies a considerable extension of the 7-8 years average for the promissory notes. As a result, the current Irish redemption profile (Figure 2.12) is less challenging.

On 13 March 2013, the NTMA launched its second syndication of a new benchmark bond maturing in March 2023. EUR 5 billion was raised at a yield of 4.15% with total bids amounting to around 13 billion.

These syndications were important not only for the successful elimination of a so-called "funding cliff" (representing a scheduled bond repayment of almost EUR 12 billion in mid-January 2014) but also for a smooth exit from the EU/IMF Programme. Ireland aims to raise in 2013 a total of EUR 10 billion (so as to have covered in advance a full year's funding needs). After those operations the NTMA decided to suspend its monthly Treasury Bills auctions for the final quarter of 2013, while further medium/long-term bond issuances were postponed until the early part of 2014.

Figure 2.12. **Recent Irish redemption profile of government bonds, multi-(bilateral)-, and EFSF/EFSM loans**

Billion euro

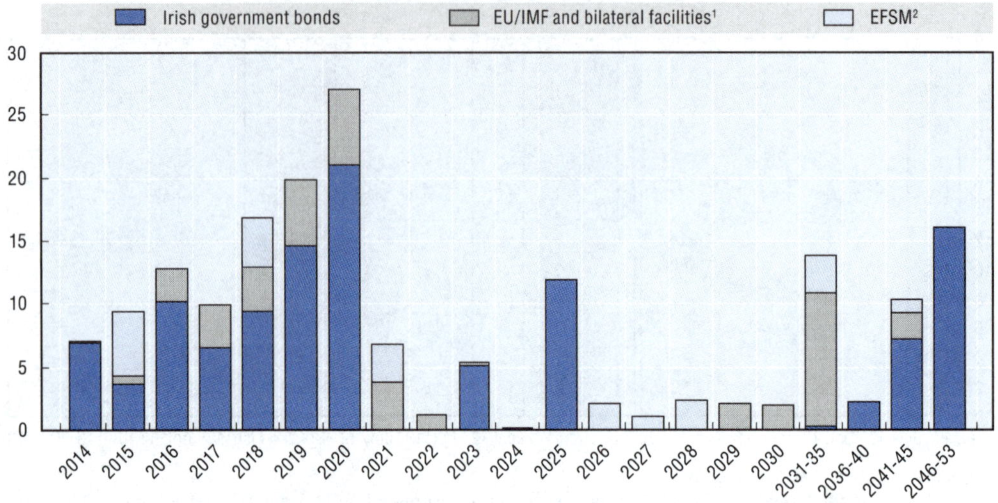

Notes: The figure is a snapshot and does not incorporate expected future borrowing operations. It does not include T-bills and commercial papers. Cut-off date is 30 November 2013.

1. EFSF loans (reflecting the maturity extensions agreed in June 2013) are included in bilateral facilities.

2. EFSM loans are also subject to a seven-year extension that will bring their weighted average maturity from 12.5 years to 19.5 years. It is not expected that Ireland will have to refinance any of its EFSM loans before 2027. However, the revised maturity dates of individual EFSM loans will only be determined as they approach their original maturity dates. EFSM loans with original maturity dates are represented by the light blue portion of the "EU/IMF and bilateral facilities" column in the graph above. It is possible that individual EFSM loans will be extended more than once in order to achieve the objective of increasing the weighted average maturity to 19.5 years.

Source: NTMA and OECD staff calculations.

StatLink http://dx.doi.org/10.1787/888932993921

2.6. Changes in the aggregate demand for and supply of safe sovereign assets

Safe sovereign assets are characterised in this report by their relatively high liquidity while they are also considered virtually default-free in nominal terms. Clearly, safe nominal government bonds are not necessarily risk free in all respects (e.g. inflation risk), because, in reality, no asset is absolutely risk free. Hence, sovereign assets are not absolutely secure but they can be considered as relatively safe or secure in terms of the (near) absence of one or more key risk dimensions.

The supply of safe sovereign assets ("information-insensitive" instruments that can serve as secure stores of value) is crucial for the functioning of the financial system. These functions include traditionally the allocation of resources (savings) and the pricing of (risk) benchmarks. But they also involve the growing importance of safe sovereign assets as a collateral (re)source in a financial landscape with a greater emphasis on its collateral intermediation function. Collateral underpins an increasing range of transactions such as hedging, securities lending, and secured funding (Claessens, Pozsar, Ratnovski and Singh, 2012).

This increase in the demand for high quality collateral is in part driven by new regulations in response to the global financial crisis. OECD Sovereign Borrowing Outlook 2013 notes that the demand for safe sovereign assets has increased due to regulatory changes, non-conventional monetary policy, greater use of high grade collateral (partly in response to regulatory measures), the build-up and management of foreign exchange reserves by central banks, the holding by the BIS of safe cash products for central banks globally, and the strong demand for liquid sovereign assets from institutional cash flows (Pozsar, 2011).[15] Accordingly, a recent report by the Committee on the Global Financial System (CGFS) estimates that the "structural" demand for safe assets can globally increase by about $4 trillion (3.1 trillion) over the next couple of years.[16] At the same time, it has been argued that the supply of "safe" sovereign assets seemingly has fallen, after credit rating agencies (CRAs) began to downgrade OECD governments. This seems to have created a widespread concern that there is a (growing) structural "shortage" of safe assets (also referred to as High Quality Assets or HQA). For example, the IMF (2012) noted that "the shrinking set of assets perceived as safe, now limited to mostly high-quality sovereign debt, coupled with growing demand, can have negative implications for global financial stability."[17] An industry group argues that there is the possibility of a (high-quality) collateral crunch.[18]

But how serious is this "shortage" issue in reality? In Chapter 2 of the OECD Borrowing Outlook 2013 critical questions were raised about the information value of sovereign credit ratings and the alleged impact of rating changes on the safety status of sovereign assets. The 2013 OECD report also argued that changes in the ratings of OECD governments have at times conflicted with price signals from markets, while concluding that it is far from obvious how rating agencies can integrate into a single consistent framework both "underlying fundamentals" (to justify changes in sovereign ratings) and "market indicators" (that, according to CRAs, may prove to be fundamentally unjustifiable). For these reasons, the argument that downgrades have led to a reduction in the supply of safe sovereign assets (and its total outstanding stock), will be more closely scrutinised.

2.7. Is there a structural shortage in the supply of safe sovereign assets?

Sovereign issuers are the largest suppliers of safe assets. Our calculations show that the supply of safe sovereign assets has increased significantly since the crisis. For example, between 2007 and 2014 the outstanding amount of AAA-rated longer-term central government debt securities data for OECD countries is projected to increase by more than $ 6 trillion.

However, as a result of downgrades, the AAA share of the total outstanding stock of OECD long-term marketable government debt is expected to fall from around 43.9% in 2007 to around 41.7% in 2014. For the calculations it is assumed that an AAA sovereign rating is a reliable measure of the "safest" sovereign assets. A sovereign issuer is then classified as "AAA" when two out of three of the major CRAs assign a triple-A rating to its government bonds. According to this calculation rule #1, French government debt lost its AAA-status in 2012, thereby reducing the triple-A fraction of the total outstanding (longer-term) marketable government debt in the OECD area from around 52.3% in 2011 to 48.2% in 2012 (see Figure 2.13). The triple-A share was further reduced in 2013 to 41.4%, due to the downgrade of the United Kingdom by two CRAs.

Presumably, this type of calculations has been used to justify the idea that there is a structural shortage in the supply of safe sovereign assets. However, there are good reasons not to take this calculation - and its underlying assumptions - too seriously.

As explained in OECD Borrowing Outlook 2013, both the concept of sovereign risk and market measures of this risk, are ill-defined. As a result, because of the link of this risk with the notion of "safe assets", these market measures are not clearly and consistently defined either. In fact, these problems in defining and measuring the degree of safety of sovereign assets also affect the definition (and measurement) of eligible collateral. For example, a recent report by the Committee on the Global Financial System (CGFS) notes that even a consistent definition of the "eligibility of (high quality) collateral assets" is

Figure 2.13. **Supply of long-term safe (AAA) sovereign assets – Rule#1**

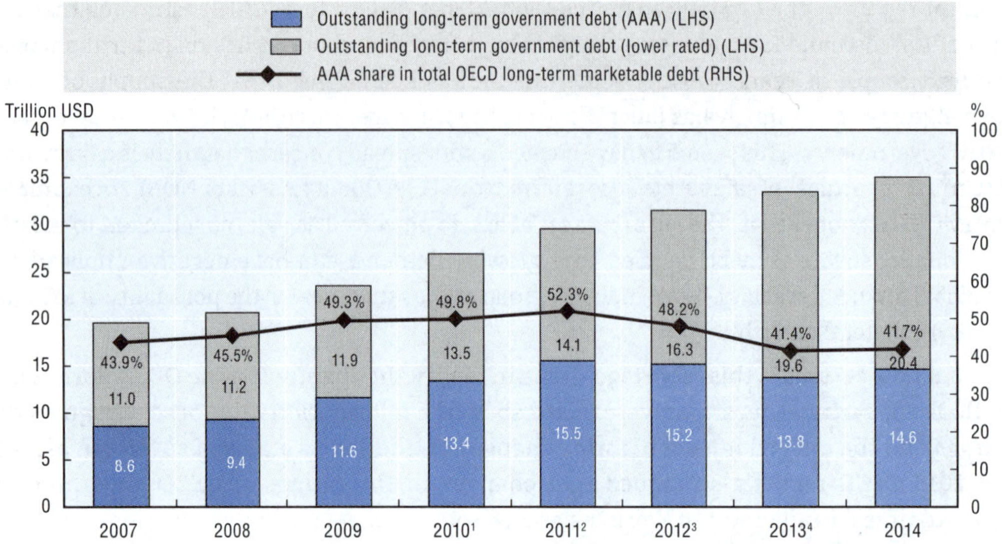

Notes: The data used for the credit rating country groupings are from the three main credit rating agencies: Moody's, Fitch and Standard and Poor's.

The classification of an issuer as AAA is based on two of three best rating grades, that is, if a sovereign issuer has been attributed triple-A by two rating agencies, the country is classified as triple-A. See for details the table with sovereign ratings in Annex B on "Methods and Sources". The cut-off date for credit ratings is 30 November 2013.

1. Downgrade of Greece (to BBB from A) and Ireland (to AA from AAA).
2. Downgrade of Ireland (to BBB from AA), Portugal (to A from AA), Spain (to AA from AAA) and Greece (to non-investment from BBB).
3. Downgrade of Italy (to BBB from AA) and Portugal (to BBB from A).
4. Downgrade of Spain (to BBB from AA), France (to AA from AAA), Portugal (to non-investment from BBB), Slovenia (to A from AA) and Hungary (to non-investment from BBB). Downgrade of United Kingdom and France (to AA from AAA).

Source: 2013 Survey on central government marketable debt and borrowing by OECD Working Party on Debt Management; credit ratings from Moody's, Fitch and Standard and Poor's and OECD staff estimations.

StatLink http://dx.doi.org/10.1787/888932993940

missing. A solution to these problems is complicated by the absence of a clear standard, while "different definitions of collateral assets exist among regulators, central banks and market participants."[19]

2.8. Reasons why the triple-A standard for assessing the alleged shortage in the supply of safe sovereign assets is not very reliable

Clearly, lack of consistency and unclear or multiple definitions are important obstacles in properly measuring and pricing the "safety" of sovereign assets (or, its counterpart, sovereign risk). Using sovereign ratings and existing market measures of this risk is therefore hazardous. For that reason, one should be very cautious in concluding that the sovereign debt of an OECD country has indeed lost its "risk-free" or "safe asset" status.

Moreover, the different measures are giving conflicting signals. The market reaction to sovereign downgrades in recent years has been quite extraordinary. Many sovereigns experienced lower bond yields in the wake of a downgrade (see Figure 2.18 in OECD's Sovereign Borrowing Outlook 2013). Naturally, also these conflicting signals (together with ill-defined concepts for sovereign risk and high-quality collateral) are raising fundamental questions about the information value of sovereign credit risk ratings and, quite crucially, the reliability or usefulness of the AAA-standard to calculate the structural shortage in the supply of safe sovereign assets.

Relying exclusively on the so-called "triple-A standard" to reliably measure the safety of sovereign assets seems, indeed, perilous. In view of these considerations, we have re-calculated the change in the supply of safe sovereign assets by relaxing the two out of three rule. The revised calculation rule #2 is the following: If a sovereign is rated by one of the major agencies as AAA or AA or A, then the asset is considered as "safe".

Using this new rule, the outstanding stock of (longer-term) triple-A-rated + double-A-rated + single-A-rated OECD government debt is estimated to reach 86.4% of total OECD long-term marketable debt in 2013 and a projected 86.7% in 2014. Figure 2.14 shows the evolution of the outstanding stock of longer-term AAA+AA+A marketable government debt in the period 2007-2014, including as a share of total longer-term marketable debt.

This data also shows that between 2007 and 2014 the outstanding amount of triple-A + double-A-rated + single-A-rated longer-term central government debt for OECD countries is estimated to increase by more than $ 11 trillion!

Not as gloomy an outlook on the "decline" in safe sovereign assets, and related alleged shortages in the supply of these assets, as some may imagine. Moreover, we are not implying that sovereign assets rated lower than A are necessarily "unsafe".

Figure 2.14. **Supply of long-term safe (AAA+AA+A) sovereign assets – Rule#2 for bonds**

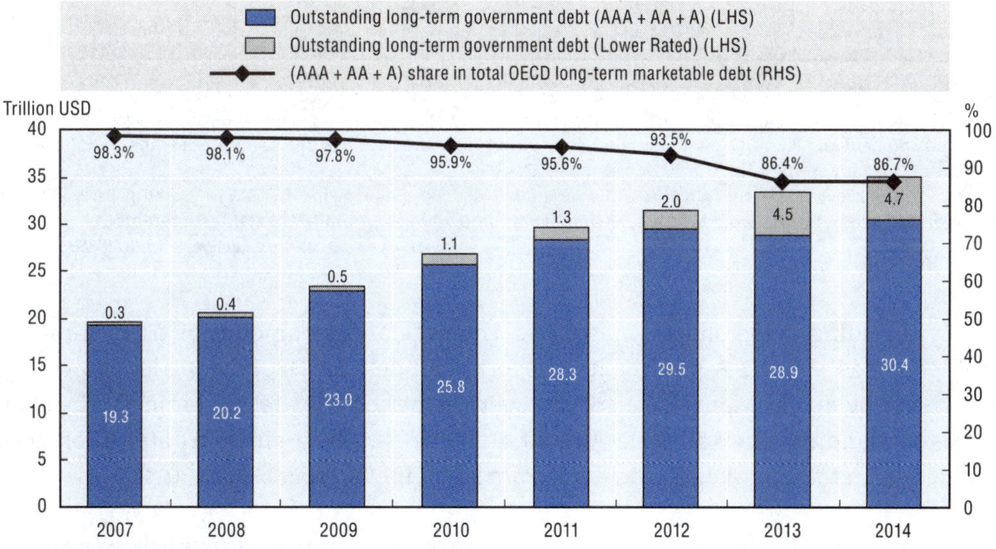

Notes: The data used for the credit rating country groupings are from the three main credit rating agencies: Moody's, Fitch and Standard and Poor's. The cut-off date for credit ratings is 30 November 2013.

Source: 2013 Survey on central government marketable debt and borrowing by OECD Working Party on Debt Management; credit ratings from Moody's, Fitch and Standard and Poor's and OECD staff estimations.

StatLink http://dx.doi.org/10.1787/888932993959

2.9. Importance of the supply of T-bills

The following considerations weaken further the notion that there is indeed a structural shortage in the supply of safe sovereign assets. T-bills play an important role in debt management (see Chapter 1 for details) as well as in cash or liquidity management by governments and central banks. The core purposes for issuing T-bills from the perspective of liability management are (1) cost effectiveness, (2) relative ease of market access and (3) investor diversification. The supply numbers in Figure 2.15 include therefore short-term instruments, largely T-bills.

Figure 2.15. **Supply of short-term safe (AAA+AA+A) sovereign assets – Rule#2 for bills**

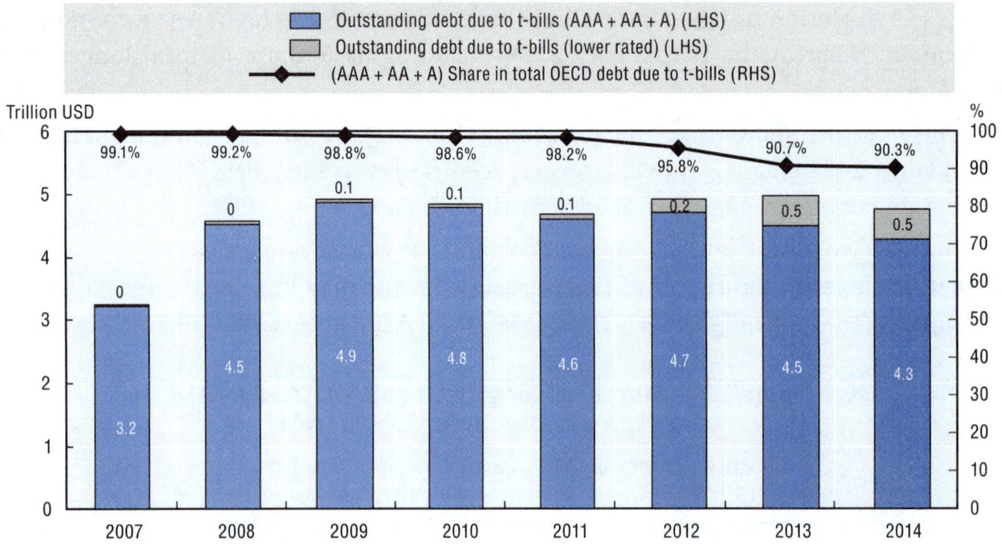

Notes: The data used for the credit rating country groupings are from the three main credit rating agencies: Moody's, Fitch and Standard and Poor's. Outstanding short-term government debt is measured as the stock at the end-of-the-year. The cut-off date for credit ratings is 30 November 2013.

Source: 2013 Survey on central government marketable debt and borrowing by OECD Working Party on Debt Management; credit ratings from Moody's, Fitch and Standard and Poor's and OECD staff estimations.

StatLink http://dx.doi.org/10.1787/888932993978

By including these shorter-maturities, the outstanding amount of triple-A-rated + double-A-rated + single-A-rated central government debt for OECD countries is projected to increase by an additional $ 1.1 trillion over the period 2007-14. Accordingly, the share of the outstanding stock of triple-A-rated + double-A-rated + single-A-rated short-term (T-bill) debt in total marketable debt fell from 99.1% in 2007 to 90.3% in 2014.

2.10. Local imbalances in the supply and demand for safe sovereign assets

The above discussion shows that there is no decisive evidence for supporting the belief that there is a lasting, structural shortage in the aggregate supply of safe sovereign assets. Nonetheless, given the uneven distribution of safe asset holdings, local and temporary supply-demand imbalances are possible. For example, market pressures at times did not so much reflect an insufficient quantity of HQAs in the aggregate but "local" collateral shortages of a temporary nature.

However, these local imbalances and associated price changes are likely to generate endogenous reactions. Endogenous policy responses are an important way for addressing real or perceived distributional imbalances of collateral (for example, via liquidity backstops by central banks). But also endogenous market responses reflect key pricing and incentives mechanisms for addressing any (perceived) local shortage of HQAs[20] For example, the more effective utilisation of available HQAs via an increase in the rehypothecation of collateral[21].

Notes

1. Benoît Cœuré (2013), The implications of bail-in rules for bank activity and stability, Opening speech at the Conference on "Financing the recovery after the crisis- the roles of bank profitability, stability and regulation", Bocconi University, Milan, 30 September.
2. Hans J. Blommestein (2013), Le Futur de L'emprunt Souverain dans un Paysage Bancaire Européen en Évolution: Moteurs, Liens et Rétroactions, in: Les Systèmes Bancaires Européens, 1. État des lieux, Revue D'économie Financière, N° 111, Septembre 2013.
3. C. Thompson (2013), Recovery hopes boost Eurozone money markets, Financial Times, 7 November.
4. IMF (2013), Global Financial Stability Report (Transition Challenges to Stability), October.
5. US Treasury (2013), Treasury Assistant Secretary for Financial Markets Matthew Rutherford, November 2013 Quarterly Refunding Statement.
6. R. Leong (2013), Analysis –Debt fight dings US Treasury bills' status, Reuters, October 17.
7. See OECD Sovereign Borrowing Outlook 2012 and 2013 for details.
8. For example, in 2011 and 2012 several governments in the euro area had to face periods with ultra-high yields (See Chapter 2 in OECD Sovereign Borrowing Outlook 2013 for details).
9. Carlo Cottarelli did a similar exercise for three groups of countries to show progress made in terms of debt ratios and deficits. [Carlo Cottarelli (2012), Taking Stock: Public Finances Now Stronger in Many Countries, Posted on his IMF blog on 9 October 2012 by iMF direct.] The figures in this report include additional OECD countries, more recent data and additional information on average maturity and gross borrowing needs (both in relation to GDP) for (cumulative) changes since 2007.
10. H.J. Blommestein and P. Turner (2012), eds., Threat of fiscal dominance?, BIS Papers No 65, BIS/OECD Publishing. See also Chapter 3 in OECD Sovereign Borrowing Outlook 2013.
11. See *www.imf.org/external/pubs/ft/scr/2013/cr13241.pdf*
12. *www.imf.org/external/pubs/ft/scr/2013/cr13324.pdf*
13. The European Commission is empowered to contract borrowings on behalf of the European Union for the purpose of funding loans made under the EFSM (Article 2 of Council Regulation 407/2010). The Commission is allowed to borrow up to a total of 60 billion in financial markets on behalf of the Union under an implicit EU budget guarantee. Under the EFSM, the borrower is the European Union. The EU enjoys an AAA credit rating from the major rating agencies. The Commission is the institution that manages the borrowing on behalf of the EU. The Commission's role in this respect is comparable to a government finance agency contracting borrowing on behalf of the country. See *ec.europa.eu/economy_finance/eu_borrower/efsm/*
14. See *www.igcp.pt/gca/index.php?id=1334*.
15. Z. Pozsar (2011), Institutional Cash Flows and the Triffin Dilemma of the US Banking System, IMF Working Paper, WP/11/190.
16. Referred to as high-quality assets (HQA) in the report by the Committee on the Global Financial System (2013), Committee on the Global Financial System (CGFS) Papers, Asset encumbrance, financial reform and the demand for collateral assets, No 49, May.
17. IMF (2012), Global Financial Stability Report.
18. S. Vecchiato (2013), Collateral crunch?, International Capital Market Association (ICMA) Quarterly Report, Issue 28, First Quarter 2013.
19. Committee on the Global Financial System (2013), CGFS Papers, Asset encumbrance, financial reform and the demand for collateral assets, No 49, May.

20. Committee on the Global Financial System (2013), CGFS Papers, Asset encumbrance, financial reform and the demand for collateral assets, No 49, May.
21. This mechanism would then increase the velocity of pledged collateral [M. Singh (2011), Velocity of Pledged Collateral: Analysis and Implications, IMF Working Paper No. 11/256.]

References

Blommestein, H.J. (2013), "Le Futur de L'emprunt Souverain dans un Paysage Bancaire Européen en Évolution: Moteurs, Liens et Rétroactions", in Les Systèmes Bancaires Européens, 1. État des lieux, Revue D'économie Financière, No. 111, September.

Blommestein, H.J. and P. Turner (2012) (eds.), "Threat of fiscal dominance?", BIS Papers, No 65, BIS/OECD Publishing.

Blommestein, H.J. and Turner P. (2012), "Interactions between sovereign debt management and monetary policy under fiscal dominance and financial instability", in H. J. Blommestein and P. Turner (2012), (eds.), Threat of Fiscal Dominance?, BIS Papers No 65, BIS-OECD Publishing.

Cœuré, B. (2013), "The implications of bail-in rules for bank activity and stability", opening speech at the conference on financing the recovery after the crisis- the roles of bank profitability, stability and regulation, Bocconi University, Milan, 30 September.

Committee on the Global Financial System (2013), "Asset encumbrance, financial reform and the demand for collateral assets", CGFS Papers, No 49.

Cottarelli, C. (2012), "Taking Stock: Public Finances Now Stronger in Many Countries", IMF blog on October 9 2012 by iMF direct.

International Monetary Fund (2013), Global Financial Stability Report (Transition Challenges to Stability), October.

Leong, R. (2013), "Analysis: Debt fight dings US Treasury bills' status", Reuters, 17 October.

OECD (2013), OECD Sovereign Borrowing Outlook 2013, OECD Publishing.

Pozsar, Z. (2011), "Institutional Cash Flows and the Triffin Dilemma of the US Banking System", IMF Working Paper, No. 11/190.

Singh, M. (2011), "Velocity of Pledged Collateral: Analysis and Implications", IMF Working Paper, No. 11/256.

Thompson, C. (2013), "Recovery hopes boost Eurozone money markets", Financial Times, 7 November.

US Department of Treasury (2013), "Treasury Assistant Secretary for Financial Markets Matthew Rutherford", Quarterly Refunding Statement, November 2013.

Vecchiato, S. (2013), "Collateral crunch?", ICMA Quarterly Report, Issue 28, first quarter 2013.

Chapter 3

Challenges for public debt management: The use of, and exit from, central bank asset purchase programmes

Sovereign debt management offices need to deal with the challenges of changes in unconventional monetary policy; a tightening of fiscal policy; and market dynamics associated with the various exit paths from Quantitative Easing (QE).

The complications generated by the increase in global volatility and long-term rates associated with confusion about the timing of the QE exit and tapering by the US Federal Reserve, constitute additional challenges for government issuers. This global volatility-cum-yield shock provides arguments for assessing carefully the potential impact of exit strategies and procedures on debt management and sovereign borrowing decisions.

The challenges for debt managers during the early stages of the monetary and fiscal exit strategy are framed against the question that bedevils almost every government: how to continue to raise smoothly new funds at a reasonable cost, while managing rollover risk and the risks associated with a still growing debt stock.

The statistical data for Israel are supplied by and under the responsibility of the relevant Israeli authorities. The use of such data by the OECD is without prejudice to the status of the Golan Heights, East Jerusalem and Israeli settlements in the West Bank under the terms of international law.

3.1. Background and Introduction

The response of governments to the global financial crisis set the stage for a surge in government deficits and (contingent) state liabilities. As a result, the issuance of government debt increased rapidly.

The rapid acceleration in sovereign borrowing needs was further boosted by the fiscal response to concerns about the possibility of a severe economic slump. In addition, the Federal Reserve (FED) and other major central banks undertook unprecedented monetary policy actions covering both extensive traditional liquidity actions and non-standard or unconventional monetary policy (UMP) measures. Central banks implemented UMP operations to affect a broad easing in financial market conditions that was aimed at providing additional stimulus to contain the fall-out of the global financial crisis and to support the economic recovery.

Now, more than five years after the Lehmann moment, there are early but still tentative signs of an economic recovery in the advanced markets. However, there is continued uncertainty about the pace or strength of the recovery and the associated asset price outlook with the degree of this outright uncertainty differing by country or region. The confusion and uncertainty about the start of FED tapering earlier in the year has shown that many emerging markets have become over reliant on loose monetary policies in advanced markets and the associated extraordinary inflows of capital.

For now, in November-December 2013, the FED and other internationally important central banks continue with both extensive traditional liquidity actions and UMP measures. Forward guidance by, among others, the FED, the European Central Bank (ECB) and the Bank of England (BOE) that policy rates will remain extraordinary low as long as the outlook for the recovery remains relatively weak,[1] plays an important role in influencing investors' expectations of future short-term interest rates.[2]

However, when Chairman Bernanke and the FED began to signal that a further and decisive improvement in economic fundamentals may (or will) prompt the FED to start tapering its monthly $85 billion bond purchases, it became apparent that these communications are more problematic than anticipated. Last year's tapering and exit signals led to extraordinary turbulence in global financial markets, especially in emerging markets (EM). Moreover, when this tapering signal was reversed to some degree by the Federal Open Market Committee (FOMC) decision on 18 September 2014, it led, initially, to even more uncertainty among market participants. The decision surprised markets, while the FED acknowledged that its communication strategy was facing new and complex challenges. Chairman Bernanke noted during his press conference that "[w]e are dealing with tools that are less familiar and harder to communicate about."[3]

Later in the year, on 18 December 2013, the FOMC meeting decided that the FED will start to taper its bond buying from January 2014.[4] This time the "tapering" decision did not lead to significant turbulence in government bond markets due to a small selloff (also in stocks). The FOMC also noted regarding future Quantitative Easing (QE) actions that: "If incoming information broadly supports the Committee's expectation of ongoing improvement in labour market conditions and inflation moving back toward its longer-run objective, the Committee will likely reduce the pace of asset purchases in further measured steps at future meetings."[5]

The negative signals from emerging economies contrasted with positive news about advanced economies, in particular the United States and some countries in Europe.

Japan announced on 4 April 2013 the new Quantitative and Qualitative Monetary Easing (QQE) framework with the radical objective to raise the inflation target to 2%. The Bank of Japan (BOJ) has also strengthened its communication strategy including through its forward guidance via its pre-commitment to continue with QQE for as long it is necessary for achieving the inflation target.[6]

The chapter will first summarise the implications and challenges of the actual use of UMP measures for (1) public debt management operations (in particular for borrowing strategies) and (2) the functioning of government securities markets.[7]

The remainder of the Chapter will then analyse in some detail the (potential) challenges for debt managers during the exit phase of the current accommodative stance of unconventional monetary policy (UMP).

3.2. Policy response to the worst global financial crisis on record

The origin, severity, and global nature of the financial shock and its aftermath made the 2007–09 global financial crisis the worst financial crisis on record. The policy response by governments set the stage for a surge in government deficits and (contingent) state liabilities.

In parallel, central banks implemented UMP operations to affect a broad easing in financial market conditions that was aimed at providing additional stimulus to contain the fall-out of the global financial crisis and to support the economic recovery. UMP programmes led to a massive expansion of Central Bank's balance sheets (see Figure 3.1).

Figure 3.1. **Central bank balance sheets for selected countries**

Percentage of GDP

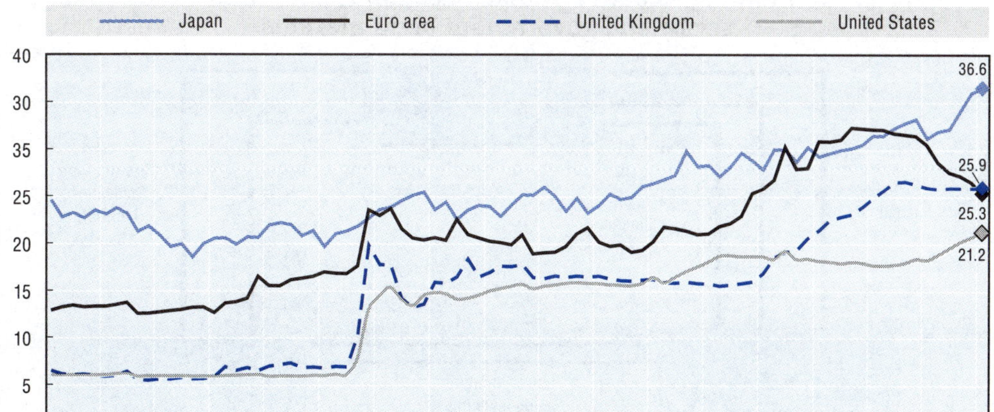

Note: Cut-off date is 28 June 2013.
Source: Datastream and IMF.

StatLink http://dx.doi.org/10.1787/888932993997

3.3. UMP operations and the demand for government securities

"Quantitative easing" (QE or LSAP),[8] "Operation Twist" (or MEP)[9] and the ECB's Outright Monetary Transactions (OMT) programme are examples of UMP operations that are having a (direct) impact on government securities markets and the broader economy.[10]

The macro framework in Figure 3.2 can be used to discuss various scenarios (or real events and policy actions) by showing key links between macroeconomic conditions, policies, the banking sector and government bond markets.

For example, the framework can be used to discuss the impact of the use of unconventional monetary policy (UMP) in response to a deteriorating macroeconomic environment, leading to lower government bond yields. One such policy action is the impact of the use of the FED's maturity extension programme (MEP; more often referred to as operation Twist) on government securities markets, whereby the US central bank sold or redeemed a total of USD 667 billion of shorter-term Treasury securities by the end of 2012[11] and used the proceeds to buy longer-term Treasury securities. This will extend the average maturity of the securities in the Federal Reserve's portfolio (while reducing the average maturity of the securities held by the public). By reducing the supply of longer-term Treasury securities in the market, this action should put downward pressure on longer-term interest rates,[12] including rates on financial assets that investors consider to be close substitutes for longer-term Treasury securities.

Figure 3.2 can also be used to show the dramatic turbulence in government bond markets since 22 May 2013 (Bernanke's testimony). The speculation about tapering (i.e., the anticipation by markets that demand by the FED will slow down due to an expected change in UMP) led to a sudden, strong upward pressure on rates (Figures 3.8 and 3.9). As noted, the FOMC decision on 18 September 2013 not to start tapering, surprised markets. Initially, yields on government bonds dropped sharply, before rebounding somewhat. Clearly, this volatility in government bond markets is complicating the funding strategies of DMOs and the management of outstanding sovereign debt.

The increase in bond yields has also produced significant capital losses[13] in banks' portfolios (see Figure 3.2).

Figure 3.2. **Main linkages between macroeconomic conditions, the banking sector and government bond markets**

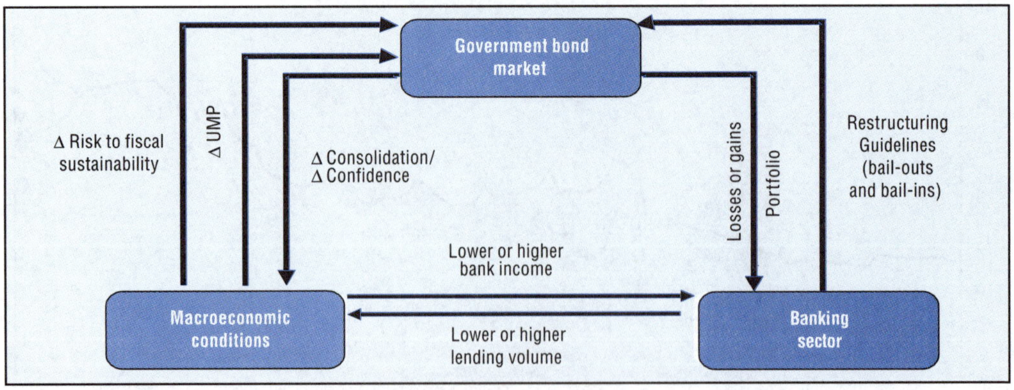

Notes: Arrows indicate the channel through which changing conditions in one area affect the other two areas.
Δ means "changes in".
Source: ECB Monthly Bulletin, August 2012 and Blommestein (2012[14] 2013[15]).

Since 2008, the demand for government securities by domestic central banks had a major direct impact on local currency government securities markets (Figure 3.2). For example, in 2011, the FED purchased 60.2% of the total net Treasury issuance (up from very small amounts prior to 2008).

Total FED Treasury holdings stand now at nearly USD 2.15 trillion (as of 20 November 2013) or 18.4% of total marketable US Treasuries (Figure 3.3).

Figure 3.3. **US Treasury securities held by the Federal Reserve**

Trillion USD

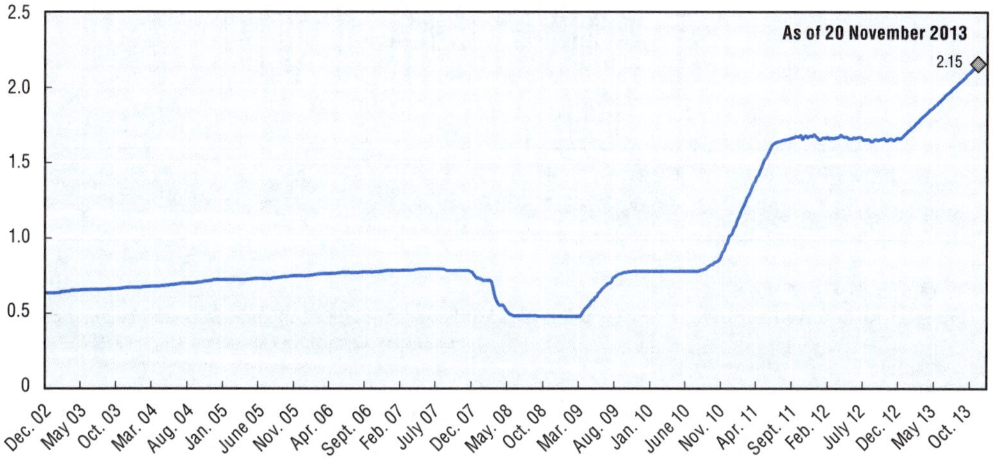

Note: Cut-off date is 20 November 2013.
Source: Board of Governors of the Federal Reserve System and OECD Staff calculations.

StatLink http://dx.doi.org/10.1787/888932994016

How much the FED owns of each Treasury maturity is shown in Figure 3.4. The US Federal Reserve owns a fairly large part of nominal Treasuries that mature in more than five years (5+). In absolute terms there are about USD 3.276 trillion Treasury issues with 5+ maturities on 20 November 2013 (the FED owns around USD 1.308 trillion of these issues or almost 40%). There is a self-imposed limit of 70% ownership for each maturity. As of 20 November 2013, the average overall ownership share of nominal issues with 5+ maturities is almost 45% (Figure 3.4). For (the much less liquid) Tips with 5+ maturities this share is almost 17%.

The new government in Japan announced in April of this year a "new phase" in their QE Programme (the new QQE regime)[16] that involves buying over Yen 7 trillion per month, equivalent to roughly 70% of total new government issuance.[17] As a result of such purchases, the amount of outstanding Japanese Government Bonds (JGBs) held by the BOJ will increase from 89 trillion yen at end-2012 to around 143 trillion yen at end-2013 and to 190 trillion yen at end- 2014 (this is a more than doubling in two years) (see Figure 3.5). In addition, the BOJ decided to more than double its average remaining maturity of JGB purchases, from slightly less than three years to about seven years.

The start of Japan's new QE phase was followed, first, by yield volatility and, then, by unexpected spikes in yields, in part related to the initial confusion about (the start of) tapering by the US Federal Reserve. This was followed by a downward trend, with the 10-year JGB yielding around 60 bps at the end of November (see Figure 3.6).

Figure 3.4. **Federal Reserve notes and bonds holdings**

Percentages

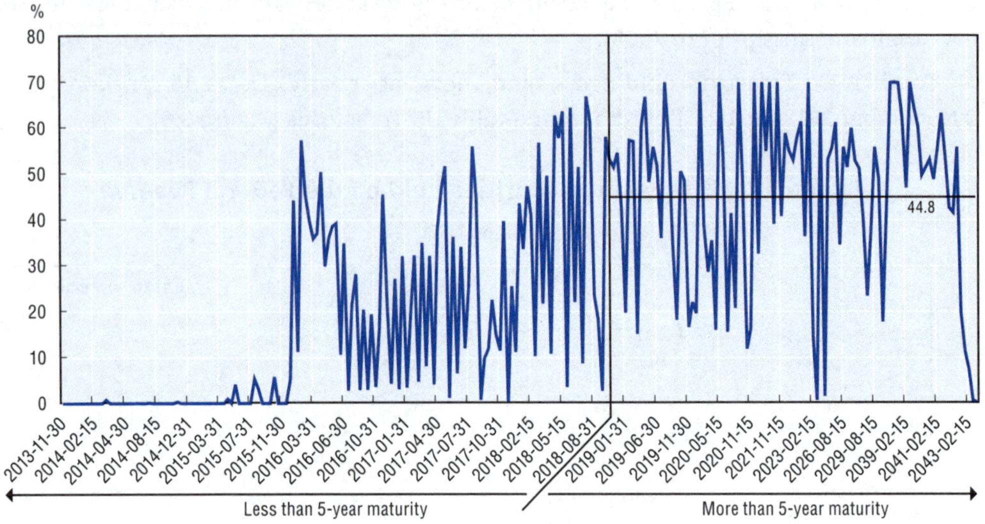

Note: Cut-off date is 20 November 2013.

Source: Federal Reserve Bank of New York (System Open Market Account (SOMA)) and OECD staff calculations.

StatLink http://dx.doi.org/10.1787/888932994035

Figure 3.5. **JGB holdings of BOJ**

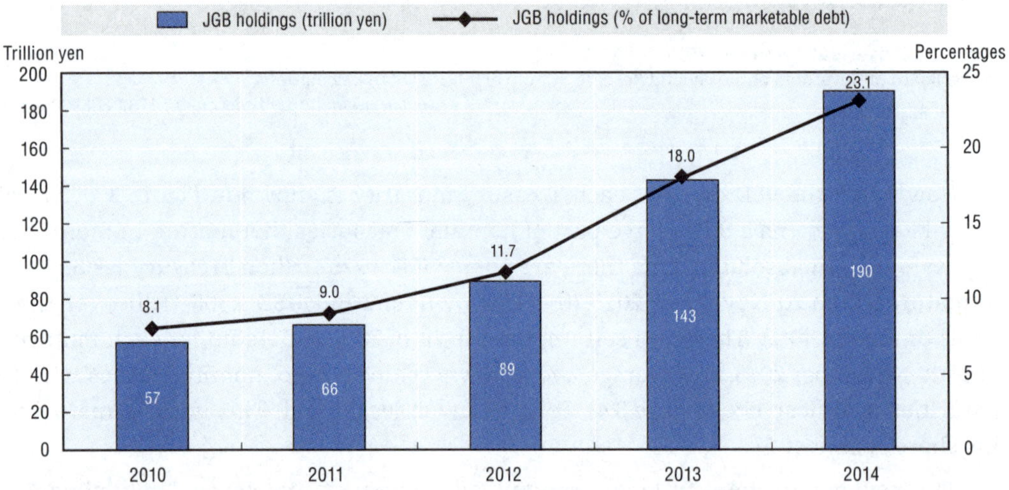

Note: Cut-off date is 10 December 2013.

Figures cover only holdings of Japan Government Bonds (JGBs). Figures for 2013 and 2014 are projections.

Source: Bank of Japan, Ministry of Finance of Japan; and OECD staff estimates.

StatLink http://dx.doi.org/10.1787/888932994054

3.4. Conflicts between UMP, sovereign issuance and market functioning?

There are potential conflicts of interest in implementing QE or MEP on the one hand, and the sovereign issuance strategy, on the other. For example, research indicates that the FED's asset purchase programmes were countervailed by the US Treasury's public debt management strategy.[18] In fact, the US Treasury's extension of the average maturity of outstanding debt during the Large-Scale Asset Purchase (LSAP) programmes pushed the 10-year government bond yield up by 27 basis points during the first stage of the programme (LSAP1) and by 14 basis points during the second stage (LSAP2).[19] In other

Figure 3.6. **10-year JGB benchmark yield and volatility**

Percentages

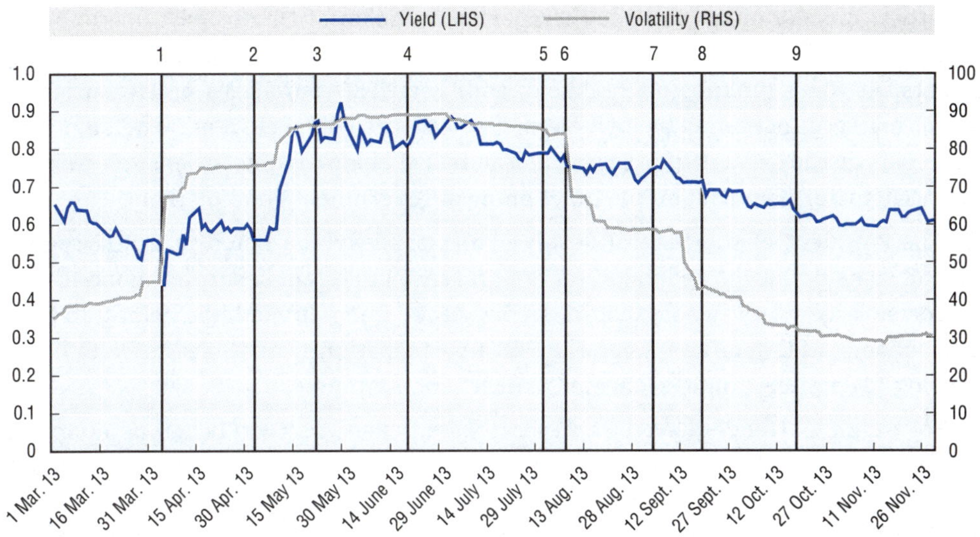

Notes: Cut-off date is 30 November 2013.

1) BOJ Aggressive QE (4 April 2013); 2) Non-farm payroll data (3 May 2013); 3) Bernanke's testimony on the US economy (22 May 2013); 4) FOMC statement (19 June 2013); 5) FOMC statement (31 July 2013); 6) ECB and BOE forward guidance announcement (7 August 2013); 7) ISM manufacturing index data (3 September 2013); 8) FOMC statement (18 September 2013); 9) US Government reopens (17 October 2013).

Historical volatility is the annualized standard deviation of the change in daily yields of 10-year benchmark government bonds. Calculation uses 90 day moving standard deviation. Yield volatility is an indicator of risk arising from movements in interest rates. High volatility suggests less predictability of daily movements in bond yields. A number near zero indicates that daily bond yields are clustered around the average yield.

Source: Datastream and OECD staff calculations.

StatLink http://dx.doi.org/10.1787/888932994073

words, the effectiveness of QE and Twist operations are constrained or limited by the public debt management strategy.

In other words, central banks and DMOs have different policy goals that sometimes may conflict. Blommestein and Turner (2012)[20] show that in the past there has been quite a strong empirical link between actual debt management choices and two simple measures of both fiscal policy and monetary policy. They provide prima facie evidence that debt management choices (in the United States at least) have been endogenous with respect to macroeconomic policy.

Also Hoogduin et al (2010, 2011) found an endogenous link in the euro area: a steepening in the yield curve leads euro area national debt managers to shorten the duration of their issuance.

From this we derive the key policy point that debt management choices seem not in practice have been independent of monetary policy.[21]

The policy tensions between the US Treasury and the Federal Reserve have been clear in the minutes of the quarterly meeting of the Treasury Borrowing Advisory Committee. On 2 November 2010, for instance, the Committee noted:

"Overall, the Committee was comfortable with continuing to extend the average maturity of the debt ... The question arose regarding whether the FED and the Treasury were working at cross purposes... It was pointed out by members of the Committee that the FED and the Treasury are independent institutions, with two different mandates that might sometimes appear to be in conflict".

Other considerations that may temper the benefits of QE or Twist operations are worries that the FED (and other central banks) will affect the efficient functioning of markets. At some (unknown) threshold, additional FED purchases of Treasuries may disrupt market functioning by lower liquidity. The size of the current ownership shares of the FED in the 5+ maturity segment (Figure 3.4) seem significant enough to have a (potential) material impact on the functioning of government bond markets.

The President of the Federal Reserve Bank of Cleveland noted in a 2012 speech[22] "that, at some point, the Federal Reserve's presence in certain securities markets would become so large that it would distort market functioning. It would be helpful to have a better understanding of how large the FED's participation would have to be to cause a meaningful deterioration in securities market functioning."

For example, traders have at times expressed concerns that Twist operations may reduce liquidity in the short-term funding market. Since operation Twist was launched on 21 September 2011, primary dealer holdings of Treasury paper have increased significantly; most of it with a short maturity (3 years and lower). Figure 3.7 shows the upward trend of total holdings since the first week of October 2011 till the end of December 2012; in that same period, short-term holdings as a percentage of total primary dealer holdings increased from 76% on 12 October 2011 to 89% on 26 December 2012; this percentage was 97% on the 11th of December 2013. On the other hand, the amount of short term holdings began to decrease starting from the end of 2012 to December 2013 (on 11 December this was around USD 24 billion).

Twist operations mean that the Central Bank will no longer buy newly issued government bonds at US Treasury auctions. The implication is that these on-the-run issues could trade at a premium in the repo market, thereby posing a challenge to

Figure 3.7. **Primary dealer net outright position in government securities**

Billion USD

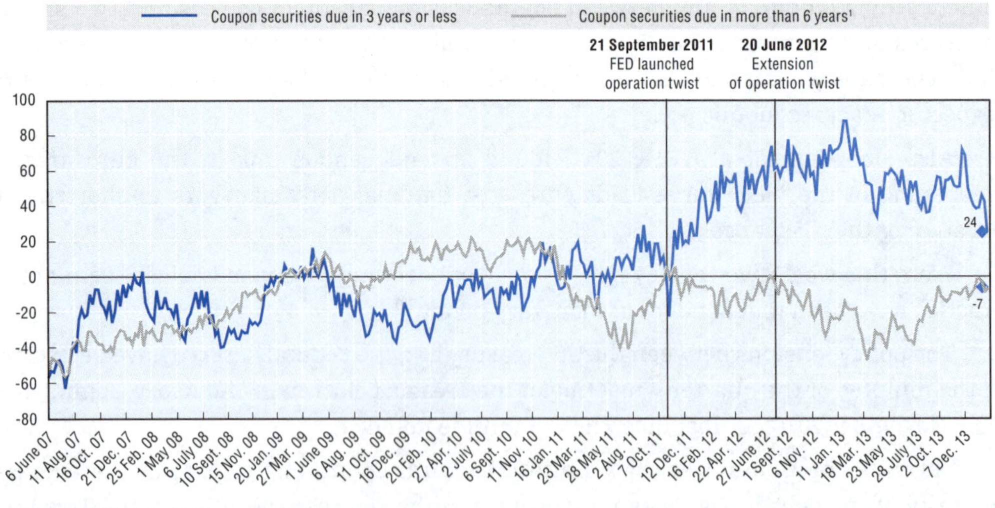

Note: Cut-off date is 11 December 2013.

1. But less than or equal to 11 years.

Source: Federal Reserve Bank of New York (FRBNY) and OECD staff calculations.

StatLink http://dx.doi.org/10.1787/888932994092

market liquidity. A second implication of Twist for market liquidity is that after end of this operation (at the end of 2012), the FED held few short-dated Treasury securities that mature through to January 2016 in its System Open Market Account (SOMA). Without SOMA as a backstop in the repo market, the repo market may become more volatile. Moreover, the FED will be hampered in its function of rolling over any maturing securities into (new) on-the-runs. Hence, Twist reduces the FED's role in helping alleviate liquidity pressures for off-the-run (older) Treasury securities.

3.5. Sovereign borrowing and future exit policies create a new set of challenges

Some of last year's exit signals (first given by Bernanke in his speech with Q&A session on the 22nd of May 2013 and repeated and highlighted during the FOMC meeting on 19 June 2013) led to turbulence and significant repricing in global bond markets, especially in emerging markets (EM) and perceived "safe haven" markets. Borrowing costs in these economies climbed to the highest since October 2011 as investors continued to fret that the end of US monetary stimulus would exacerbate sluggish economic growth in the developing world. Most emerging market currencies fell against the US dollar, while yields drifted upward. However, after the FOMC meeting of 18 September 2013, where it was decided that tapering will be postponed, emerging market assets recovered somewhat.

The OECD[23] indicated in its Interim Economic Assessment that unconventional monetary policy remains key to supporting demand in advanced economies (with differentiation in policy settings reflecting differences in progress towards recovery). Although the OECD notes that it would be appropriate for the FED to gradually reduce the rate of bond purchases (while keeping policy rates low in line with existing forward guidance), monetary easing in Japan should continue and supportive monetary conditions should be maintained in the euro area.

The IMF observes that some parts of UMP (such as forward guidance and the rate of future asset purchases) are likely to be adjusted well before any assets are sold. Hence, "the exit from UMP is likely to be slower and longer than is often portrayed..."[24]

Fiscal exits, in the form of fiscal consolidation programmes, have started. Highly indebted governments that are facing significant market pressures in the form of ultra-high borrowing costs have little choice but to proceed rapidly with the implementation of consolidation plans. Other indebted countries need to implement austerity measures as part of medium-term fiscal adjustment programmes so as to avoid (or minimise) exacerbating adverse feedback loops with the real economy.

The functional link between fiscal policy and Public Debt Management (PDM) means that fiscal consolidation has a direct quantitative impact on the borrowing operations by DMOs. Borrowing needs will decrease, thereby reducing the pressure on the funding strategies of DMOs. However, DMOs have to tackle additional and specific policy issues in the market for government securities (see below).

3.6. DMOs have a great interest in a smooth exit

A looming challenge for DMOs is the risk that when the recovery gains traction and risk aversion falls further, yields will start to rise significantly. Market stress may be further aggravated by the exit implications of monetary policy shifts, creating additional complications for the debt management strategy. Exit measures, via unwinding of unconventional monetary policy measures, reverse repos, or raising official rates, must therefore be carried out with great prudence. Recent experiences have also shown that ensuring proper communications about these unwinding measures is a great challenge. Misunderstood messages can lead to a premature increase in longer-term borrowing rates triggered by shifting market expectations (see the discussion below). Central banks are facing extraordinary expectation-formation challenges.

In sum, the sovereign borrowing strategy would be very much complicated when sovereign issuers would have to face disorderly shocks and market stress as a result of the exit. DMOs have therefore a great interest in a smooth exit strategy (that includes the proper management of highly sensitive communications via forward policy guidance) as this shapes importantly the issuance conditions.

3.7. The challenge of higher US rates and impact on borrowing conditions elsewhere

The termination of central bank purchase programmes, and the associated selling of assets acquired by central banks during quantitative easing programmes, would mean that continued strong government issuance would take place without market support by the central bank, leading to an upward pressure on market rates (which may of course be desirable from a monetary policy point-of-view). Especially where unwinding (tapering of future asset purchases or selling of public assets) is executed in situations where continued strong government debt issuance in the near future can be expected (i.e. especially at the start of the recovery and/or when fiscal exit strategies are postponed or take more time than expected to execute them),[25] sovereign issuers may face significant challenges.

What happens with borrowing rates in individual countries is dependent on underlying fundamentals (including the stance of monetary and fiscal policy) and market dynamics not related to changes in fundamentals including fluctuations in market psychology (animal spirits). For example, a recovery and associated return to (more) normal market circumstances would probably mean that prevailing ultra-low rates in so-called flight-to-safety countries will increase (Figure 3.9), while ultra-high rates would fall (see Figure 2.9 section 2.5).

However, (expectation about imminent) exits could also rock (government) securities markets by pushing-up longer-term rates in government bond markets more strongly than desirable or warranted. The recent turbulence (in May/July) in financial markets highlights the crucial role of central banks in shaping expectations and market performance. Indeed, recent FED communications have led to a significant shift in global market expectations.

Figure 3.8 shows the impact of the 19 June 2013 FOMC meeting in which Governor Bernanke indicated that the pace of asset purchases would probably be moderated later in the year (usually referred to as FED tapering). This message was already hinted at during the May 22nd testimony by the FED Chair. The resulting increase in longer-term rates, however, was considered as premature (and higher than warranted based on standard estimates).[26] An increase in interest rates could already be detected in early May in the wake of better economic news starting with stronger non-farm payrolls' data[27] (Figure 3.8).

Figure 3.8. **US Treasury bond yields (2-year and 10-year)**

Percentage

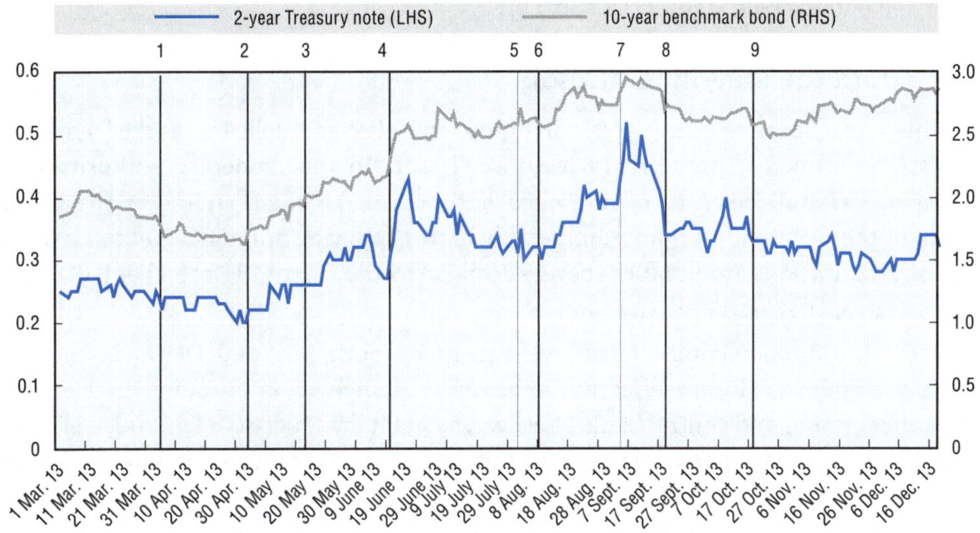

Notes: Cut-off date is 18 December 2013.

1) BOJ Aggressive QE (4 April 2013); 2) Non-farm payroll data (3 May 2013); 3) Bernanke's testimony on the US economy (22 May 2013); 4) FOMC statement (19 June 2013); 5) FOMC statement (31 July 2013); 6) ECB and BOE forward guidance announcement (7 August 2013); 7) ISM manufacturing index data (3 September 2013); 8) FOMC statement (18 September 2013) 9) US Government reopens (17 October 2013).

Source: Datastream.

StatLink http://dx.doi.org/10.1787/888932994111

Figure 3.9. **Government bond yields (France, Germany, Italy and United Kingdom) 10-year benchmark bond**

Percentage

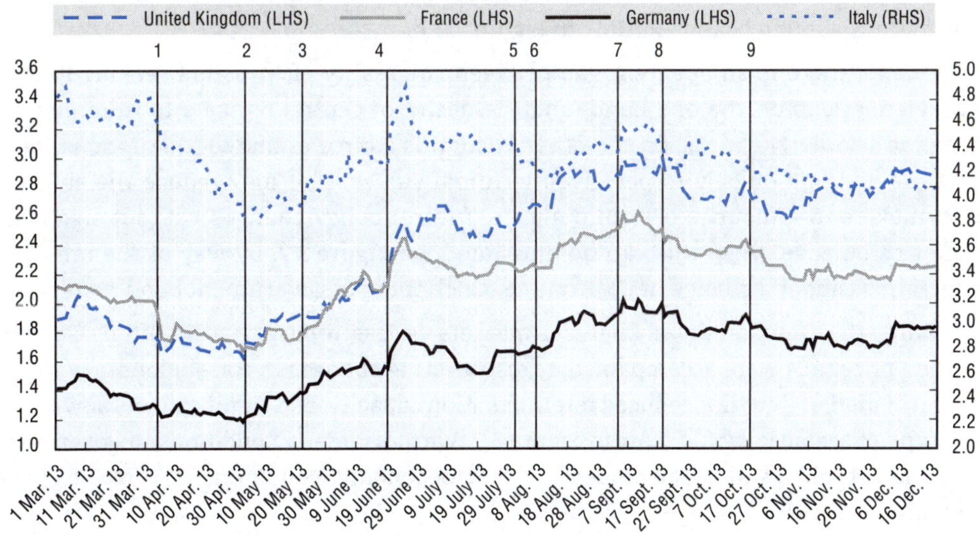

Notes: Cut-off date is 18 December 2013.

1) BOJ Aggressive QE (4 April 2013); 2) Non-farm payroll data (3 May 2013); 3) Bernanke's testimony on the US economy (22 May 2013); 4) FOMC statement (19 June 2013); 5) FOMC statement (31 July 2013); 6) ECB and BOE forward guidance announcement (7 August 2013); 7) ISM manufacturing index data (3 September 2013); 8) FOMC statement (18 September 2013); 9) US Government reopens (17 October 2013).

Source: Datastream.

StatLink http://dx.doi.org/10.1787/888932994130

FED tapering communications (including the FOMC decision on 18 September 2013) had both a major impact on financial markets and borrowing conditions inside the United States and outside (See Figures 3.8 and 3.9).

3.8. Lessons from the May-June turmoil

This increase in volatility, reflecting quite complex and delicate market dynamics, suggests a number of preliminary lessons. First, both the monetary authorities and market participants need to have a clear and common understanding of the market impact of the different exit programmes (including tapering announcements). It seems that communications around the tapering decision by the FED of 18 December (2013) were more effective than earlier in the year.

Second, a proper communication strategy by both CBs and DMOs is therefore essential, supported by an effective two-way exchange of information between the government issuer and central bank. However, as noted by Chairman Bernanke, effective communications with markets is a great challenge as tapering and exit strategies are less familiar tools.

With proper planning, effective exit tools,[28] good communications, and a transparent borrowing strategy with issuance calendar, tapering and asset sales by CBs are not necessarily disruptive. However, the recent turmoil in government securities markets prompted by heightened expectations of imminent tapering in the rate of asset purchases by the US central bank is a warning that the exit may not be as smooth as hoped for.

In this context, there are three additional lessons from the market disruptions in the May-June period for the functioning of government securities markets. First, confusions about expectations by market participants may reduce the ability of policymakers to announce or communicate (future) policy changes without generating considerable market turmoil. (This can be interpreted as a government bond market reaction to expectations about a change in UMP in Figure 3.2.)

Second, there is an apparent gap between the reality of investors seeking to price final destinations on the one hand, and the desire of central bankers to minimise the scope for disorderly shocks, on the other. Also, this source of market disruptions, "with investors jumping quickly to perceived terminal values....",[29] may reduce the ability of policymakers to announce or communicate (future) policy changes without significant market turbulence. (Also this can be illustrated via Figure 3.2. by way of the impact of expectations about a change in UMP on the functioning of government bond markets.)

Third, the functioning of financial markets is less robust than is often assumed. "Sudden price falls were accompanied by discomfiting changes in correlations, a worrying erosion of market liquidity, reduced intermediation capacity, and significant outflows ....".[30] This type of scenario would start in Figure 3.2. with disorderly conditions in government bond markets followed by an impact on macroeconomic conditions (a threat to lower economic activity.)

Clearly, these lessons are not only important for central bankers, but also for debt managers (since they are operating in the same markets).

Against the backdrop of these market challenges it is of interest to note that, at a relatively early stage, Bernanke (2010) had commented on (additional) securities purchases and noted that "substantial further expansions of the [FED's] balance sheet could reduce public confidence in the FED's ability to execute a smooth exit from its accommodative policies at the appropriate time."[31] For this reason, the FED has developed a suite of tools to ensure (or at least contribute to) a smooth exit,[32] while providing maximum clarity about how and when these exit methods will be used, including state-contingent forward guidance.

3.9. Sound sovereign debt management needs to be part of a credible overall exit strategy

The overall exit strategy is focused on a return to a normal policy stance regarding fiscal policy,[33] monetary conditions and public debt management and borrowing operations. Exit challenges (for CBs and fiscal policymakers) are to an important degree a function of (i) its starting point (e.g. the size of the balance sheets of CBs, levels of interest rates, size of government deficits and sovereign debt), (ii) expectations about the timing and pace of the monetary and fiscal exit, and (iii) market dynamics during the exit.

DMOs, operating in the same markets as CBs, need to deal with the implications of both changes in the monetary and fiscal policy stance as well as market dynamics associated with the exit paths for their borrowing strategy. As noted, this may be quite challenging. Moreover, the sovereign borrowing outlook in each year since 2007 was surrounded by an unusually high degree of uncertainty because the exact timing and strength of the recovery remained highly indeterminate. This in turn affected (uncertainties around) the fiscal policy stance and the size of government borrowing requirements.

Sound sovereign debt management will need to be part of the overall macroeconomic exit strategy in order to (i) contain the acceleration in market fears about the alleged increase in sovereign risk, (ii) mitigate possible contagion dangers, and (iii) contribute to the overall consistency of the macro policy mix. In other words, skilful debt management (supported by a transparent monetary exit[34] and a prudent fiscal strategy[35]) is needed to address overly negative market sentiments and uncertainties surrounding fears about an increase in sovereign stress. Failure to do so may not only affect adversely the credibility of the overall monetary and fiscal exit strategy, but it may also prompt a return to dysfunctional markets, including higher stress in inter-banking markets and sovereign debt markets.

The challenges for debt managers during the early stages of the monetary and fiscal exit strategy are framed against the question that bedevils almost every government: how to continue to raise smoothly new funds at reasonable cost, while also managing rollover risk and the risks associated with a still growing debt stock?

3.10. Return to a more transparent and predictable issuance framework aimed at lower rollover risk

DMOs are not only facing challenges due to the (potential) impact of the monetary and fiscal exit measures on markets. They may also have to exit themselves from policies and procedures introduced during crisis periods. DMOs need to worry about when and how quick to reverse opportunistically introduced issuance procedures. In other words, when and how rapidly should DMOs return to a more transparent and predictable issuance framework? (A structure at least as transparent and predictable as before 2008 or perhaps even more so.[36])

In response to liquidity pressures, rapidly rising borrowing requirements and strongly risk-averse investor behaviour, debt managers were initially forced to modify their fund raising strategies.[37] Most notably, many DMOs have become more flexible and opportunistic. This shift, while understandable, creates risks. Issuance programmes became less predictable, which is not desirable in the long term. The exit strategies for DMOs need therefore to include a return to a less opportunistic issuance strategy. A transparent debt management framework and a strong communication policy are instrumental in reducing the type of market noise that can unnecessarily lift borrowing costs.[38]

The other key challenge is rollover risk. Initially, governments responded to their rapidly increasing borrowing needs by tapping to an important degree the short term debt markets. Almost 60% of gross borrowing needs for 2009, for example, were covered using short-term debt instruments. This trend lowered average maturities and created more challenging repayment schedules. In response, many OECD DMOs began to rebalance the profile of their issuance programmes by selling more long-term instruments. This shift reflects the need to create a more sustainable and balanced medium-term issuance profile. However, as explained above, this shift to the supply of longer-term paper may constitute a conflict with the objectives of non-standard monetary policy. This policy tension is likely to abate when CBs seriously begin to exit UMP and reduce the size of their balance sheets.

Notes

1. Earlier this year (in July 2013) also the BOE has adopted forward guidance as a policy tool [C. Giles and R. Wigglesworth (2013), Bank of England tries out "forward guidance" earlier than expected, Financial Times, 4 July.] Also the unprecedented pledge by the ECB to keep the key rates at or below their current record lows is a recent (in July 2013) major intellectual shift in their communication policy [M. Steen (2013), Federal Reserve pioneers prompt ECB to get experimental, Financial Times, 4 July]. Forward guidance by the Bank of Japan (BOJ) and the BOE is based, broadly speaking, on the FED strategy whereby policy guidance is linked to specific variables (targets) in the economic news flow (improvements in labour markets and economic activity; expectations of continued low inflation; benign financial conditions).
2. B. S. Bernanke (2013), Communication and monetary policy, Speech at the National Economists Club Annual Dinner, Herbert Stein Memorial Lecture, Washington DC, 19 November.
3. Transcript of Chairman Bernanke's Press Conference on 18 September 2013 (FOMC Meeting). However, a few months later Bernanke noted that the September 2013 decision by the FOMC ".. appears to have strengthened the credibility of the Committee's forward rate guidance..." [B. S. Bernanke (2013), ibid.]
4. The press release following the 18 December 2013 FOMC meeting stated: "Beginning in January [2014], the Committee will add to its holdings of agency mortgage-backed securities at a pace of $35 billion per month rather than $40 billion per month, and will add to its holdings of longer-term Treasury securities at a pace of $40 billion per month rather than $45 billion per month."
5. The press release also noted the following conditions regarding future QE actions: "However, asset purchases are not on a pre-set course, and the Committee's decisions about their pace will remain contingent on the Committee's outlook for the labour market and inflation as well as its assessment of the likely efficacy and costs of such purchases."
6. IMF (2013) 2013 Article IV Consultation with Japan, Concluding Statement of the IMF Mission.
7. Hans J. Blommestein (2012), "Challenges for Debt Managers during the Entry and Exit of Standard and Non-Standard Monetary Policy", Lecture at the seminar on "Government Debt Management: New Trends and Challenges" organised by Central Banking Publications, Christ's College, Cambridge University, United Kingdom,11–14 September.
8. The FED refers to QE as the Large-Scale Asset Purchase (LSAP) Programme.
9. Also referred to by the FED as the Maturity Extension Program (MEP).
10. The reduction in longer-term interest rates, in turn, will contribute to a broad easing in financial market conditions that will provide additional stimulus to support the economic recovery. [Source: Website of The Board of Governors of the Federal Reserve System: Maturity Extension Program and Reinvestment Policy (accessed on 1 August 2012).]
11. USD 400 billion over the period ending in June 2011 and a USD 267 billion extension through the end of 2012.

12. Via the direct impact on the term premium.
13. For example, estimates by the US Federal Reserve suggests capital losses of around 10% for US bond holders through early summer 2013 (ECB, Financial Stability Review, November 2013).
14. Hans J. Blommestein (2012), Challenges for Debt Managers during the Entry and Exit of Standard and Non-Standard Monetary Policy, Lecture at the seminar on Government Debt Management: New Trends and Challenges, held on 11-14 September 2012, at Christ's College, Cambridge University, United Kingdom, and organised by Central Banking Publications.
15. Hans J. Blommestein (2013), Challenges for Debt Managers during Central Bank Exit Strategies, Lecture at the seminar on Government Debt Management: New Trends and Challenges, held on 10-14 September 2013, at Christ's College, Cambridge University, United Kingdom, and organised by Central Banking Publications.
16. This new quantitative and qualitative monetary easing (QQE) programme has both a quantitative aspect (such as increasing the monetary base and the amount outstanding of the Bank's JGB holdings) and a qualitative aspect (such as extending the average remaining maturity of the Bank's JGB purchases). (Haruhiko Kuroda (2013), Japan's economy and monetary policy – toward overcoming deflation, Speech by the Governor of the Bank of Japan, at a meeting held by the Naigai Josei Chousa Kai (Research Institute of Japan), Tokyo, 29 July 2013.
17. J. Noble (2013), Bank of Japan acts to stem rising JGB yields, Financial Times, May 15.
18. T. Ehlers (2012), The effectiveness of the Federal Reserve's Maturity Extension Program – Operation Twist 2: the portfolio rebalancing channel and public debt management, in: H.J. Blommestein and P. Turner (2012), eds., Threat of fiscal dominance?, BIS Papers No 65, BIS/OECD Publishing.
19. Jack Meaning and Feng Zhu (2012), The impact of Federal Reserve asset purchase programmes: another twist, BIS Quarterly Review, March 2012.
20. Blommestein, H. J. and P. Turner (2012), "Interactions Between Sovereign Debt Management and Monetary Policy Under Fiscal Dominance and Financial Instability", in: H.J. Blommestein and P. Turner (2012), eds., Threat of fiscal dominance?, BIS Papers No 65, BIS/OECD Publishing.
21. Public Debt Management (PDM) is by definition not functionally independent of fiscal policy, although DMOs possess in most OECD countries operational independence or autonomy. See for details Chapter 6 in OECD (2002), Debt Management and Government Securities Markets in the 21st Century (Paris: Organisation for Economic Cooperation and Development).
22. Sandra Pianalto (2012), Monetary policy in Challenging Times, Speech given by the President of the Federal Reserve Bank of Cleveland, on July 17, at the Economic Research Institute of Erie (ERIE), Pennsylvania State University-Erie Erie, Pennsylvania.
23. OECD, Interim Economic Assessment, 3 September 2013.
24. Christine Lagarde, The Global Calculus of Unconventional Monetary Policies, Federal Reserve Bank of Kansas City Economic Policy Symposium, Jackson Hole, 22-24 August 2013.
25. Vito Tanzi discusses compelling reasons why a reversal of stimulative fiscal policies may be more difficult than often assumed. [Comments on Recent Fiscal Developments and Exit Strategies, CESifo Forum 2/2010].
26. Such as standard estimates of the effect of asset purchases on yields (see Report to the Secretary of the Treasury from the Treasury Borrowing Advisory Committee of the Securities Industry and Financial Markets Association of 30 July 2013).
27. This may have led to a change in expectations regarding future overnight interest rate policy.
28. This includes, most recently, the announcement of a fixed-rate, full allotment overnight reverse repurchase agreement facility. By being available not just to the primary dealers this tool allows the FED to tighten its control over money market rates while also reducing the volatility of short-term interest rates. Moreover, the full allotment feature of the reverse repo facility would increase the availability of a risk-free asset. [William C. Dudley (2013), Reflections on the Economic outlook and the Implications for Monetary Policy, Remarks at Fordham Wall Street Council, Fordham University Graduate School of Business, New York City, 23 September.]
29. Mohamed El-Erian (2013), Fundamentals vs. the FED: which will win? FT Markets Insight, Financial Times, July 30th.
30. Mohamed El-Erian (2013), ibid.
31. Bernanke, B.S. (2010), The economic outlook and monetary policy, Speech at the Federal Reserve Bank of Kansas City Economic Symposium, Jackson Hole, Wyoming, 27 August 2010.
32. As noted, this includes the recently announced fixed-rate, full allotment overnight reverse repurchase agreement facility [William C. Dudley, (2013), ibid.].

33. Fiscal consolidation implies an exit path for fiscal policy by changing the fiscal position of governments. Clearly, the strength of the recovery (the pace of economic growth) has a major impact on this exit path.
34. Jeremy C Stein (2013), Research on the monetary transmission mechanism, Speech by Mr Jeremy C Stein, Member of the Board of Governors of the Federal Reserve System, at the "Banking, Liquidity and Monetary Policy", a Symposium sponsored by the Centre for Financial Studies, Frankfurt am Main, 26 September 2013.
35. Although a clever debt management strategy could potentially reduce turbulence in markets during the exit (thereby also moderating the potential rise in government borrowing costs) sound public debt management is under no circumstances a substitute for a sound fiscal policy. Over time, (a return to) a prudent medium-term fiscal strategy would be an essential element of any credible exit strategy to bring or keep debt service costs under control.
36. For example along the lines of the forthcoming report by the OECD Task Force on Transparency of Debt Statistics, Operations and Policies.
37. See for details the various issues of the OECD Sovereign Borrowing Outlook, in particular OECD Sovereign Borrowing Outlook 2012 and 2013 and chapter4.
38. It is against this backdrop that a Task Force of the OECD Working Party on Debt Management is discussing suggestions for making additional parts or details of the public debt and issuance strategy (and related operations) more transparent.

References

Bernanke, B. S. (2013), "Communication and monetary policy", speech at the National Economists Club Annual Dinner, Herbert Stein Memorial Lecture, Washington DC, 19 November.

Bernanke, B.S. (2010), "The economic outlook and monetary policy", speech at the Federal Reserve Bank of Kansas City Economic Symposium, Jackson Hole, Wyoming, 27 August.

Blommestein, H.J. (2012), "Challenges for Debt Managers during the Entry and Exit of Standard and Non-Standard Monetary Policy", lecture at the seminar on "Government Debt Management: New Trends and Challenges" organised by Central Banking Publications, Christ's College, Cambridge University, United Kingdom, 11–14 September.

Dudley, W.C. (2013), "Reflections on the Economic outlook and the Implications for Monetary Policy", remarks at Fordham Wall Street Council, Fordham University Graduate School of Business, New York City, 23 September.

Ehlers, T. (2012), "The effectiveness of the Federal Reserve's Maturity Extension Program – Operation Twist 2: the portfolio rebalancing channel and public debt management", in: H.J. Blommestein and P. Turner (2012) (eds.), Threat of fiscal dominance?, BIS Papers No 65, BIS/OECD Publishing.

El-Erian, M. (2013), "Fundamentals vs. the FED: which will win?", FT Markets Insight, Financial Times, 30 July.

Kuroda, H. (2013), "Japan's economy and monetary policy: toward overcoming deflation", speech by the Governor of the Bank of Japan, at the Naigai Josei Chousa Kai (Research Institute of Japan), Tokyo, 29 July.

Lagarde, C. (2013), "The Global Calculus of Unconventional Monetary Policies", Federal Reserve Bank of Kansas City Economic Policy Symposium, Jackson Hole, 22-24 August.

Meaning, J. and Z. Feng (2012), "The impact of Federal Reserve asset purchase programmes: another twist", BIS Quarterly Review, March 2012.

OECD (2002), Debt Management and Government Securities Markets in the 21st Century, OECD Publishing.

Pianalto, S. (2012), "Monetary policy in Challenging Times", speech given by the President of the Federal Reserve Bank of Cleveland at the Economic Research Institute of Erie (ERIE), Pennsylvania State University-Erie, Erie, Pennsylvania, 17 July.

Stein, J.C. (2013), "Research on the monetary transmission mechanism", speech by Mr Jeremy C Stein, Member of the Board of Governors of the Federal Reserve System, at the Banking, Liquidity and Monetary Policy Symposium, Frankfurt am Main, 26 September.

Chapter 4

Challenges in primary and secondary markets

Challenges for sovereign issuers are analysed, based on surveys of OECD debt managers, including the impact of direct bidding, syndication practices and the expected impact of (new) regulations. The way a more challenging issuance environment has affected the functioning of secondary government securities markets is also considered.

Issuance conditions vary from issuers without full market access, to sovereigns suffering from the consequences of relatively unsuccessful auctions, to the fairly large group that had more or less unchanged issuance conditions.

Many sovereign debt management offices adjusted their issuance procedures and introduced new types of instruments in response to a challenging issuance environment. Moreover, with the greater role of central banks (foreign and domestic) in government bond markets, maintaining a diversified investor base has become more difficult.

Challenges also include the pressure on existing primary dealer systems and the impact of forthcoming regulations on primary markets.

The statistical data for Israel are supplied by and under the responsibility of the relevant Israeli authorities. The use of such data by the OECD is without prejudice to the status of the Golan Heights, East Jerusalem and Israeli settlements in the West Bank under the terms of international law.

4.1. The need to adjust issuance procedures and techniques in different groups of countries[1]

OECD debt management offices (DMOs) are using broadly similar issuance procedures and policies with a high degree of transparency and predictability that facilitate and encourage liquid markets.[2] Broad and deep primary and secondary markets, in turn, are instrumental in lowering the cost of borrowing for the government.[3]

The global financial and economic crisis had, and is having, an important impact on sovereign debt markets and borrowing activities and has led to changes in (the use of) issuance procedures and techniques (see, for example, OECD Sovereign Borrowing Outlook 2012 and 2013 and Chapter 4.3 below). As shown in Chapters 1 and 2, OECD debt managers are facing ongoing funding challenges in meeting elevated borrowing needs, including an increase in longer-term redemptions in 2013 and 2014.

However, since issuance conditions vary among countries, sometimes significantly, issuance policies and funding strategies may differ, leading to changes in the use of issuance techniques and instruments. For some issuers, the challenge was how best to deal with sometimes high yields, lower bid-to-cover ratios and greater auction tails (reflecting relatively unsuccessful auctions).[4] Others had lost full market access (although different degrees of access can be distinguished when returning to markets; see Chapter 2.5). Some OECD sovereign issuers experienced at times (especially in 2011 and 2012) very strong ("flight-to-safety") demand at auctions resulting in some instances in negative yields. However, quite a few issuers had more or less unchanged issuance conditions.

Against this backdrop this chapter provides an overview of changes made in issuance procedures and techniques. In response to at times challenging issuance environment, many debt management offices adjusted their issuance procedures (such as more flexible auction calendars, increasing the size of non-competitive subscriptions and greater reliance on syndications) and introduced new types of instruments (like linkers and floaters). Moreover, with the greater role of central banks (foreign and domestic) in government bond markets, maintaining a diversified investor base has become more difficult than before.

The chapter also analyses how a more challenging issuance environment has affected secondary government securities markets. Also this part of the analysis is informed by survey responses by OECD debt managers, including the role of primary dealer systems in secondary markets and the impact of (new) regulations on secondary market liquidity.

4.2. Results from an OECD survey on the current use of issuance procedures and policies

The principal issuing procedure in use is auctions (Table 4.1). The responses show that 29 OECD countries (88%) use auctions for issuing long-term, while 28 DMOs (85%) also use auctions for issuing short-term debt. 23 OECD countries (70%) show that the preferred auction type is the multiple-price format.[5] However, single-price[6] auctions run a close

Table 4.1. **Overview of issuing procedures in the OECD**

	Auctions		Auction type		Tap issues		Syndication
	Long-term	Short-term	Single-price	Multiple-price	Long-term	Short-term	
Australia	X	X		X			X
Austria	X			X	X	X	X
Belgium	X	X		X	X	X	X
Canada	X	X	X	X			X
Chile	X		X				
Czech Republic	X	X	X	X	X		X
Denmark	X	X	X		X		X
Finland	X		X		X	X	X
France	X	X		X	X	X	X
Germany	X	X		X	X	X	X
Greece[1]		X	X				
Hungary	X	X		X	X	X	X
Iceland	X	X	X				X
Ireland[2]	X	X	X	Possible	X	X	X
Israel	X	X		X	X	X	
Italy	X	X	X	X	X	X	X
Japan	X	X	X	X			
Korea	X		X	X			
Luxembourg							X
Mexico	X	X	X	X	X	X	X
Netherlands	X	X	X	X	X	X	
New Zealand	X	X		X			X
Norway	X	X	X				
Poland	X	X	X	X			X
Portugal		X		X	X	X	X
Slovak Republic	X	X	X	X	X	X	X
Slovenia		X	X		X		X
Spain	X	X	Mixture	Mixture	X	X	X
Sweden	X	X		X		X	X
Switzerland	X	X	X				
Turkey	X	X		X			X
United Kingdom	X	X	X	X	X	X	X
United States	X	X	X				
Total	**29**	**28**	**21**	**23**	**18**	**16**	**25**

Notes:

Australia	Syndication is used on a selective basis. It is typically used for the first issue of new linkers and long-dated bonds (15 years), although in May 2013 syndication was used for the initial issue of a bond maturing in 2025. It has also recently been announced that consideration will be given to issuance via syndication into existing linker lines. Nominal debt is sold via multiple-price auctions.
Austria	Syndication for portion of each issue. Existing issues are regularly tapped via scheduled auctions.
Belgium	Auctions are done through the "Bloomberg Auction system (BAS system)" for two standard products: short-term Treasury Certificates and long-term Linear Bonds. Issuance through CP - and Schuldschein programmes is done via tap sales. Under the Euro Medium-Term Note (EMTN) programme, both syndications and tap sales are possible.
Canada	Syndication used for foreign currency debt issuance (for foreign exchange reserve funding purposes only). A single price auction format is used only for issuance of inflation-linked bonds.
Chile	Bonds with a maturity less than 365 days are considered short term instruments.
Czech Republic	Syndication is used for long term foreign currency debt issuance. Single-price auction is used for T-bills, multiple-price auctions for bonds and tap sales, while fixed price is employed for buy-backs.
Denmark	Primary dealer obligations do not require primary dealers to participate in auctions for a specified amount. Syndication is used for long term foreign currency debt issuance only, while short-term foreign paper is issued via Commercial Paper (CP) programmes.

Table 4.1. **Overview of issuing procedures in the OECD** *(cont.)*

Notes:

France	Syndication is usually used once a year, essentially for the first issuance of a new line of long duration nominal bonds or long-term indexed bonds.
Germany	Syndication for the first issuance of a linker and its first re-opening (2006) as well as for the first issuance of the Bund-Länder-Anleihe (2013). Syndication is used for USD bonds.
Greece[1]	Switch to single price auctions for T-bills on a monthly basis (instead of quarterly). Since May 2011, Greece is funded via an EU/IMF adjustment programme. The DMO issues only T-bills.
Hungary	Some T-bills and bonds are sold via tap sales or via subscription to retail investors. Syndication is used for bond issuances in foreign currency.
Iceland	Single price format used for T-bills and T-bonds. Syndication or private placement is used for bond issuance in foreign currencies.
Israel	Issuance of T-bills, nominal bonds and CPI-linked bonds. Issuer also uses switch auctions (redemption of short-term bonds and issuance of long-term bonds according to a conversion ratio) and buy-back auctions. Introduction of the use of primary dealers for CPI-linked bonds. More emphasis on investor relations, particularly on strategic investors from Asia. A 30-year fixed rate bond was issued for the first time in the beginning of 2012.
Ireland[2]	There have been no regular bond auctions for some time since Ireland was in an EU/IMF adjustment programme.
Italy	Syndication used for the first tranche of long-term bonds and global (USD) bonds. The single-price auction format is employed for all kinds of bonds as well as tap issues except for BOT (Buoni Ordinari del Tesoro) for which the multiple-price auction format is used.
Korea	Syndication for the first issuance of inflation-linked bonds and foreign exchange stabilisation bonds. Switch from single-price to multiple-price auctions. Buy-back auctions use the multiple-price format.
Japan	Single-price auction is currently used only for 40-year Bonds. Since October 2013, single-price auctions are used for 10-year Inflation-Indexed Bonds (JGBi).
Mexico	Syndication is used to launch new benchmarks of Fixed-Rate and Inflation-Linked Bonds with a maturity longer than three years. Tap issues are executed through single-price auctions (for Fixed-Rate and Inflation-Linked bonds), while multiple-price auctions are used for Cetes and Floating-Rate Bonds (Bondes D).
Netherlands	For the new issuance of longer dated bonds, the DSTA uses a Dutch Direct Auction (DDA) system. The DDA system is implemented as a rule-based auction in which the DSTA is the book runner. End investors have the ability to participate directly in this auction.
New Zealand	The major change was the use of syndication for the first time. Previously all debt was raised via competitive-bid bond tenders. New Zealand undertook the first syndication in October 2012 where a $2.5 billion issue of inflation-indexed bonds was syndicated. New Zealand offered the first tender of inflation-indexed bonds since the 1990's on 7 February 2013.
Poland	Single-price auction is used for T-bills and T-bonds and in supplementary auctions. The multiple-price format is used in switch and buy-back auctions. Syndication is used for the issuance of external debt.
Portugal	Portugal is currently in the transition phase from being in an EU/IMF Financial Assistance Programme to a return to full bond market access (see Chapter 2.5 for details). At the short-end of the market Portugal is issuing short-term instruments using a regular auction calendar, while two syndications have been employed for the issuance of bonds.
Slovak Republic	Syndication is used for (1) the opening of new benchmark bond lines and (2) for issuing internationally (Switzerland, United States, and Japan). Auctions are used for the tapping of all available lines of T-bonds and T-bills. The single-price auction format is used only for T-bills.
Slovenia	The syndication method has been used for the new issuance of government bonds since 2007. Uniform price auctions are used for T-bills. Tap issues of 12-month T-bills were introduced in the beginning of 2012 (but were not used in 2013). Tap issues of bonds have been approved as an alternative funding instrument, but have not been used thus far.
Spain	Spanish auctions follow a "Spanish-style" system (similar to a "modified-Dutch" system), involving a format that is a mixture of single-price and multiple-price auction formats. Bids at a price above the weighted average price are awarded at the weighted average price, while bids at a price below the weighted average (but above the marginal price) are awarded at the bid price.
Sweden	Syndications are used for public issues in foreign currencies and, occasionally, for domestic currency bonds.
Switzerland	Since the global financial market crisis and the resulting flight to safety, T-bills have been issued regularly with tender prices above par (enabling the Swiss government to raise money against negative yields).
Turkey	Eurobond issuances are syndicated offerings arranged by book runners on a best-effort basis. Direct sales to banks and institutional investors take place.
United Kingdom	Auctions are the primary method of issuance for gilts across the maturity curve. Index-linked gilts are issued using a single price format while nominal and T-bills are issued via bid-price auctions. Taps for market management are reserved for exceptional circumstances only. Taps are distinct from mini-tenders, which were introduced in October 2008 as one of the supplementary methods for distributing gilts. A programme of syndications was introduced in the 2009-10 financial year and has been used every year since then.
United States	US Treasury reopens issues, but does so through regular and predictable auctions.

1. At the cut-of date of this publication (5 December 2013), Greece had no access to long-term funding markets (see Chapter 2.5 for details).
2. Ireland regained full market access when it formally exited the EUR 67.5 billion bail-out programme (agreed with the EU, IMF and ECB in 2010) in December 2013 (see Chapter 2.5 for details).

Source: Responses to the 2013 survey on primary markets developments by OECD Working Party on Debt Management.

second. Moreover, 12 OECD countries use both single and multiple prices, depending on the maturity or type of debt instruments. For example, some countries issue index-linked bonds using the single price format (e.g. Canada, Japan, Mexico and United Kingdom) while nominal bonds are issued via multiple price auctions.

Table 4.1 indicates that syndication is a commonly used issuance procedure (25 OECD countries are currently using syndications). The notes to the table indicate that syndication is used for (i) international bond issues (e.g. Canada, Czech Republic, Denmark, Hungary, Iceland, Italy, Korea, Poland, Slovak Republic, Sweden and Turkey), (ii) the first-time issuance of new instruments such as linkers (e.g. Australia, France, Korea, Mexico and New Zealand) or long-dated bonds (e.g. Australia, Italy and France) and/or the sale of first tranches of benchmark issues, and (iii) targeting and directly placing securities among specific investor groups.

Syndications are likely to yield better results (higher placing certainty) in difficult market conditions. On the other hand, syndications are less transparent than auctions. (Additional details on the use of syndications can be found in Section 4.5.)

Tap issues are less frequently used, with 16 OECD DMOs (48%) using taps for issuing short-term debt and 18 DMOs (55%) for issuing long-term debt. In addition, a few countries use other techniques like private placement (e.g. Italy and Iceland).

As noted, several OECD debt managers had to face at times considerable funding challenges (Chapter 2), while others may do so in the future. Issuance conditions may become tougher with the possibility that some DMOs may be faced with weaker demand at auctions (lower cover ratios) and greater auction tails reflecting relatively unsuccessful auction results.

Relatively high funding needs together with at times unfavourable market conditions and sovereign stress are raising important policy issues such as:

- How to deal with lower cover ratios and greater auction tails?
- What are the policy implications for DMOs of lower liquidity in secondary markets (with sometimes decoupling of secondary market prices from sovereign funding costs)?
- How to respond to the adverse impact of new financial sector regulations on the functioning of primary markets (including primary dealer systems)?

Against this backdrop, many DMOs have adopted changes in issuance procedures so as to address (some of) these issuance challenges. More specifically, delegates from the OECD Working Party on Public Debt Management confirmed the following trends and developments:

(a) Changes in issuance methods and procedures, including more flexible auction calendars (weekly or monthly instead of quarterly/annual), an increase in the number of instruments issued at each auction date, and using other distribution methods than "regular" auctions including mini-tenders, syndication, Dutch Direct Auction (DDA) procedures and private placement (see Table 4.4 for a country-by-country overview).

(b) Introduction of new funding instruments such as (higher) linker issuance, variable rate notes, and ultra-long instruments (Table 4.2 and Figure 1.12).

In the period September 2012-October 2013 almost 47% of OECD issuers (15 countries) have introduced new funding instruments (see Table 4.2).

Table 4.2. **Introduction of new types of funding instruments**

Inflation linked bonds	Variable rate notes	Longer dated securities	Others
Czech Republic	Ireland	Austria	Germany
Hungary	Sweden	Chile	Hungary
New Zealand		Israel	Ireland
		Korea	Mexico
		New Zealand	Slovak Republic
		United Kingdom	Turkey

Notes:

Austria	Ultra-long Schuldschein.
Chile	BTP-30: nominal Treasury Bonds (USD denominated) with maturity 30 years.
Czech Republic	Inflation linked savings bond for retail sector.
Germany	Bund-Länder-Anleihe (first joint issue of the Federal Government and ten German Federal States).
Hungary	3-year domestic EUR bond with coupon linked to euro area Consumer Prices Index (CPI) and "Residency bond" (5-year zero coupon in EUR).
Ireland	Floating rate bonds linked to Euribor (used to pay the Central Bank for promissory notes); and amortising bonds which make annuity-style payments of principal and interest (aimed at domestic investors).
Israel	In January 2013, the DMO implemented the State of Israel's first ever dual tranche sovereign issuance in global markets.
Mexico	Introduction (in November 2012) of Segregated Inflation-Linked Bonds (an innovative facility to simultaneously strip coupons from the principal and from interests of Udibonos). The objective is to issue instruments whose cash flows and duration characteristics allow a more efficient management of portfolio by institutional investors such as pension and insurance funds.
New Zealand	Issue of a 2025 Index-linked bond (ILB).
Slovak Republic	Issue of a Samurai bond (JPY denominated).
Sweden	Issuance of a FRN in foreign currency.
Turkey	In September 2012, issuance of first USD Denominated bond and later (in October 2012), the first issuance of TRY denominated lease certificates (sukuks).
United Kingdom	In May 2012, the UK DMO launched a market consultation on the case for issuance of gilts with maturities in excess of 50 years and/or perpetual gilts. Respondents to the consultation suggested that there may be demand for gilts with maturities slightly longer than those currently in issue (e.g. 60 years) from a sub-set of investors looking to hedge liabilities in excess of 50 years, but that demand for gilts with much longer maturities would be more limited. In December 2012, based on feedback received in response to the consultation, the Government decided to remove the current maturity cap on gilt issuance set at around 50 years, to look to launch new issuance in the 50-60 year area in 2013-14, subject to demand and market conditions and not to introduce new perpetual gilts at the current time. In June 2013, supported by strong demand, the UK DMO extended the gilt curve modestly by launching a 55-year gilt (maturing in July 2068) via syndication. The DMO raised £4.8 billion of 2068 gilts from the transaction. Potential demand for both conventional and index-linked gilts in the 50-60 year area had been identified; however, there were some calls from the market for the DMO to establish a conventional benchmark as a first step – a gilt which could be used as a pricing reference for a potential 50-60 year index-linked gilt issue.

Source: Responses to the 2013 survey on primary markets developments by OECD Working Party on Debt Management.

Moreover, there are seven DMOs (22%) that are planning to issue new types of securities like inflation linked bonds, variable rate notes and longer dated securities (see Table 4.3). For example, Austria may issue a bond with maturity of up to 70 years, New Zealand is planning to issue a 2030 index-linked bond, while the United States will start to issue floating rates notes (FRNs) in 2014 (see for details section 4.4).

In sum, higher borrowing needs have led to a greater diversification in the use of funding instruments, in particular via an increase in the issuance of inflation-linked bond issuances. This in turn has broadened the investor base. Continued funding challenges have led to a situation where a broad and diverse investor base is more essential than before. This means that it is more important to take into account the preferences of both foreign and domestic investors when making changes in issuance procedures and introducing new instruments. In this regard, most countries mention that they give a higher priority to maintaining good investor relationships.

Table 4.3. **Planning of the issuance of new types of funding instruments**

Inflation linked bonds	Variable rate notes	Longer dated securities	Others
Belgium	United States	Austria	Slovak Republic
Japan		New Zealand	
New Zealand		Turkey	

Notes:

Austria	Possible issuance of bonds with a maturity of up to 70 years.
Belgium	Possible sale of inflation linked bond as part of the EMTN-programme.
Japan	Possible issuance (and reopening) of a new Inflation-Indexed Bonds (JGBi).
New Zealand	Possible sale of a 2030 Index-linked bond (IIB).
Slovak Republic	Bond issues in other currencies through private placements will be considered.
Turkey	Possible issuance of longer term TRY denominated bonds.
United States	Introduction in 2014 of FRNs (floating rate notes) tied to the weekly high rate of 13-week Treasury bill auctions. First FRN auctions are projected to take place in Q1 2014.

Source: Responses to the 2013 survey on primary markets developments by OECD Working Party on Debt Management.

4.3. Overview of changes in issuance procedures and techniques in OECD primary markets

As noted, issuance strategies and associated procedures are broadly similar (Table 4.1). However, they may vary greatly in terms of operational and technical details. Moreover, as a result of the crisis, many countries have changed one or more (technical or operational) features of their issuance procedures Table 4.4 provides a country-by-country overview of important changes made in issuance procedures and techniques.

Against this backdrop, the following can be noted. In response to uncertainty and volatility, auction calendars have become more flexible in most jurisdictions, auctions were held more frequently (e.g. Belgium, Denmark, Iceland, Norway and Poland) and multiple series per auction were introduced (e.g. France and Iceland).

Some countries increased the offer amounts (for example, Norway has increased the number of auctions in response to larger financing needs).

In order to smooth the redemption profile during a period with higher financing needs, some countries (re)introduced new maturities:

- Germany introduced a new structure of maturities for 10- and 30-year Federal bonds.
- Austria extended the maximum tenor for issuance from 50 years to 70 years.
- Chile issued for the first time a 30-year USD denominated bond.

Some countries also issue more frequently off-the-run bonds in order to provide liquidity and create smooth redemption flows. For example, Belgium, France and Japan have increased the number of re-openings (of off-the-run bonds that have sufficient market demand) so as to reduce market volatility, and (in the case of Japan) to enhance liquidity of the JGB market.

Other changes in issuance strategies include (1) a stronger emphasis on retail issuance (e.g. Italy) so as to broaden and to increase the stability of the investor base, (2) better co-ordination and more regular meetings with Primary Dealers, and (3) more active investor relations (e.g. Czech Republic, Finland, France and Iceland).

Table 4.4. Overview of changes in issuing procedures and techniques in OECD countries

	Changes in issuing procedures and techniques
Australia	Auctions for linkers were conducted on a single price basis up until June 2013. Auctions for all debt securities issued by the Australian Government are now conducted on a multiple price basis. The change to multiple-price auctions for linkers followed feedback from linker market participants which indicated a preference for multiple-price auctions.
Austria	Maximum tenor for issuance has been extended from 50 years to 70 years.
Belgium	As from 2009, as a result of crisis conditions, the issuance strategy was adapted to offer more flexibility in combination with predictability and transparency. As such, the number of auctions increased from six to 11, switching from bi-monthly to monthly auctions. More points of issuance offer more flexibility as to the size per auction and maturities offered. If sufficient market demand is identified, then off-the-runs can be reopened at regular auctions. As from 2012, the Treasury has created more flexibility by adding two new issuance techniques: 1) Syndicated taps on longer term "Linear bonds (Obligation Linéaire Ordinaire or OLO)" benchmarks, 2) Optional Reverse Inquiry Auctions (ORI auctions) of off-the-run OLOs at predetermined dates. These additional issuance possibilities will only be used in situations with sufficient market demand and at times that secondary market liquidity is not able to meet that demand. OLO issuance will be supplemented by alternative financing instruments: hedged foreign currency issuance and/or structured products issued under the EMTN programme, possibly including inflation linked notes, or other funding instruments, in particular Schuldscheine.
Canada	To help smooth the cash flow profile of upcoming maturities over the medium term, the maturity dates of the 2-, 3-, 5- and 30-year nominal bonds have been changed. Benchmark target range sizes in the 2-, 3- and 5-year sectors have been increased to facilitate the transition to the adjusted maturity dates in those sectors. For 2011–12, buyback operations on a cash basis were reintroduced for longer-dated bonds. In addition, weekly cash management buybacks are being held to reduce peak maturities. Discontinued cash buybacks in 10Y sector as part of broader goal of increasing net longer-term issuance. Discontinued 2Y switch buybacks, which had been used to transition to new benchmark dates in this sector.
Chile	Local market: From 2003, nominal and inflation indexed bonds are on offer. From 2007, annually preannounced calendars for fixed amounts (with the flexibility to reduce amounts by 20% or, alternatively, no allocation), while using uniform price auctions (single price/Dutch auctions). International market: In 2010, the first global issuance of local currency bonds and USD denominated securities took place. In 2011 there was another issuance of USD denominated bonds and the re-opening of the globally issued local currency bonds. USD denominated bonds with, respectively, 10-year and 30-years maturities, were issued in 2012. It was the first time that Chile issued 30-year USD denominated bonds.
Czech Republic	The situation is similar to last year. The use of flexible auction calendars (monthly), double-bond auctions with volume range, regular meetings with PD, indicative calendars, and longer deadline for the non-competitive part of T-notes auctions.
Denmark	T-bill programme re-opened in 2010. Auctions used as the primary issuance method supplemented by tap sales. Auctions are held more frequently. Normally two auctions are held each month. Multiple series per auction were introduced in Q4 2010 and auctions are held without a maximum amount sale. Inflation linked bond introduced in May 2012.
Finland	Diversification of funding sources. More emphasis on investor relations. More co-ordination with PD's. Active use of demand-supply windows.
France	The following measures to increase flexibility were introduced (since the end of 2007) to deal with volatile market conditions: 1) more "off the run" issuances, 2) more papers issued at each auction, 3) more flexibility regarding issuance size with wider range announced for the total amount to be issued, 3) two-optional auction dates (in Aug. and Dec.) and 4) changes in syndication vs. auction practices: less linkers (15-years), more new issues of long-term (more than 30-years) bonds. Since 2012, negative bids for bills are technically possible. The volume of to be auctioned T-bills is announced as a (volume) range. Emphasis on more active investor relations.
Germany	a) Introduction of a new maturity structure for the 10- and 30-year Federal bonds. b) Introduction of monthly issuance of inflation-linked Federal securities (except in August and December). c) Revision of the auction date of inflation-linked Federal securities (auctions are held on Tuesdays at 11:30 a.m.)
Greece	Since August 2010, a change in the frequency of T-bill auctions was introduced (from quarterly to monthly). Since May 2010, when the EU/IMF adjustment programme for Greece was started, long term funding is provided as bilateral (intergovernmental) loans and as financial support from supranational organisations (EFSF, European Investment Bank (EIB)). (See Chapter 2 for details.)
Hungary	More flexible auction calendar (bi-weekly bond auctions with dates but without mentioning tenors in calendars). More flexibility in the amounts offered. Introduction of top-up auctions (non-competitive subscription) and auction fees. More frequent use of re-openings of off-the-run bonds and buyback auctions. Introduction of regular (monthly) bond exchange auctions. Introduction of regular (face-to-face) meetings with institutional investors.
Iceland	During the last couple of years, greater emphasis on investor relations, notably regular (face-to-face) meetings with institutional and foreign investors. The co-ordination with Primary Dealers (PDs) has been improved. Introduction of a more flexible auction calendar. Normally, two bond auctions per month instead of one. The number of series offered in each auction was increased from one up to three. Introduction of longer dated bonds. Since 2011, annual publication of the medium term debt strategy.
Ireland	Change from multi-price to single-price for the auctioning of Bills. Bloomberg Auction System is still the main tool. Reverse Enquiry on amortising bonds.

Table 4.4. **Overview of changes in issuing procedures and techniques in OECD countries** *(cont.)*

	Changes in issuing procedures and techniques
Israel	Issuance of off-the-run bonds via switch auctions. Introduction of PDs for CPI-linked bonds. More emphasis on investor relations. Extended T-bill programme.
Italy	Since the end of 2011, CTZs (2-year zero coupon bonds or Certificato del Tesoro Zero Coupon) auctions are now priced with the discretionary pricing model already adopted for all single-price auctions, whereby the issuer sets discretionally the amount placed (and the corresponding marginal clearing price) within a range previously communicated as part of the auction announcement. In addition, from the second quarter of 2012, there is a 5% increase of re-openings reserved for Government Bond Specialists (Primary Dealers). Previously, there were two separate announcements for medium and long-term bonds (i.e. a first announcement of the bonds to be auctioned and the second one the auction amounts) has been replaced by a single announcement. Moreover, T-bills, auctioned on the basis of yield, are no longer offered together with CTZs (as they are auctioned on the basis of price; the latter are offered together with BTP is). Starting from 2013, floating rate notes (CCTeu) are issued on a monthly basis instead of quarterly (as during 2012). As regards the retail segment, from March 2012, the Italian Treasury has issued the first Italian government security indexed to the Italian inflation rate (Buono del Tesoro Poliennale or BTP Italia), with semi-annual coupons and a maturity of four years. The new bond is issued through a special platform for the retail sector.
Japan	The government of Japan is resuming the issuance of 10-Year Inflation-Indexed Bonds (JGBi) starting in October 2013 (its issuance was suspended in October 2008). The new JGBi will be equipped with a deflation floor. An increase in volatility has been observed since the start in April 2013 of the QQE programme of the BOJ. In response, the following two measures were introduced in July-August for securing more liquidity in the JGB market: a) increased issuance of off-the-run bonds (re-openings), so as to supplement the volume of each issuance (e.g. 10- and 20-Year Bonds) b) increasing the targeted issues of the Auctions for Enhanced-Liquidity (e.g. 40-Year Bonds).
Korea	Since June 2013, introduction of a 10-year Korea Treasury Bond (KTB) as benchmark bond (instead of the 5-year KTB). Since March 2013, issue rates are calculated in three decimal places (instead of two decimal places). Market rates are scheduled to be changed in 2014.
Luxembourg	Luxembourg has only issued syndicated bonds in the last couple of years and for the moment there are no plans to change this.
Mexico	Tap issues of both short and long term bonds. The use of syndications as a funding tool began in 2010. In July 2011, the scheme was changed from syndication based on book building to a syndication auction mechanism.
Netherlands	Introduction of a new long-term bond and a new facility, the "reverse tap tender". Monitoring of foreign markets for finding attractive foreign borrowing opportunities. In 2012, a USD denominated bond was introduced and a Dutch State Loan (DSL) with a maturity of 20 years was issued for the first time. On the money market, the Dutch state introduced issuance of commercial paper denominated in Norwegian Kroner. Since Dutch Treasury Certificates (DTC) were auctioned at negative yields, DTC auctions were based on prices rather than yields.
New Zealand	Syndication of two bonds, raising $4.5 billion of funding. Continuous release of bond tender scheduled prior to each new quarter. The bond tender schedule contains the dates on which tenders (auctions) will be held and the amount of bonds that will be offered at each tender. This approach allows to plan each quarter's funding requirements ahead of time, taking into account the approved bond tender programme for the fiscal year, funding which has already been raised and any syndication that it might be planning to undertake in the upcoming quarter. The frequency of tenders has been reduced. Essentially from July 2013, New Zealand will hold only one nominal and one inflation-indexed tender per month.
Norway	The number of auctions has been increased in recent years due to higher borrowing needs.
Poland	Modification of auction rules. From the beginning of 1 January 2012, the model for conducting auctions has changed. All T-bond and T-bill sales are carried out using the uniform or single price model instead of the previously used multiple price model. The change applies to sales auctions only. Switching and buy-back auctions are based on the multiple price model. However it is envisaged use the uniform price model for switching auctions. Non-competitive bids for T-bond and T-bill auctions were introduced on 1 January 2012. The share of non-competitive bids in the total sales value of a given auction cannot exceed 15% (this share was increased in April 2013, up from 5%). Supplementary auctions are open for all auction participants.
Portugal	Portugal has not changed its issuance techniques for the T-bills market, since the last survey. The DMO (IGCP) has tapped for the first time bonds via syndication. In the current circumstances, syndication is judged a better technique for regaining full market access.
Slovak Republic	The current auction system (the Reuters in-house developed Auction System) was replaced on January 2013 by the standardised Bloomberg auction system. New agreements with primary dealers were introduced (thereby replacing the previous PD system). The auction day is set on the third Monday of the month, while more bonds can be auctioned simultaneously (usually two bond lines). The new settlement day for auctions is now three (3) days, both for bonds and T-bills.
Slovenia	Syndication used for bond issues, while auctions have been used for T-bills. Tap issues of 12 month T-bills were introduced at the beginning of 2012. Tap issues of bonds and other instruments may be used depending on market conditions. Additional flexibility with respect to the timing and size of issues via the use of a mandate for prefunding government debt repayments that will mature in the following two budget years. The maximum size of a single government bond issue is set at 1.5 billion in order to manage better the concentration of repayments and refinancing risk. The group of primary dealers was enlarged and the number of the Lead Managers of individual transactions was increased. More emphasis on managing investor relations.

Table 4.4. **Overview of changes in issuing procedures and techniques in OECD countries** *(cont.)*

	Changes in issuing procedures and techniques
Spain	Spain has not changed its issuance techniques. Syndications are reserved for (1) new issues of 10-, 15- and 30-year nominal Euro benchmarks, (2) for foreign currency EMTN benchmarks, and for (3) "niche" public operations (e.g. FRNs). Auctions are used for T-bills (new issues and taps) and taps of all Euro benchmarks. However, special auctions have been introduced for small taps of "off-the-run" bonds; they are outside the regular auction calendar, with no Primary Dealer obligations. These operations are designed to provide liquidity in certain parts of the yield curve. Private placements are used for small allocations of so-called "niche" products.
Sweden	Following the increase in borrowing needs in 2009, the DMO issued long-dated bonds as well as tapped the international market in EURO. In both cases, syndications were used (relatively large in size). At the same time, bond auction volumes were of roughly the same size as before in order to ensure stability in the Sweden Government Bond (SGB) market.
Switzerland	Recently, the window (subscription time) for auctioning T-bonds was standardised (by shortening it by one hour), making it identical to the window for T-bills. Auction participants have now the same window to submit bids (from 9.30 am till 11.00 am). The response to this change has been very favourable. Since August 2011, bids with prices above 100% have been allowed. The financial market crisis and the resulting flight to safety saw tender prices regularly rising above par, enabling the Swiss government to raise money with negative yields.
Turkey	The domestic borrowing strategy, previously announced monthly, is now announced via rolling three-month periods starting in January, 2010. In addition, 10-year Turkish Lira (TL) denominated fixed coupon bonds and 10-year CPI-indexed bonds were added as new instruments in 2010. Since December 2011, two year TL denominated fixed coupon bonds have been issued every month and have been set as a benchmark instead of the 22-month zero coupon bonds. In addition, from the beginning of 2013, 5- and 10-year fixed coupon bonds are also issued every month and have been set as benchmarks. In September 2012, the first USD Denominated bond was issued and in October 2012, the first TRY denominated lease certificates (sukuks). Sukuks will be regularly issued in February and August (started in 2013).
United Kingdom	Auctions are the primary method of issuance for gilts across the maturity curve. A post auction option facility, that allows successful bidders to purchase additional stock of up to 10% of the amount allocated at auction, was introduced with effect from June 2009 and has been in use to date. It is anticipated that there will be fewer syndications overall in 2013-14, although at least four transactions during the year (one per quarter) are planned, and will be used only to launch new long conventional and index-linked gilts or to re-open existing high duration gilts. Additional transactions may be held after consultation with the market at the quarterly consultation meetings on the basis of end-investor demand. This strategy allows syndications to remain "unique" events as well as enables the DMO to maintain flexibility in aligning demand with supply. Mini-tenders, which were introduced with effect from October 2008 as a more flexible supplementary distribution method, are used to accommodate variations in proceeds from syndicated offerings. A slightly larger mini-tender programme is assumed for 2013-14 with scheduling of mini-tenders taking place during the year depending on market demand and the progress of the syndication programme.
United States	More frequent (monthly) issuance of Treasury Inflation-Protected Securities (TIPS).

Source: Responses to the 2013 survey on primary markets developments by OECD Working Party on Debt Management.

Some of these changes, while understandable, are creating some risks. To the extent that debt managers are becoming more opportunistic, issuance programmes will be less predictable. That situation may not be desirable in the longer term. DMOs emphasise therefore that they aim at using a transparent debt management framework supported, by a strong communication policy. Transparency and predictability are instrumental in reducing the type of market noise that may unnecessarily increase borrowing costs.

4.4. Floating Rate Notes (FRNs)

The use of variable rate instrument (like Floating Rate Notes – FRNs) is currently not widespread among OECD DMOs, only 10 countries (Czech Republic, Hungary, Israel, Italy, Japan, Mexico, Poland, Slovak Republic, Slovenia and Turkey) currently issue variable rate instruments.

The use of FRNs has not (yet) returned to pre-crisis levels but an increase is projected for 2013-14 (see Chapter 1, Table 1.3 and Figure 1.12). In this context it is of importance to note that the United States is planning to start a programme in January 2014. During the recent meeting of the US Treasury Borrowing Advisory Committee, held on the

6th of November 2013, it was observed that this new programme would be a replacement for Treasury bill issuance.[7]

The FRN is the first new product that the US Treasury has introduced in 17 years (Tips were launched in 1997). The FRN will have a maturity of two years and the Treasury anticipates that the size of the first auction (in January 2014) will be between $10 and $15 billion.

The US Treasury published amendments to its marketable securities auction rules to accommodate the auction and issuance of Floating Rate Notes (FRNs).[8] The notes will be auctioned off at par, with the premium (or discount) built into the spread. These FRNs are notes with quarterly payments based on the 13-week T-bill plus (or minus) some small spread. Specific terms and conditions of each FRN issue, including the auction date, issue date, and public offering amount, will be announced prior to each auction.

FRNs will add a new level of diversity to Treasury's existing suite of securities, thus providing Treasury debt managers with additional capability to expand the Treasury investor base and extend the weighted average maturity of marketable debt outstanding. The demand for "floaters" is judged as strong by market participants, as fixed income investors grapple with rising rates. Moreover, the US Treasury believes that the issuance of FRNs will contribute to the mission of financing the government at the lowest possible cost over time.

FRNs pose similar risks to Treasury as Treasury bills. For example, an FRN that allows the interest payment to change on a weekly basis would expose Treasury to the same interest rate risk as issuing a series of weekly Treasury bills. However, FRNs allow Treasury to better manage its debt by issuing securities with longer maturities than Treasury bills.

4.5. Syndication[9]

Syndication is used by both advanced and less advanced sovereign debt markets (see Table 4.1 for an overview). This sales channel is considered as especially beneficial for the latter countries as the development of their sovereign bond markets is at a relatively early stage where new instruments need to be introduced as part of market development. In those circumstances, syndications may constitute a cost-effective issuance channel, while minimising placement risk. More generally, syndications can be beneficial for the placement of bonds in specific market segments where a deeper dialogue with investors and a more interactive price discovery process may be required than for well-established instruments such as benchmark bonds (see Figure 4.1. for more details).

Various aspects of the use of syndications were discussed during the last annual meeting of the OECD Working Party on Public Debt Management (WPDM) held on 30-31 October 2013. As background the Italian Treasury circulated a policy note based on responses by OECD debt managers to a questionnaire.

The 26 survey responses show the following developments or trends (see Table 4.5). First, the number of sovereigns using syndications increased from 17 in 2008 to 22 in 2010, before falling to 19 in 2013. Second, over the period 2008-13, only nine countries (or nearly 35%) are using syndications on a regular (annual) basis (Austria, Belgium, Canada, Denmark, Finland, Poland, Slovenia, Spain and Sweden). Third, the average OECD share of syndications in gross borrowing and issuance operations increased from 25% in 2008 to 30% in 2013. However, individual shares show large variations.

Table 4.5. **Overview of the use of syndications as a percentage of total gross issuance in OECD countries**

	2008	2009	2010	2011	2012	2013*
Australia	0%	7%	2%	5%	8%	16%
Austria	16%	19%	13%	22%	37%	23%
Belgium	31%	37%	33%	35%	28%	33%
Canada[1]	16%	16%	16%	16%	16%	16%
Czech Republic	27%	17%	20%	0%	22%	0%
Denmark	17%	35%	9%	20%	10%	10%
Finland[2]	40%	46%	34%	36%	50%	45%
France	2%	3%	2%	1%	0%	3%
Germany[3]	0%	0%	0%	0%	0%	0%
Greece	91%	76%	20%	0%	0%	0%
Hungary	7%	5%	9%	22%	0%	22%
Iceland	0%	0%	0%	50%	62%	0%
Ireland	100%	68%	25%	0%	0%	90%
Italy	2%	3%	4%	1%	0%	4%
Korea	0%	0%	0%	2%	10%	0%
Luxembourg	74%	0%	100%	0%	100%	100%
Mexico	0%	0%	3%	5%	4%	0%
New Zealand	0%	0%	0%	0%	32%	0%
Poland	7%	15%	14%	13%	22%	6%
Portugal	45%	46%	32%	47%	0%	100%
Slovak Republic	0%	28%	41%	38%	41%	68%
Slovenia	78%	78%	78%	78%	78%	78%
Spain	19%	21%	28%	11%	4%	23%
Sweden[4]	0%	53%	0%	0%	19%	0%
	0%	100%	100%	100%	100%	70%
Turkey[5]	100%	100%	100%	100%	100%	94%
United Kingdom	0%	13%	16%	19%	20%	13%
OECD average of syndications as percentage of gross issuance	25%	29%	26%	23%	28%	30%
Number of countries with syndications	17	21	22	20	19	19

Notes: Cut-off date of this survey is September 2013 (*The data for 2013 are therefore provisional.)
1. There was no domestic (currency) syndicated issuance by Canada in the period 2008-2013. The figures refer to foreign-currency syndicated issuance comprising an average of around 16% of foreign-currency funding.
2. Finland: total issuance includes long- and short-term issuance.
3. Germany: the figure for 2009 is 0.01%.
4. Sweden: the first line refers to SBG, the second to foreign currency issuance.
5. Turkey: the percentages refer only to international bond issues.

Source: Responses to the 2013 survey on syndication design and implementation prepared by the Italian Treasury.

As noted, relative to auctions, syndications allow higher placement certainty and other advantages such as (1) facilitating the subscription of larger amounts in a very short time, (2) achieving a more appropriate distribution of subscriptions in terms of geography or investor type, (3) a better performance in price execution, and (4) better liquidity in secondary markets (Figure 4.1).

However, there are also disadvantages (relative to auctions) such as higher intermediation costs. Only a few debt managers reported more difficulties in reaching potential buyers, while lack of transparency seems to be only a problem for a few issuers (Figure 4.2).

Figure 4.1. **Advantages of syndications**

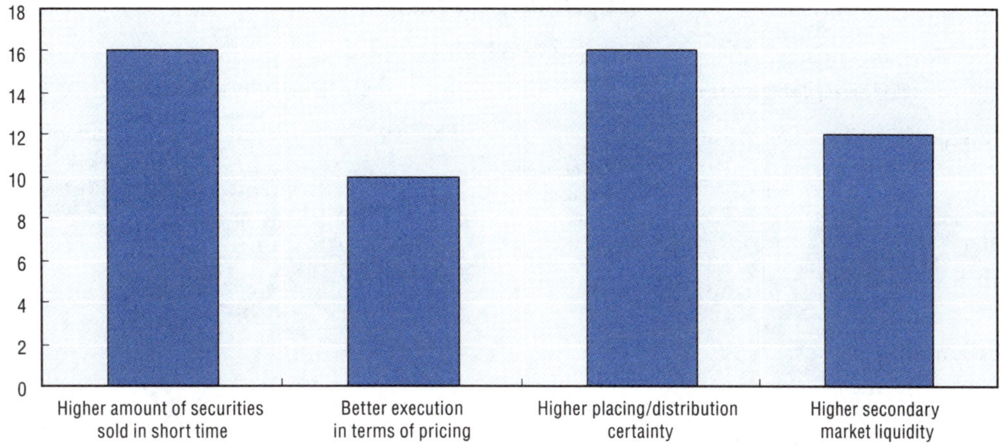

Source: Responses to the 2013 survey on syndication design prepared by the Italian Treasury.

Figure 4.2. **Disadvantages of syndications**

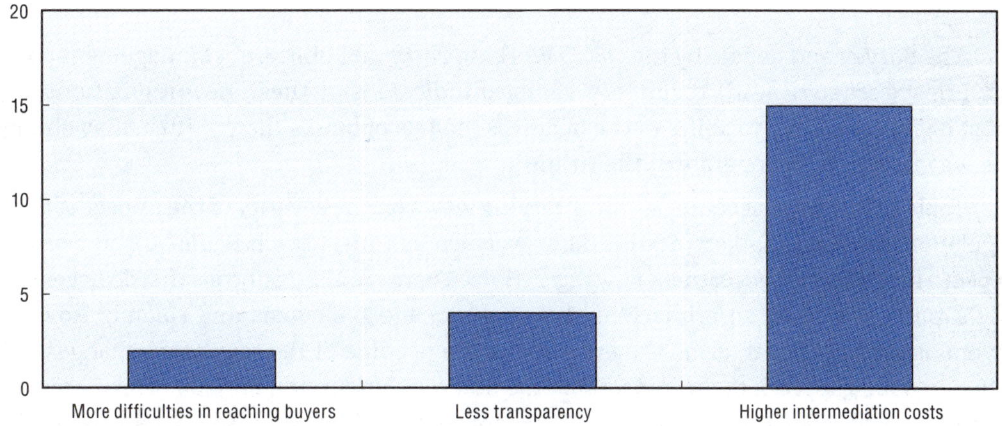

Source: Responses to the 2013 survey on syndication design prepared by the Italian Treasury.

4.6. Impact of forthcoming regulations on the functioning of primary markets[10]

Sovereign issuers have expressed on various occasions their concern about the impact (positive and negative) of new or future financial reform measures, arguing that this could affect (1) the overall balance of incentives for primary dealers to participate actively in sovereign bond markets and (2) the demand for government securities by end-investors.

For example, regulatory changes could reduce the profitability (and thus the attractiveness) of being a primary dealer in sovereign bond markets or reduce the ability of Primary Dealers (PDs) to participate actively in primary issuance or maintain sufficient inventories in government bonds (and thus provide liquidity in individual sovereign bond markets).

Table 4.6 provides a country-by-country overview of impact of new regulations and their (potential) effects on the functioning of primary markets, including Basel III, Financial Transactions Tax (FTT) and Volcker rule. The 2013 survey responses show that the tax on financial transactions (48%) and Basel III (28%) are the regulations with potentially the biggest impact on primary markets (see Figure 4.3). Interestingly, last year only 10% of the DMOs considered the FTT as having the biggest impact, while 30% of the respondents associate the Volcker rule with having potentially the biggest impact (dropping to 10% in this year's survey).

Figure 4.3. **Biggest (potential) impact of new regulations on the functioning of primary markets**

Percentage

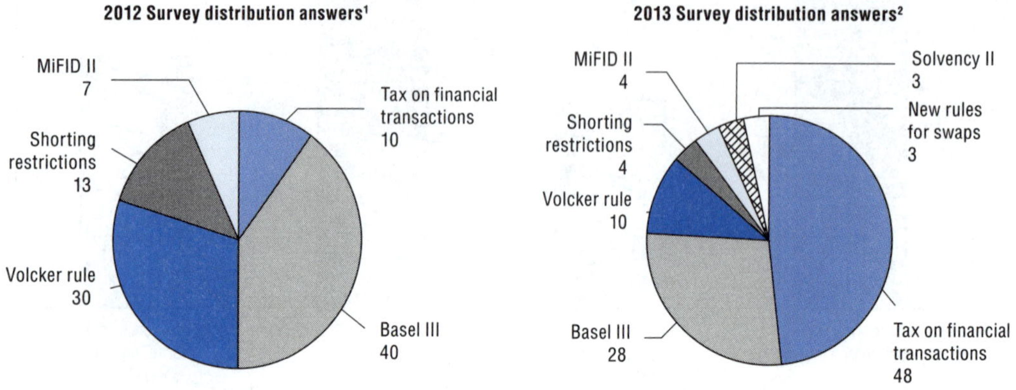

1. 30 OECD countries out of 34 answered this question.
2. 29 OECD countries out of 34 answered this question.

Source: Responses to the 2012 and 2013 surveys on primary markets developments by OECD Working Party on Debt Management.

The Survey and debate by the OECD Working Party on Public Debt Management about the impact of (envisaged) regulatory changes indicate that these new regulations will most likely contribute to shifts in the business models of banks that, in turn, may change the way in which PDs operate in the future.

Table 4.6 shows that countries have varying views on the severity of the impact of these regulations on their markets. Some countries (such as Chile, Czech Republic and Norway) expect a moderate impact of these new regulations. There are also countries that do not expect any significant impact on primary market operations (e.g. Slovenia and Poland). However several issuers note that, given the evolving nature of some of the regulatory changes, it is difficult to fully appreciate the impact that the new regulations will have on primary market operations. Moreover, many of the rules have not yet been implemented, thereby increasing the difficulty in ranking the impact of these new regulations.

Table 4.6. **Regulations with the biggest impact on Primary Markets**

Tax on financial transactions	Basel III	Volcker Rule	Shorting Restrictions	MiFID II	Solvency II	New rules for swaps
Austria	Australia	Japan	Netherlands	Mexico	Switzerland	Norway
Belgium	Belgium	New Zealand				
Czech Republic	France	United Kingdom				
Denmark	Netherlands					
Germany	New Zealand					
Hungary	Portugal					
Ireland	Spain					
Italy	United States					
Luxembourg						
Portugal						
Slovak Republic						
Slovenia						
Sweden						
United Kingdom						

Table 4.6. **Regulations with the biggest impact on Primary Markets** *(cont.)*

Notes:

Australia	This is difficult to judge at this time. Registered bidders (primary dealers) seem to be most focused on the Basel III implications on their balance sheet size.
Austria	The introduction of a financial transaction tax – though primary markets could presumably be exempted – can have a secondary effect on primary markets as Austria uses a primary dealer system to distribute its bonds to the end investor who would have to pay this tax and thus could affect his/her decision to purchase Republic of Austria Government bonds. Basel III and Solvency II could have a positive impact on the demand for high credit quality bonds with high liquidity. New rules for swaps have already led to higher costs for hedging issuance in foreign currencies. As a result, the windows for issuing in foreign currencies have become smaller and their issuance less frequent. Shorting restrictions do not have a large impact on primary markets apart from potentially motivating dealers to take larger sizes at issuance for warehousing purposes. The Volcker rule does not have a significant impact on the primary market of RAGB as it mainly affects US-banks and their non-market-making activities.
Belgium	The Financial Transaction Tax (FTT) as it is drafted now will have a serious impact on the cost of issuance. It ignores the link between primary and secondary markets. (The secondary market plays a crucial role in providing reference prices for primary issuance of sovereign debt.) The FTT-proposal should be carefully designed in order not to jeopardise liquidity and hence cause an increase in the cost of issuance for the sovereign. It would cause a further fragmentation of the sovereign debt market in the Euro area, as the smaller and less liquid markets will suffer more from the reduction in volumes and liquidity. It does not differentiate between the different maturities of the bonds transacted, and therefore may have some unintended consequences on the maturity profile of the sovereigns. In particular, there could be a disproportionate impact on some specific maturities and this could therefore be especially damaging for DMOs seeking to maintain liquidity along the entire yield curve. It does not take into account the potential impact that the taxation of derivatives will have on the tapping of new foreign currency bond markets by sovereigns, as cross currency swaps will become more expensive. Hence, issuers will be either forced to limit their funding instruments to issuance in domestic currency only or to take currency risks. Both options have a potentially negative impact on the cost of funding. Basel III and especially the LCR will basically have a positive impact on the demand by banks.
Canada	Given the evolving nature of some of the regulatory changes, it is difficult to fully appreciate the impact that the new regulations will have on primary markets/operations in the debt management space. Many of the rules have not yet been implemented and, as such, are not observable. This means that the ranking of the impact of these new regulations is not feasible at this time. However, the information provided below is intended to elucidate the potential effects of new regulations on our primary markets. Volcker Rule: The draft Volcker rule restricts proprietary trading. The proposed rule contains an exemption for market making as well as for the trading of US government, state and municipal bonds. However, Canadian government, provincial and municipal bonds are not exempted from the draft rule. To the extent that there is a reduction in proprietary trading of Government of Canada securities in association with this rule, there may be an impact to some extent on the demand for the Government of Canada securities in the primary bond market. Basel III (Capital Requirements Directive (CRD) IV): The future implementation of Basel III has increased the demand for safe assets, such as cash and high quality sovereign assets. Government of Canada debt securities are AAA-rated, and as such in high demand for collateral posting purposes. Basel III implementation is likely to increase the demand for the Government of Canada securities in the primary market and secondary market. Tax on financial transactions (e.g. Tobin-tax): Recently introduced financial transaction taxes (FTTs) in France and Italy have not and will not have any direct impact on the primary market operations for Canadian sovereign debt issuance. The adopted taxes in both jurisdictions are on equity instruments, not debt instruments. The proposed European Union FTT that encompasses transactions on debt instruments is still under negotiation with a possibility that primary market transactions will be exempt. However, even if primary market transactions are exempt, the adopted tax may decrease secondary market trading of Government of Canada debt by EU entities, which could indirectly impact the demand for Government of Canada securities in the primary market. The scale of this impact depends on the level of trading activity of Government of Canada debt by EU entities. New rules for swaps: Currently no impact. Potential impact may arise as new rules take hold. For example, the forthcoming margining rules for non-cleared derivatives will require the exchange of initial margin, therefore increasing the demand for high-quality securities, such as Government of Canada debt. This would increase the demand for Government of Canada securities in the secondary and primary markets. Other regulations: Single-Counterparty Credit Limits (s. 165 (e) of the Dodd-Frank Act) – Domestic Rules. s. 165 (e) (SCCL) prohibits an entity from having over a certain percentage credit exposure to any unaffiliated company. SCCL may affect the ability of US bank holding companies to hold Government of Canada securities. This could reduce the demand for Government of Canada securities.
Chile	The impact of these regulations on Chilean markets is very moderate.
Czech Republic	These regulations may increase the issuance costs.
Denmark	The increase in capital charges through for instance CRD IV, Cash Reserve Ratio (CRR) and Incremental Risk Charge (IRC) will ensure that primary dealers are better capitalised. However, this will likely also raise the costs of warehousing government securities, and may cause changes in the primary dealer model. Although Denmark is currently outside of a potential FTT-zone, the Danish government bond market may still be adversely affected. As liquidity in secondary markets is intentionally reduced by introducing an FTT, one should expect higher investor premiums in primary markets. This will raise funding costs in many markets, including for government debt.
Finland	It is extremely difficult to rank these regulations, as the content for all of them are not yet finalised – e.g. the final format of the FTT remains unknown. It is clear, however, that all of them have a potential impact, including on the market making environment for banks. This development, in turn, would affect both primary and secondary markets for Finnish government securities. Some regulations have a (potentially) bigger impact on smaller markets (like Finland) than on larger ones.
France	Volcker rule: impact depends whether the exemption is limited to US sovereign bonds or is expanded to all sovereign markets. If the rule does not exempt all sovereign markets, the participation by US banks on French and other domestic markets will be limited. Solvency II: less demand on instruments at the very long run of the yield curve (after 20 years). However, there might be an increase in the structural demand for long-term government bonds due to a need to fill duration gaps by insurance companies. Basel III (CRD IV): more constraints on primary dealer balance sheets to warehouse bonds, which, in turn, would imply higher market volatility, especially around auctions. Shorting restrictions: no impact. New rules for swaps: maybe more demand for bond to manage duration risk when compared to swaps.
Germany	Two main effects (of the new regulations) on Germany primary market operations can be distinguished: 1) Some regulations (e.g. Volcker rule, Tax on Financial Transactions, Markets in Financial Instruments Directive (MiFID) II) may reduce the demand for German Federal securities. The liquidity in the cash market for German Federal securities (as well as in the repo and the futures markets) may decrease. As a consequence, the activities in the primary market may become more challenging. 2) New rules for swaps can affect the activities with regard to the debt portfolio. As the management of the portfolio via swaps may become more complex and expensive, primary market activities have to replace or support swap activities in order to reach the targeted portfolio.

Table 4.6. **Regulations with the biggest impact on Primary Markets** *(cont.)*

Notes:

Hungary	Financial Transactions Tax could be severely harmful for the sale of short term instruments (T-bills).
Iceland	Foreign exchange transactions have been subject to capital controls since the autumn of 2008. However, there is a strategy in place for the liberalisation of capital controls. However, when the restrictions are relaxed there could be an outflow of capital leading to a large impact on the cost of servicing government debt. The demand from investors can also change during this liberalisation process. This may affect, in turn, the issuance strategy of the government.
Ireland	Apart from FTT which looks most negative, Ireland have assessed the above in qualitative terms concerning both Primary and Secondary Markets operations: 1) Volcker Rule: The potential separation of "high-street" and "merchant-banking" functions will likely lead to a decrease in the pool of capital available for primary dealer market-making. Short-run, and viewed in isolation (ignoring any systemic benefits that may accrue on a global basis), this would diminish the appetite for inventory/position taking among the bulk of NTMA's market-makers. 2) Solvency II While initial estimates were that it would be positive for investment-grade bonds, at the expense of both equities and non-investment grade issuance, an emerging concern is that too much power may be handed to the rating agencies (and backward-looking risk models). Given Ireland's deteriorated credit rating in the last five years, this could lead to further flows out of IGBs into higher-rated paper, based on considerations more of existing ratings and box-ticking than on prospective outlook. Insofar as data is available on the fund dispositions of Irish insurers at present, it might be hard to spot the difference that this would make. 3) Basel 3: The downstream impact of this is difficult to quantify but likely to have a negative impact on the ability of banks which act as primary dealers to dedicate capital to sovereigns. It may also impact the ability to hedge positions with these banks. 4) Shorting Restrictions: No specific impact assessed. 5) FTT: While primary issuance from sovereign issuers is to be exempt, the introduction of FTT in its current form is potentially catastrophic, on a systemic basis. Primary market issuance is heavily reliant on properly functioning liquid secondary markets. The level of tax proposed, along with the cascading effect will render current market making models uneconomic, leading to significant deterioration in market liquidity. In effect FTT seeks to raise revenues based on existing behaviour, and to simultaneously render this behaviour economically unfeasible. As proposed it would destroy private sector money transmission mechanisms, and force all money market transactions into the ECB and National Central Banks (NCBs). 6) Swap Rules: No direct adverse impact assessed for sovereign due to exemption from reporting and clearing especially with established 2-way collateral arrangements such as Ireland has in place – however this impact assessment may change depending on how the market adapts to the new regulations.
Italy	It is difficult to evaluate the impact of these new regulations on the primary market. However, Primary Dealers may be affected by these new regulations (primarily Basel III- CRD IV, Solvency II, Short Selling Regulation and Volker rule) by having less capital available (credit lines) to absorb new issuances supply while managing the associated risks. There might also be more difficulties in delivering government securities to final investors, especially the auctioning of bonds with a lower rating or in situations with higher volatility. Even the anticipation of these adverse effects may make the issuance of bonds more expensive. Italy has at times experienced this situation, although not to an important degree. However, even if the Italian government is not able to quantify precisely the impact of this higher cost, there is no doubt that the participation strategy in auctions has evolved over time, in particular expressed by more hedging activities before auctions or more prudent behaviour during bidding at auctions. Moreover CRD IV and Solvency II (both European Regulations will enter into force on 1 January 2014) will strengthen the capital requirement for banks and insurers, making it more costly to hold lower-rated bonds in their books. This may imply, in turn, a reduced capacity for PDs to distribute government bonds. Two final considerations. First, the forthcoming new regulations related to the FTT will also apply to government bonds' transactions, thereby having a major negative impact on the participation of Primary Dealers in auctions. This will significantly increase the cost-at-issuance. The resulting higher cost of trading will have an adverse impact on borrowing costs. In addition, the FTT will have an adverse influence on liquidity in the secondary market, thereby further increasing the borrowing costs for governments. Second, the new EMIR Regulations may have negative consequences resulting from the new risk management rules envisaged by the regulation for the interoperability of CCPs. The Italian government bond repo market operates with interoperable CCPs. The new rules may make trading with CCPs more costly, thereby pushing repo traders to switch back to bilateral repo trading. As a result, the liquidity of the repo market will be affected and, indirectly, the liquidity of the secondary cash market.
Japan	The Volker rule prohibits "proprietary trading", allowing only allow certain types of transactions. When JGB transactions are viewed as "proprietary trading", then some of the major JGB market participants' (which are defined as "banking entities" in the rule) in primary market operations would be restricted to "underwriting", etc. Basel III may have a mixed impact on the functioning of the JGB primary market. On the one hand, capital requirements and LCR are treating low risk assets such as JGBs as favourable. These regulations promote JGB holdings and are in principle favourable to JGB primary market operations. On the other hand, leverage ratios limit the leverage and this, in turn, may restrict asset holdings, including JGBs.
Netherlands	DSTA is closely monitoring all regulatory changes that could impact our debt management operations. However, most of the above mentioned regulatory frameworks have not yet been finalised. Therefore, the potential impact is difficult to assess. Furthermore, it is very hard to assess whether certain regulatory changes will have a direct or indirect impact. As regards the pending FTT, it is highly uncertain how this tax will actually be implemented.
New Zealand	The Volcker Rule has had little or no impact on us as our previous flexible issuance approach meant that intermediaries did not warehouse bonds for us as they could generally access the bond maturity and the volumes of bonds that they required in our tenders. As a result, US investment banks have not held large amounts of our bonds for some years. Since 2008, domestic investors have bought more of our bonds for liquidity purposes so it is these banks that tend to sell bonds to foreign investors who want to buy in the secondary market. Solvency, shorting restrictions and tax on financial transactions are not applicable for New Zealand. Basel III and the proposed central clearing for swaps have also had little to no impact to date however with central clearing we believe the impact is just delayed as their counterparties move towards compliance.
Norway	Uncertain, probably small, effects.
Poland	No impact.
Portugal	Regarding the Volcker Rule, European debt should have a similar exemption as for US sovereign debt. Otherwise it will shrink the investor base and change the primary dealership model. The FTT will have a material impact on the costs of issuance.
Slovak Republic	Generally, each new regulation will affect the balance of market incentives.

Table 4.6. **Regulations with the biggest impact on Primary Markets** *(cont.)*

Notes:

Slovenia	Primary market operations will predominantly be affected by the tax on financial transaction (FTT). Even though the current proposal excludes primary market operations, there will still be an indirect impact on primary market operations and sovereign funding costs due to the influence of the FTT on the secondary market trading of government securities. Other new regulations are not expected to have a significant impact on primary market operations in Slovenia.
Spain	CRD-IV restricts the amount of bonds that a PD can warehouse on its own balance sheet (due to increasing capital charges for volatile and lower-rated bonds. Moreover, the uneven application of Basel III in Europe and the US could create a non-level playing field and thereby affect the ability of Spanish banks to buy debt in the primary market. This has a pro-cyclical effect on instability. The Financial Transactions Tax could have a very destructive effect on the execution of auctions (through secondary market volatility); although this will be mitigated if all public debt and all repos on public debt are excluded. Volcker Rule would affect most Spanish banks through the extraterritorial effects of the Dodd-Frank Act. Solvency II could have a positive effect on the demand for longer-duration Spanish public debt by certain types of buy-to-hold investor (pension funds, insurance companies).
Sweden	The most important impact on the primary market is indirect, namely via the detrimental impact on the secondary market. Solvency II will have a direct effect on the primary market.
Switzerland	New regulations regarding capital requirements and risk management may affect market liquidity and demand for particular securities. For example, solvency regulations for insurance companies (in particular regarding life insurance products) may increase the demand for longer dated government securities (and such a change in market conditions would then have to be taken into account when formulating issuance strategies). Currently, such market effects are in line with the current issuance strategy of the Swiss government. Taxes on financial transactions may also have an adverse market impact. In contrast, Switzerland abolished the issuance tax on domestic money and capital market securities, with a positive impact on primary market operations.
United Kingdom	The DMO is very mindful of regulatory developments in Europe and internationally and realises that there are potentially significant impacts these can have on the sovereign debt markets. The DMO has a role in providing advice and analysis to HM Treasury on the implications of these regulatory initiatives, in particular for the gilt market, in order to ensure that any concerns for the gilt market/sovereign bonds are raised and given due consideration by the appropriate authorities. In addition, the UK DMO provides its view and participates in discussions on the impact of regulatory issues in various forums such as the EFC sub-committee on EU sovereign debt markets (ESDM) and other platforms for public sector borrowers. During the period of regulatory change, the performance of the DMO's issuance operations has remained sound. We believe that ongoing strong performance is partly due to: (i) the size, depth and liquidity of the gilt market; (ii) the consequently relatively smooth adjustment of prices to allow supply to be taken down across maturities and types of gilts; and (iii) competition between primary dealers that consequently offer fine pricing to investors. A key priority for the UK DMO is to support the smooth functioning of the gilt market because we see that as an important contributory factor in ensuring the DMO can continue to fund the Government in the face of developments in the external environment (e.g. regulatory change). With regard to specific regulatory initiatives that are forthcoming or are already in practice, the degree of relevance for the gilt market of each has varied. Sovereign debt primary market transactions are exempt under certain regulations, for example, the restriction on short selling and this therefore, haven't had a meaningful impact on primary market operations. The financial transaction tax, as it stands (although not implemented yet), also exempts primary market operations; however, the potential impact of the tax on the secondary market in gilts could have a knock-on effect on primary market operations and a potentially significant rise in the cost of issuance of gilts. Implementation of the Capital Requirements Directive (CRD IV) in the United Kingdom, as part of the Basel III regulation, is expected to be from 1 January 2014. With certain provisions in the regulation, such as liquidity requirements, being phased in between 2014 and 2019, we do not expect that banks or other relevant institutions will materially alter their holdings in gilts (which have already increased significantly in the last few years in anticipation of CRD IV) directly as a result of the regulation in the near term. New rules for swaps markets, including standardised OTC derivative contracts being traded on exchanges or electronic trading platforms and being centrally cleared, could have the potential to impact demand for gilts, and other sovereign bonds, as the requirements could significantly increase demand for high quality assets for use as collateral in derivative contracts.
United States	All else equal, Basel III and derivatives clearing regulations should increase demand for high-quality collateral. Accordingly, our primary market operations should see more competitive and/or increased investor participation. Conversely, although the Volcker rule and proposed taxes on financial transactions exempt new government issuance from its purview, the impact that these regulations will likely exert on our secondary market operations (please see below) would adversely impact demand for our securities in the primary market.

Source: Responses to the 2013 survey on primary markets developments by OECD Working Party on Debt Management.

4.7. Impact of (new) regulations on liquidity in secondary markets

Debt managers (and market participants) have expressed concerns that some of the regulatory changes in response to the global financial crisis may have an adverse impact on liquidity in secondary markets for government bonds, leading to a likely rise in borrowing costs. For example, in response to a 2013 OECD survey several debt managers have noted that in its current form, the financial transactions tax (FTT), given its wide scope and extra-territorial nature, has the potential of having material implications for the secondary market in government bonds. It is feared that the costs associated with the FTT could significantly widen bid offer spreads in government bonds. These costs are likely to ultimately result in a rise in borrowing costs since primary market issuance is likely to be priced at higher yields (see United Kingdom response in Table 4.7).

The Volcker rule has led to worries by debt managers outside the US since the rule does not provide exemptions for sovereign debt (aside from US sovereign debt). This means that,

Table 4.7. New regulations and their (potential) effects on secondary market operations

	Country views
Belgium	In its current form, the FTT will seriously impact secondary market liquidity and price transparency. The FTT does not take into account the specific business model in sovereign debt markets based on market making (as a cornerstone of liquidity), thereby under-estimating the adverse impact of the proposal on market liquidity, transaction costs and price formation. The FTT is likely to increase volatility and bid-offer spreads in government bond markets, thereby substantially reducing the attractiveness of sovereign bonds.
Canada	As far as impact of new regulations on secondary markets, during the annual consultation process market participants commented that increased liquidity and requirements for collateral resulting from new developments in regulatory frameworks, such as the Liquidity Coverage Ratio standard under Basel III, as well as reforms to the over the counter derivatives market, may increase demand for Government of Canada securities. The implementation of new regulatory frameworks was viewed by market participants as affecting the ability of dealers to use their balance sheets for market making and risk taking activities. While this was described as not having a direct impact on the on the run Government of Canada securities, dealers mentioned a migration away from principal based market making, where dealers hold large bond inventories, toward a hybrid, agency based "order driven" model for less liquid securities.[11]
Chile	The impact of new regulations on secondary market operations is likely to be moderate, especially for external bonds.
Czech Republic	Especially FTT is likely to have a significantly negative effect on the secondary sovereign debt market (including repo market operations).
Denmark	One of the lessons of the financial crisis is that liquidity is crucial. A tax on financial transactions is effectively a tax on market liquidity. The FTT will harm liquidity in the secondary market, especially on trades with a small margin, and reduce the general efficiency of capital markets. Moreover, the tax cannot be expected to reduce undesirable speculative trades, since potential rewards are far larger than the cost of this type of trades.
France	Volcker rule: If the rule does not exempt non-US sovereign markets, then the participation by US-based banks to make an effective market in foreign sovereign debt markets will be affected (thereby reducing the liquidity). Solvency II: less demand at the very long run of the yield curve (after 20 years) (i.e.in the current financing conditions and according to current regulatory parameters). On the other hand, Solvency II may lead to an increase in structural demand for long term government bonds due to the need by insurance companies to tackle duration gaps. Basel III (CRD IV): reduced ability by primary dealers to warehouse bonds, implying higher market volatility, especially around auctions. Shorting restrictions: no impact. New rules for swaps: this may lead to an increase in the demand for bond due to the greater need to manage duration.
Hungary	FTT could have a very negative impact on the repo market. A significant decrease in repo market liquidity may, in turn, have a negative impact on the market making activity by PDs. Short selling restriction has not had any negative impact thus far.
Iceland	Liberalisation of capital controls can lead to higher yields in secondary markets, especially at the shorter end of the yield curve (because this is the part where most of the bonds are held by foreign investors who are locked-in). Relaxation of the controls can create uncertainty for market participants.
Italy	The Treasury is not very active in secondary markets (only for buybacks and exchanges). In other words, the direct impact for the Treasury of new regulations on secondary markets is very limited.
Japan	The Volker rule restricts "proprietary trading" activities, limiting admissible transactions to specific transactions such as hedging activities, market-making-related activities, etc. The Japanese DMO has concerns that the rule in its current form may reduce liquidity in the JGB market.
Netherlands	The secondary market operations of the DSTA are limited. However, the impact of regulatory changes on secondary markets could very well have a pass-through effect on the primary market operations by the DSTA. The Volcker rule could impact the primary dealer activities of certain banks. Shorting restrictions might create a lower degree of liquidity in bond markets and the FTT might impose an unequal level playing field for primary dealers in certain regions.
New Zealand	New regulations have had little or no impact to date. However, FED tapering will have some effect on the demand from sovereign wealth funds, central banks and other investors for New Zealand's bonds.
Norway	Regulations are likely to have uncertain, but probably small, effects on the functioning of secondary markets.
Poland	New Basel III regulations may increase the rates quoted by banks in swap transactions. Maintaining cash collateral as required by CSA agreements would cause higher debt servicing costs.
Portugal	Basel III: impact on the capacity of banks to hold debt. The zero risk weighting exemption for sovereign debt under the IRB option will be more difficult to achieve for bigger banks. Short selling regulations: adverse impact on liquidity. It is more difficult to hedge in less liquid markets (due to the prohibition of cross-border hedging using Credit Default Swaps, CDS). FTT: material impact on the liquidity in secondary markets, leading to an increase in funding costs.
Slovak Republic	FTT has an adverse impact on liquidity management by the Slovak Republic.
Slovenia	Secondary market operations will predominantly be affected by the tax on financial transactions (FTT), with a negative impact on secondary market pricing and liquidity. As far as other new regulations are concerned, at this moment Slovenia does not foresee any significant impacts arising from them on our secondary market operations.
Spain	Both the CRD –IV and the Financial Transactions Tax (unless sovereign debt and repo activities are excluded) are likely to increase volatility, because they penalise market-making activities.
Sweden	FTT will make hedging becomes more difficult and expensive. This, in turn, is likely to have a negative impact on cross-border transactions, thereby strengthening the demand for domestic (Swedish) bonds.
Switzerland	The Swiss DMO is not active in secondary markets.
United Kingdom	In its current form, the financial transactions tax, given its wide scope and extra-territorial nature, has the potential of having material implications for the secondary market in gilts. Market participants have highlighted to the DMO that the costs associated with the tax could significantly widen bid offer spreads in gilts and may render whole businesses at investment banks uneconomical, e.g. the repo market. These costs are likely to ultimately result in a rise in borrowing costs for the United Kingdom and primary market issuance being priced at higher yields. The Volcker rule, which does not provide exemptions for sovereign securities (aside from US sovereign debt) in its current form, is likely to impact the ability of US-based banks to make an effective market in gilts. Under the MiFID II regulation, proposed post trade transparency requirements, if not well calibrated, could have the impact of damaging liquidity in the gilt market. The inability of banks to effectively make a market in gilts, the potential closure of the repo market and damaged liquidity could consequently lead to an increase in the issuance cost of sovereign debt for the United Kingdom. Summary: While the initial impact of some of the regulatory initiatives is likely to be limited, the cumulative effect may well have a disproportionate longer term consequence for the well-functioning of the secondary and primary markets.
United States	The argument has been made that the Volcker rule will adversely impact our primary dealer system by not exempting Treasury futures and options from its purview. The concern being that futures and options are crucial to the investor community as they attempt to hedge their exposure to this or that security. The financial transactions tax (FTT), meanwhile, has inspired a variety of concerns, one of which is its effect on liquidity. Additionally, taxes on derivative financial instruments have the potential to adversely impact hedging activities.

Source: Responses to the 2013 survey on primary markets developments by OECD Working Party on Debt Management.

in its current form, the rule is likely to impact the ability of US-based banks to make an effective market in foreign sovereign debt (see Table 4.7). But even within the United States the argument has been made that the Volcker rule may adversely impact the US primary dealer system by not exempting US Treasury futures and options from its purview. The concern being that futures and options are crucial to the investor community as they are used to hedge their exposure to the various securities (see US response in Table 4.7).

Table 4.7 provides a country-by-country overview of country responses to a survey about the likely impact of new regulations on secondary market operations. Although countries have varying views on the severity of the (likely) impact of new regulations, DMOs have expressed common concerns that lower liquidity in secondary markets is likely to affect primary market issuance in the form of a rise in borrowing costs. However, it was also pointed out that increased liquidity and requirements for collateral resulting from new developments in regulatory frameworks, such as the Liquidity Coverage Ratio standard under Basel III, as well as reforms to the over the counter derivatives market, may increase demand for government bonds (see, for example, the Canadian response in Table 4.7).

Notes

1. The policy information in this section is based on a Survey among OECD DMOs as well as the October 2013 proceedings of the OECD Working Party on Public Debt Management (WPDM).
2. It is widely recognised that issuers, investors, dealers and tax payers have benefited from transparent, efficient, robust and reliable issuance procedures for government debt [Hans J. Blommestein (2002), editor, Debt Management and Government Securities Markets in the 21st Century, OECD].
3. Supporting domestic capital markets is therefore an indirect debt management objective. It is an indirect one as it is a means to achieving the direct objective of minimising borrowing costs subject the preferred level of risk.
4. This group of issuers include peripheral sovereigns from the euro area.
5. At a multiple-price auction, bonds are sold at the actual bid price of successful bidders.
6. At a single-price (uniform-price or Dutch) auction, all bonds are sold at the same lowest accepted price.
7. See "Report to the Secretary of the Treasury from the Treasury Borrowing Advisory Committee of the Securities Industry and Financial Markets Association", 6 November 2013.
8. See Amendments on Floating Rate Notes on 31 July 2013. US Treasury published a Final Rule to accommodate the auction and issuance of floating rate notes. *www.treasurydirect.gov/instit/statreg/auctreg/auctreg.htm*.
9. This topic was discussed at the 30-31 October meeting of the OECD Working Party on Public Debt Management. The session was prepared and moderated by the Italian Treasury.
10. This topic was discussed at the 30-31 October meeting of the OECD Working Party on Public Debt Management. The session was prepared and moderated by the UK DMO.
11. More information on 2013–14 Debt Management Strategy Consultations: *www.bankofcanada.ca/wp-content/uploads/2013/03/DMS-2013-14-Consultations-Summary.pdf*.

References

OECD (2002), *Debt Management and Government Securities Markets in the 21st Century*, OECD Publishing. doi: *10.1787/9789264176003-en*

US Department of Treasury (2013), "Report to the Secretary of the Treasury from the Treasury Borrowing Advisory Committee of the Securities Industry and Financial Markets Association", November 6.

OECD Sovereign Borrowing Outlook 2014

Chapter 5

The pros and cons of direct bidding

This chapter summarises OECD members' responses to the OECD survey on the direct bidding in auction systems. Bidders in sovereign debt auctions typically fall into one of three categories: Primary Dealers or authorised dealers, dealer clients or indirect bidders, and direct bidders. In particular, direct bidders include both large institutional bidders who submit competitive bids and smaller retail investors who submit non-competitive bids.

The Borrowing Outlook investigates the participation of primary dealers and large institutional direct bidders under different auction mechanics, based on the responses from 22 OECD debt managers.

- *The survey results are analysed from multiple perspectives.*
- *The prevalence of direct bidding under different auction formats.*
- *Potential benefits and disadvantages of allowing direct bidding in the auction process.*
- *Potential risks imposed by direct bidders.*

Impact of direct bidding on the bidding behaviour of other investors (mainly Primary Dealers), risk transfer costs, auction results, and secondary market liquidity.

The statistical data for Israel are supplied by and under the responsibility of the relevant Israeli authorities. The use of such data by the OECD is without prejudice to the status of the Golan Heights, East Jerusalem and Israeli settlements in the West Bank under the terms of international law.

5.1. Background and executive summary[1]

This chapter summarises OECD WPDM[2] members' responses to the survey on the direct bidding in auction systems. Bidders in sovereign debt auctions typically fall into one of three categories: Primary Dealers (PDs) or authorised dealers, dealer clients or indirect bidders, and direct bidders. In particular, direct bidders include both large institutional bidders who submit competitive bids and smaller retail investors who submit non-competitive bids.

The Borrowing Outlook investigates the participation of primary dealers and large institutional direct bidders under different auction mechanics, based on the responses from 22 OECD countries to the survey distributed by the Office of Debt Management of the US Treasury. Survey responses are tabulated in the Appendix.

The survey results are analysed from multiple perspectives:

- The prevalence of direct bidding under different auction formats.
- Potential benefits and disadvantages of allowing direct bidding in the auction process;
- Potential risks imposed by direct bidders.
- Impact of direct bidding on the bidding behaviour of other investors (mainly Primary Dealers), risk transfer costs, auction results, and secondary market liquidity.

The principal conclusions can be summarised as follows:

a) Primary Dealers constitute the major bidder class in all 22 sovereign auction markets. Direct bidding (by large institutional investors) is rather limited.

b) The majority of respondents believe that it is essential to focus on, maintain, and strengthen their relationship with Primary Dealers.

c) All of the respondents that currently do not allow direct bidders have no intention to allow direct bidders in the near future.

d) The impact of direct bidding needs to be better quantified and modelled. To that end, some ideas for further study are suggested.

5.2. Direct bidding and auction mechanics

Auction and syndication are the predominant primary distribution channels for sovereign debt.

- Out of 22 respondent countries, 21 utilise the auction mechanism, except for Luxembourg.
  - 6 DMOs use the single price auction format.
  - 7 DMOs use the multiple price auction format.
  - 8 DMOs use both single and multiple price auction formats.
- 17 DMOs (excluding Iceland, Israel, Netherlands, Switzerland, and United States in the 22 respondent countries) also utilise syndication.

- 8 DMOs also use other distribution mechanisms including reverse inquiries, switches, and buybacks in addition to the auction and/or syndication.

Primary Dealers constitute the major bidder class in all 22 sovereign auction markets. By comparison, direct bidding (by large institutional investors) is rather limited.

- 21 DMOs have designated Primary Dealers or a consortium of institutional investors that function similarly to Primary Dealers. Of the 21 DMOs, eight allow only Primary Dealers to participate in any type of sovereign debt offerings.
- Of the remaining 13 DMOs, eight allow institutional direct bidding. However, most of these DMOs have seen very limited competitive participation through this channel. For example:

1. In Spain, direct bidders are not active in bidding competitively, although they are very strong in the non-competitive portion.
2. France and Australia have seen no direct bidders thus far.
3. Turkey has seen rare direct bidding participation in their auctions.
4. In Mexico, direct bidding primarily occurs in the bills market, but the participation appears very volatile.
5. Based on the survey, the United States is the only country that has witnessed meaningful and relatively stable direct bidder participation. For example, during 2011 and 2013, direct bidders have been awarded an increasing proportion of nominal coupon auctions, whereas its bills awards have remained relatively constant. Direct Bidders are most active in longer-dated nominal coupon securities (7-years, 10-years, and 30-years).

- 6 DMOs allow retail investors but place additional bidding restrictions on retail investors compared to Primary Dealers. Most restrictions are related to quantity limits. For example, Greece does allow retail investors but they can only bid up to €15 000.

Requirements on Primary Dealers are more rigorous than those on Direct Bidders across all countries, especially when considering the obligation of Primary Dealers.

- DMOs impose similar requirements on PDs across countries to ensure stable and reliable funding sources. Besides certain capital requirements, PDs are usually subject to a minimum bidding requirement and may have obligations to provide liquidity in the secondary market (e.g. making markets for certain hours during the trading day, providing quotes that fall within a certain range around market prices, etc.). On the other hand, PDs enjoy certain privileges, such as participating in securities lending facility, syndications, and having Green Shoe option.
- Capital requirements for Direct Bidders are less stringent. They usually do not have the requirement to bid in each auction.
- There are no additional requirements for Indirects. Because they bid through a designated dealer, much of the risk is transferred from the DMO to the PD.

Overall, although eight out of 21 countries are open to institutions' direct bidding, most eligible direct bidders choose not to use this channel. A natural question is under what conditions Direct Bidding may work the best.

5.3. Benefit of direct bidding

From the institutional perspective, theory suggests that there might be more collusion under a multiple-price auction format than under a single-price format. The value of knowing where others are bidding can mitigate the risk of the Winner's Curse. This would lead to a hypothesis that direct bidders would be more inclined to bid as a customer of dealer in multiple price auctions than in a single price auction. In practice, there does not seem to be a bias of more direct bidding occurring under a single-price format relative to a multi-price format.

- Out of six DMOs using only Single Price Auction Format:
  - 3 allow only PDs
  - 2 allow Direct Bidders in addition to PDs
- Out of seven DMOs using only Multiple Price Auction Format:
  - 1 allows only PD 4
  - allow Direct Bidders in addition to PDs
- Out of eight DMOs using both and additional auction formats:
  - 4 allow only PDs
  - 2 allow Direct Bidders in addition to PDs

The eight countries that allow direct bidding cite various justifications:

- Enables broad and open access, and thus, greater competition.
- Allows for greater price discovery.
- Provides an additional source of demand.
- Diversifies allocation and investor base, and thus improves the efficiency of the auction.
- Provides an alternative to PDs in distribution, and it is a direct channel to reach end-investors.
- There is long-standing agreement between DMO and large institutional investors.
- There is no compelling reason to prohibit the direct bidding channel.

From the perspective of the investor, being able to bid directly and bypass financial intermediaries is beneficial too:

- Preserve tactical preference and privacy and retains anonymity.
- Saves fees on using intermediary.
- Direct Bidders do not have the same stringent requirements as Primary Dealers.

5.4. Disadvantages of direct bidding

The majority of respondents believe that it is essential to focus on, maintain, and strengthen their relationship with Primary Dealers.

- By transferring much of the responsibility including marketing, market making, and credit analysis to the Primary Dealers, many DMOs see the process as becoming more efficient and cost effective.
- By giving Primary Dealers exclusive rights to their auctions, DMOs also allow their Primary Dealers to appropriately source bonds and provide necessary functions in the secondary market.

- Direct Bidders have no obligations in the primary/secondary market and because they are likely price driven, they may have a myopic view of P&L on those particular auctions they elect to participate. The speculative move at times may be disruptive to price discovery.
- The survey results suggest that most DMOs do believe that direct bidding broadens their respective investor base. It seems that there is a particular type of direct bidders in a country. For example:
  - In Spain, public government funds tend to bid directly.
  - Mexico finds mutual/pension funds to bid directly.
  - Many DMOs cite retail investors, though their participation is inconsequential.
  - United States, which may have the most direct bidding experience, does not comment on the participation of its direct bidders.

All of the respondents that currently do not allow direct bidders have no intention to allow direct bidders in the near future.

5.5. Risks of direct bidders

Most respondents acknowledged potential risks with direct bidders, mostly operational and credit risk. On the other hand, risks in settlement and counterparty may be well mitigated by using delivery vs. payment method.

- Turkey imposes 1% collateral on total bid amounts as a further safe guard.

Most countries do not utilise any vetting process for direct bidders except when direct bidders are forced to go through a clearing house, which may have its own vetting process.

5.6. Impact of direct bidding

The impact of direct bidding needs to be better quantified and modelled.

Of particular interest is the reaction of Primary Dealers in the presence of active Direct Bidders. Respondents, in particular United States (with active interaction between PDs and DBs), advance three hypotheses: PDs become more aggressive, PDs become less supportive, PDs already factor in DBs' participation and do not alter their behaviour. Each could happen with PDs losing information advantage and/or market share.

- There is no known model in the sovereign debt market auction literature that predicts/ supports any of these directions.
- United States continues to study the recent behaviour of PDs and DBs to understand empirically the impact of direct bidding.

Besides increasing the bid-to-cover ratio, the impact of direct bidding on auction performance is perceived as minimal by most of respondent (5 out of 6). This may be due to the limited presence of direct bidders in most markets. In fact, in a funding environment with dynamic interest rates, it is difficult to pin point the impact of direct bidding on auction stop-out rate.

- A piece of anecdotal evidence is from Hungary. It allowed direct bidding 15 years ago and found slightly worse performance. It subsequently terminated direct bidding.

Most respondents perceive DBs' impact on secondary market liquidity immaterial.

- Direct Bidders may be primarily buy-and-hold investors. As such, they may remove some liquidity initially but such impact is deemed negligible.

Central banks may bid directly in auction. However, because of the non-competitive nature of their participation, the direct bidding from central banks does not have any material impact.

- 14 DMOs do not allow any type of central bank participation.
- Of the remaining 7, one DMO sets up a separate TAP arrangement for the central bank, while the others only allow non-competitive or a separate add-on for central banks.

5.7. Possible further topics for discussion

Further studies may be required to understand better the utility of direct bidding, especially with auction as the dominant distribution channel.

- What are the market and institutional factors that drive the use of direct bidding? Size of auction, depth of sovereign debt market, degree of diversification of investor base, auction format?
- How to theorise the impact of direct bidder participation in auctions from the perspective of the sovereign issuer? What are the appropriate metrics to measure the change of auction effectiveness?
- Empirically, how to collect better statistics on investor behaviour, with or without direct bidding?
- What does it take for a DMO to consider direct bidding?

Notes

1. This Chapter is based on a revised Room Document on Pros and Cons of Direct Bidding prepared for the October 2013 meeting of the OECD Working Party on Public Debt Management by the Office of Debt Management of the US Treasury.
2. Working Party on Public Debt Management (WPDM).

APPENDIX 5.A1

Survey results

Table 5.A1.1. **Distribution method**

	Security Distribution Method					
	Auctions	Syndication	Reverse Inquiry	Windows	Other	Auction Format
Australia	X	X				Multiple Price
Belgium	X	X	X			Multiple Price
Canada	X	X			X	Both Single and Multiple Price based on Security
Czech Republic	X	X				Both Single and Multiple Price based on Security
Denmark	X	X			X	Single Price
France	X	X				Multiple Price
Germany	X	X				Multiple Price
Greece	X	X				Single Price
Hungary	X	X			X	Single, Multiple, and TAP sale based on Security
Iceland	X					Single Price
Ireland	X	X				Single Price
Israel	X		X			Multiple Price
Luxembourg		X				
Mexico	X	X				Both Single and Multiple Price based on Security
Netherlands	X				X	Single, Multiple, and Dutch Direct based on Security
New Zealand	X	X				Multiple Price
Poland	X	X				Both Single and Multiple Price based on Security
Spain	X	X	X			Mixture between Single and Multiple Price
Switzerland	X				X	Single Price
Turkey	X	X				Multiple Price
United Kingdom	X	X				Both Single and Multiple Price based on Security
United States	X					Single Price

Table 5.A1.2. **Types of Investors**

	Types of Bidders					
	Primary Dealers	Other Dealers	Direct Bidders	Domestic Central Banks	Foreign Central Banks	Retail
Australia		X	X	X	X	
Belgium	X	X			X	
Canada	X	X		X	X	
Czech Republic	X					
Denmark	X					
France	X		X			
Germany		X			X	
Greece	X					X
Hungary	X					
Iceland	X					
Ireland	X					
Israel	X					
Luxembourg						
Mexico	X	X	X			X
Netherlands	X					
New Zealand	X		X			
Poland	X					
Spain	X	X	X	X	X	X
Switzerland		X	X		X	
Turkey	X	X	X			X
United Kingdom	X					X
United States	X	X	X	X	X	X

	Allow/Restrictions on Retail Investors
Australia	No.
Belgium	No.
Canada	No.
Czech Republic	No.
Denmark	No.
France	
Germany	No.
Greece	15 000 € Maximum.
Hungary	No.
Iceland	No.
Ireland	No.
Israel	No.
Luxembourg	
Mexico	All Retail Investors are consolidated into one non-competitive bid
Netherlands	No.
New Zealand	No.
Poland	No.
Spain	5M € Non Competitive Maximum. Latest bid 30 minutes before close
Switzerland	No.
Turkey	Cannot participate in buy back or switches. Deposit collateral of 1%
United Kingdom	All Retail Investors are consolidated into one non-competitive bid
United States	$5M Non Competitive Maximum

Table 5.A1.3. **Requirement on investors**

	Requirements/Privileges for PDs	Requirements for Directs
Australia		
Belgium		
Canada	Access to overnight standing PRA facility	
Czech Republic		
Denmark		
France		Affiliated to Euroclear France/Banque de France
Germany		
Greece		
Hungary		
Iceland		
Ireland	Quote prices for five hours a day within certain spreads	
Israel		
Luxembourg		
Mexico	Green-shoe options / Securities Lending Facility	
Netherlands		
New Zealand	Minimum A-/A3 credit rating	Same as primary dealers
Poland		
Spain	Can participate in second round of auction	
Switzerland		
Turkey		Deposit 1% of total bid as collateral
United Kingdom		
United States		No Requirements/Privileges

	DB Impact on other participants	What type of bidders are DBs
Australia	No experience	No experience
Belgium		
Canada		
Czech Republic		
Denmark		
France	No impact	No DB Participation since 2001
Germany		
Greece		
Hungary		
Iceland		
Ireland		
Israel		
Luxembourg		
Mexico	Infrequent Impact	Mutual/Pension Funds, Banks, Brokerage Houses
Netherlands		
New Zealand	No impact	Crown Asset Managers
Poland		
Spain	Infrequent/Insignificant impact	Governmental Institutions
Switzerland		Banks
Turkey	No impact	Retail Investors
United Kingdom		
United States	May cause PDs to bid less aggressive. Continue to study issue	No Comment

Table 5.A1.4. **Reasons for and against allowing direct bidding**

	If Direct Bidding is permitted, why?	If not permitted, Why?	Plan to allow DB in future?
Australia			
Belgium		Respect PD Involvement	No.
Canada		Current framework is effective	Issue is periodically reviewed
Czech Republic		Maintain relationship with PD	No.
Denmark		Current framework is effective	No.
France	Alternative to PDs		
Germany		Maintain relationship with PD	No.
Greece		Increase PD Involvement	No.
Hungary		Respect PD Involvement	No.
Iceland		Higher administration cost	No.
Ireland		Maintain relationship with PD	No.
Israel		Current framework is effective	No.
Luxembourg			
Mexico	Price discovery / diversified allocation		
Netherlands			Issue is periodically reviewed
New Zealand	Long standing arrangement		
Poland		Current framework is effective	No.
Spain	Additional demand		
Switzerland	Wider bidder basis		
Turkey	Only mechanism for non-institutional clients		
United Kingdom		Reduce due diligence/counter party risk	No.
United States	Greater Competition	n/a	n/a

	Estimates on DB Participation	Volatility of DB Participation
Australia	No experience	No experience
Belgium		
Canada		
Czech Republic		
Denmark		
France	0% since 2001	
Germany		
Greece		
Hungary		
Iceland		
Ireland		
Israel		
Luxembourg		
Mexico	Bills: 4% Awarded	Allocations range from 1% to 60% of auctions
Netherlands		
New Zealand		
Poland		
Spain	Bill Non Comp: 9%, Bond Non Comp: 2%	
Switzerland		
Turkey	All bids/awarded amounts < 1%	Limited to no volatility
United Kingdom		
United States		Increased Coupon Volatility. Stable Bill Volatility

Table 5.A1.5. **Risk and impact of direct bidding**

	Why DB vs. bidding through PD	Any restrictions on DB participation in auction	Risks with DBs
Australia		No restrictions	Settling through Austraclear reduces operational risk
Belgium			
Canada			
Czech Republic			
Denmark			
France		No restrictions	
Germany			
Greece			
Hungary			
Iceland			
Ireland			
Israel			
Luxembourg			
Mexico	Avoid Primary Dealer Fees	Cannot bid for more than 60% of offered amount	DVP to eliminate settlement risk
Netherlands			Counterparty, settlement, and operational risk
New Zealand	Privacy/Anonymity	No restrictions	
Poland			
Spain	Avoid Primary Dealer Fees	Max of five Million Euros except those authorised by Treasury	Settling through Iberclear reduces operational risk
Switzerland	Most prefer PDs		No.
Turkey		No restrictions	Eliminated some risk with collateral requirements
United Kingdom			
United States	Privacy/Anonymity	No restrictions	Treasury has safeguards for operational risk

	Impact of DB on auction performance	Impact of DB on secondary market performance and liquidity
Australia		
Belgium		
Canada		
Czech Republic		
Denmark		
France		
Germany		
Greece		
Hungary		
Iceland		
Ireland		
Israel		
Luxembourg		
Mexico	Increased BTC and improved price	Neutral Impact
Netherlands		
New Zealand	Neutral Impact	Neutral Impact
Poland		
Spain	Neutral Impact	Neutral Impact
Switzerland		
Turkey	Neutral Impact	
United Kingdom		
United States	Increased BTC. Price performance unsure. Still studying issue.	Increased difficulty for PDs to source bonds diminishing role in secondary market

ANNEX A

*Assessing the cost effectiveness of index-linked bond issuance: A methodological approach, illustrated using UK examples**

Sovereign index-linked bond issuance has grown significantly since the early 1980s, with nearly $2.5 trillion USD in bonds now in issue. Index-linked bonds have become a widely accepted part of the set of instruments that sovereign debt managers use for funding purposes and so the question of how to assess their cost effectiveness relative to other financing options is of increasing importance. This paper sets out a methodology for conducting such an analysis, the rationale behind it and ways in which such an approach could be further developed.

* This Annex is written by James Knight, UK Debt Management Office. The views expressed in this paper are those of the author and do not necessarily represent those of the UK Debt Management Office of HM Treasury, the OECD or the governments of its member and partner countries. The author would like to thank Mark Deacon, Gareth Aird, Tim Riddington, Gurminder Bhachu and Tom Dodd for their helpful comments.

A.1. Introduction

For those sovereigns that issue index-linked bonds, or are considering future issuance, determining their cost effectiveness is an important part in evaluating whether or not they should be included in any issuance strategy in the context of a debt management objective with a focus on cost minimisation, taking into account risk. There are a number of additional benefits[1] for an issuer that should be considered as part of this assessment (on both cost and risk grounds); however this note focuses solely on measuring the cost of index-linked issuance against alternative financing options.

In setting out a methodology for assessing the cost effectiveness of index-linked bond issuance in a debt management context, this paper focuses on (i) the rationale for this assessment, based on a comparative approach; (ii) the methodology used; (iii) the policy benefits of such an approach and the practical application of this methodology; and (iv) the limitations of the approach and potential areas for future development.

A.2. The rationale for assessing the cost effectiveness of index-linked bond issuance – a comparative approach using break-even inflation rates

For a sovereign debt manager, index-linked bonds are usually part of a wider set of issuance choices, including fixed-coupon bonds, floating rate notes (FRNs) and short-term paper (Treasury bills or sovereign Commercial Paper). Of these instruments, fixed-coupon bonds typically account for the largest part of sovereigns' issuance programmes and are therefore likely to be the most suitable benchmark against which index-linked issuance can be evaluated (in the same way in which an issuer might consider any other new financing instrument). It is nevertheless possible to evaluate the cost effectiveness of index-linked issuance against a wider set of instruments: for example, Fleckenstein et. al (2010) evaluate the cost effectiveness of US TIPS[2] by examining the potential arbitrage opportunities available from the use of Treasuries and inflation swaps. However, for debt managers to whom such strategies are not available either on a policy or practical basis, they do not necessarily serve as an appropriate benchmark for this assessment.

To evaluate the cost effectiveness of index-linked bonds against fixed-coupon bonds, the most appropriate measure to use is the break-even inflation rate. This is because it is the rate of inflation that will equalise the return on an index-linked bond with that of a conventional bond of the same maturity. In essence, the break-even rate can be seen as the average rate of inflation, over the life of an issue, that will make an issuer indifferent on cost grounds between issuing either a fixed-coupon or an index-linked bond. At its most basic, it can be calculated by subtracting the yield of an index-linked bond from that of a conventional issue of the same maturity; more precisely, it is calculated using the Fisher identity (see Appendix A.1).

While the break-even inflation rate is often interpreted as the market's expected view of inflation over a specific time period, in practice there are a number of factors that will cause it to deviate from this. Two key factors[3] are:

- an illiquidity premium: index-linked bonds are typically less liquid than conventional bonds,[4] and so investors may require a premium for this illiquidity in order to hold them – this typically causes index-linked yields to be higher relative to fixed-coupon bonds, and the corresponding break-even inflation rate to be lower; and
- an inflation risk premium: if investors attach value to protection against inflation risk then they may be prepared to pay a premium for this protection – this will typically result in lower yields for index-linked bonds relative to fixed-coupon bonds, translating into a higher break-even inflation rate.

While one can attempt to estimate the effect of these premia individually,[5] it is sufficient to take account of them in aggregate, if we consider them to be factors that can explain the overall relative demand between fixed-coupon and index-linked bonds. Assuming the existence of investor preferences (i.e. preferred habitats)[6] for specific types or maturities of bond (which may, amongst other factors, include a desire for liquidity or for inflation-linked cash flows), then yields on both fixed coupon and index-linked bonds may deviate from those based on future expectations of interest rates. In turn, break-even inflation rates will deviate from inflation expectations because they capture the relative demand between these two types of instrument (in the context of a given level of supply).

As an example, if there are investors with strong demand (a preferred habitat) for long-dated inflation-linked cash flows, then the yield on index-linked bonds may be lower than that based on expectations of real interest rates alone. In this instance, if there is not equivalently strong demand for long-dated fixed-coupon bonds, then the break-even inflation rate will be higher than it would be otherwise on the basis of inflation expectations alone. That is, if investors are willing to pay for inflation protection, and do not discount the illiquidity of index-linked bonds too heavily and/or there is strong demand for index-linked bonds relative to fixed-coupon issuance, then there may be cost benefits from issuance of the former relative to the latter.

In essence, if the break-even inflation rate on an index-linked bond is higher than the actual inflation outturn over the life of the bond, then issuance will have been more cost effective than a fixed-coupon equivalent, and vice versa.

Finally, an issuer must be aware of the potential impact of "inflation surprise" on the cost of its index-linked issuance. If inflation outturns are meaningfully different from those expected at the time of issuance, then the relative cost of fixed-coupon and index-linked bonds will alter. For example, a positive inflation surprise will increase the relative cost of index-linked bonds outstanding, while a negative surprise will have the opposite effect. However, as Dudley et al. (2009) note, "over the long run, however, inflation surprises should not matter.[7] This is because investors are likely to learn from their mistakes and not repeat their forecast errors indefinitely. If investors incorporate all known information into their prediction, inflation surprises should be unbiased, with as many downward surprises in inflation performance as upward surprises."

Nevertheless, there can be circumstances in which a policy-driven negative inflation surprise can generate significant short-run cost savings from index-linked issuance. Box A.1 sets out an example of how such a surprise resulted in considerable cost savings for the United Kingdom Government in the 1980s.

Box A.1. **Savings from the initial issuance of index-linked gilts in the United Kingdom**[1]

In 1981, the United Kingdom's first index-linked gilt was issued with a break-even inflation rate of approximately 11.5%. The level of this break-even rate reflected, in part, the market's lack of belief in the Government's ambitions for inflationary discipline in the economy – i.e. it did not believe that the Government would be successful in reducing inflation significantly (the prevailing inflation rate at the time was 12.6%). However, the Government managed to bring inflation under control and the outturn average rate of inflation over the life of the bond was just 5.9%. As such, index-linked issuance turned out to be highly cost effective for the Government relative to its fixed-coupon equivalent, a consequence of this negative inflation surprise for the market.

While the largest savings were made in the early days of the United Kingdom's index-linked issuance programme, this trend continued for much of the issuance of index-linked gilts in the 1980s and early 1990s. Figure A.1 below highlights the spread between the break-even inflation rate at issuance and the equivalent average rate of inflation (over the period from issue to maturity)[2] for each individual issue[3] of index-linked gilts and shows how the Government was able to make significant cost savings from issuance of index-linked gilts up until the late 1990s.

However, from 1997, the year in which the Bank of England was granted operational independence to set interest rates to meet the Government's inflation target, these savings have declined significantly. To the extent that the original savings made were a result of a negative inflation surprise for investors, they are unlikely to be repeated in an environment in which there is a credible central bank inflation target around which investors inflation expectations have become anchored.

1. See Deacon and Knight (2008) for a discussion of the history of index-linked gilt issuance.
2. Taking into account the indexation lag.
3. Both new issues and re-openings.

Figure A.1. **Spread between break-even inflation at issue and average inflation over the life of each tranche of index-linked gilt issuance from 1981-2001**[1]

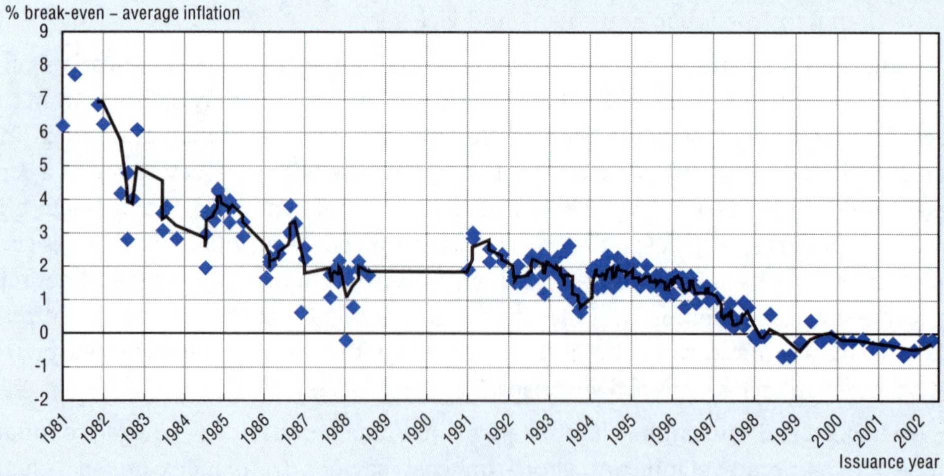

1. For those tranches of issuance that have yet to redeem, a neutral long-run inflation assumption, where inflation returns to target in two-years, and remains there indefinitely, is used.

A.3. An approach for measuring the cost effectiveness of index-linked issuance

The approach for measuring the cost effectiveness of index-linked issuance in this paper takes the methodology developed by Sack and Elsasser (2002) as its starting point.[8] It uses the break-even inflation rate on an index-linked bond (as described in section 2), to create a counterfactual bond issue against which index-linked issuance is evaluated. Appendix A.1 sets out the specifics behind the calculations discussed in this section.

This approach can be used to analyse the cost effectiveness of either (i) previous index-linked issuance (a backward-looking analysis); or (ii) potential future index-linked issuance (a forward-looking analysis). Applying the methodology involves evaluating the cost effectiveness of one tranche of index-linked issuance at a time, replicating the analysis across other issues or maturities to produce an aggregate picture of the cost effectiveness of index-linked issuance.

Starting with the counterfactual bond, its coupon is set at the same rate as that on the index-linked bond being evaluated. However, the cash flows paid on the counterfactual will grow at a constant rate determined by the break-even at issue, while the cash flows on the index-linked bond grow in line with the prevailing rate of inflation. Both the coupons and redemption payment on the counterfactual bond are indexed to a Break-even Index (BEI), which grows at the rate set by the break-even inflation rate at issue, in contrast with the index-linked bond whose coupons and redemption payment are determined by the growth in the relevant inflation index. The difference in the cash flows on the counterfactual bond and the equivalent index-linked bond will determine cost effectiveness of each index-linked bond issue. As these cash flows arise at different points in time, it is necessary to discount each back to today to calculate a net present value of the costs or savings from each issue. We consider these key inputs to the calculation next.

3.1 *Break-even Inflation Rate*

There are two inputs to the calculation of the break-even inflation rate: the respective yields on the fixed-coupon and index-linked bonds. These can be either redemption yields on bonds in the secondary market or taken from yield curve models (or a mixture of both).[9]

Using secondary market yields on index-linked bonds is appropriate when assessing the historical costs or savings from issuance of previously issued instruments, or when considering potential re-openings of existing instruments. However, for the choice of the comparator yield, depending on the precise maturity of any existing fixed-coupon issues and given potential maturity mismatches, it may be more appropriate to use a par yield derived from a nominal yield curve instead of a redemption yield on a fixed-coupon bond.

To assess the cost effectiveness of hypothetical index-linked issuance, using nominal and real yield curve data allow you to calculate the break-even inflation rate at set maturity points (e.g. examining potential 10 or 30-year index-linked issuance). Alternatively, data from an implied inflation curve can be used as a direct substitute for the break-even inflation rate.

3.2 *The rate of inflation*

One of the key inputs to the analysis of the cost effectiveness of index-linked issuance is the path of inflation itself. Depending upon whether the analysis is conducted on a forward or a backward-looking basis, a forecast of inflation may be required as one of the inputs to the calculations.

For backward-looking analysis, for those tranches of issuance that have already matured, an issuer will know exactly what inflation has been during their life and can compare this directly with the break-even inflation rate at issue to calculate savings or losses from issuance. However, for those bonds that remain in issue, a forecast of the path of inflation from the date of the calculations until their maturity will be required. Likewise for forward-looking analysis, evaluating potential future index-linked issuance will be completely reliant on an inflation forecast. The diagram below summarises this point.

The path of inflation – the degree of forecasting required

← Backward-looking analysis		Forward-looking analysis→
Matured Issuance	**Issuance Outstanding**	**Future Issuance**
Path of actual inflation is known to calculate all cash flows on index-linked bonds	Path of inflation is partially known: known for past cash flows paid, forecast required for future cash flows	Path of inflation is unknown: forecast required for all cash flows on potential issuance

Where should this forecast of inflation come from? This is what gives the model flexibility – it is possible to use either a central inflation assumption, or to undertake various scenario analyses by varying the path of future inflation to analyse the cost performance of index-linked bonds against their fixed-coupon counterparts. Using a range of inflation scenarios may also enable the model to be used for basic risk analysis, as it can show the exposure of past and future index-linked issuance to changes in inflation.

For those countries with an inflation targeting regime, setting the long-run average rate of inflation in the model equal to the central bank's inflation target[10] (provided that the central bank targets the same index that is used to uplift the index-linked bond cash flows)[11] can be considered to be an appropriate choice of inflation rate, as it implies the government assumes that the central bank will keep inflation on target on average in the long run. The use of this assumption avoids the risk of an issuer being opportunistic and seeking to out-predict the market on the future path of inflation.

3.3 *Discount rates*

The final input to the calculation is a set of discount rates to present value each cash flow to the point in time at which the calculations are performed. Cash flows occurring before the calculation date will need to be scaled up, while those in the future will need to be discounted back. Depending on the availability of data, the discount rate(s) used can either be a fixed factor or a set of rates derived from a nominal yield curve.

A.4. The policy benefits of the approach to measuring index-linked cost effectiveness

As has been noted earlier, the analysis of index-linked cost effectiveness can either be conducted on a backward or forward-looking basis. Backward-looking analysis seeks to answer the question as to whether the cost of past index-linked issuance has exceeded the cost of equivalent fixed-coupon issuance. In contrast, forward-looking analysis considers whether future index-linked issuance is likely to be a cost effective source of financing.

From a policy perspective, forward-looking analysis is likely to be a more useful tool for the debt manager than an assessment of the sunk gains or costs from past issuance, because it provides an issuer with information that can help it to decide whether or not index-linked bonds should form part of its issuance programme, how much issuance should be considered and at what maturities it should be directed. In addition, the results of backward-looking analysis may be influenced by the period over which the analysis is conducted, particularly if there is not a long history of issuance to analyse.[12]

Box A.2 illustrates the use of forward-looking analysis in the United Kingdom and how it feeds into determining the overall shape of the United Kingdom's financing remit, as well as individual index-linked gilt issuance choices.

Box A.2. **Analysing the potential cost effectiveness of index-linked gilt issuance in the United Kingdom**

The UK DMO evaluates the potential cost effectiveness of index-linked gilt issuance using the methodology set out above and this analysis is one of a number of inputs used in providing HM Treasury with advice on the appropriate amount of index-linked gilts to be issued in the year ahead.

Figures A.2 and A.3 highlight how data from the DMO's nominal and real yield curves, combined with a range of paths for inflation, can be used to estimate potential costs or savings from issuance of index-linked gilts across the maturity spectrum at a set point in time. Figure A.2 shows these potential paths of future inflation, while Figure A.3 translates them into cost effectiveness forecasts for index-linked gilt issuance by maturity, where the cost effectiveness of an index-linked gilt at any maturity point is the present value of all the future cash flows on the gilt from the date of the calculation until it matures.

In this example,[1] the figures demonstrate the potential cost effectiveness of longer-dated index-linked gilts relative to those at shorter maturities; however, they also highlight the greater dispersion in potential costs or savings from longer-dated index-linked issuance (depending on the inflation assumption used), consistent with the longer horizon over which these bonds are in issue.

Figure A.2. **Inflation: Actual and forecast**

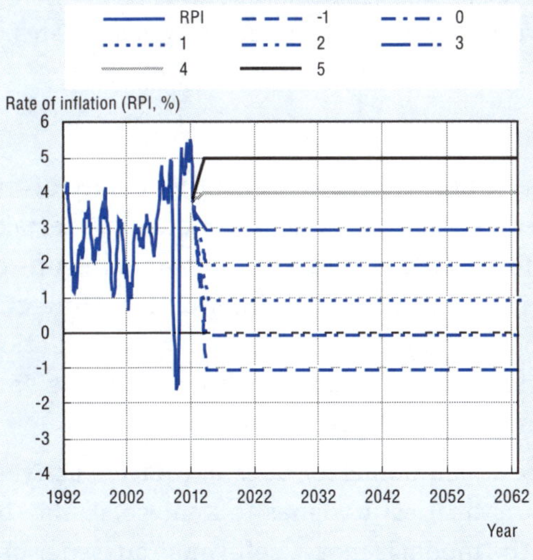

Figure A.3. **Costs/Savings from issuance (per £ bn)**

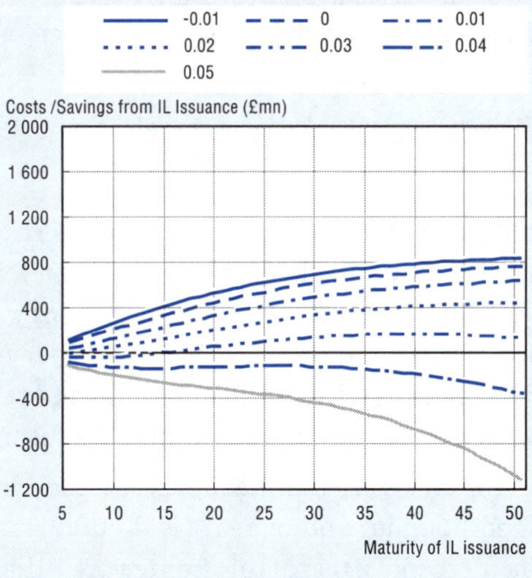

This approach can be repeated across a series of dates to show the evolution of the forecast cost effectiveness of index-linked issuance by maturity through time.

Alongside this curve-based analysis, the DMO evaluates the cost effectiveness of individual index-linked gilts. This analysis is also used, alongside other inputs, as part of the advice to HM Treasury on the potential amount of index-linked issuance for the year ahead, but also as an input throughout the year to decisions on which specific index-linked gilts to issue on a quarterly basis. Figure A.4 shows the potential costs or savings from individual index-linked gilt issues (from the date of calculation to maturity), based on a range of long-term inflation paths.

1. Data as at 21 March 2012.

Box A.2. **Analysing the potential cost effectiveness of index-linked gilt issuance in the United Kingdom** *(cont.)*

Figure A.4. **Cost effectiveness of index-linked gilts (per £ bn of issuance)**

As with the data in FigureA.3, Figure A.4 shows the potential savings to be made from index-linked issuance were generally increasing with maturity. Conducting the analysis on a bond-by-bond basis takes into account the idiosyncratic factors that may make specific issues more cost effective than others (e.g. varying degrees of liquidity, anticipated forthcoming supply, etc.).

A.5. The limitations of the model

As with most modelling exercises, the calculations rely heavily on the quality of the inputs used. As set out above, the model requires a significant amount of data to undertake the necessary calculations. In particular, for a forward-looking analysis, it requires up-to-date break-even inflation rates at differing maturities, which can either be taken directly from existing index-linked bonds in the secondary market, or from an implied inflation curve calculated from fitted nominal and real yield curves (these nominal yield curve data are also necessary for discounting the future differences in cash flows).

For an issuer that has not yet issued index-linked bonds, or does not have a actively traded nominal and/or real yield curve at the maturities it wishes to analyse, it may be difficult to make use of this framework – that is the model is most useful once an issuer has been issuing index-linked bonds and has readily available price sources in the secondary market rather than for a new issuer considering potential issuance.

One of the main limitations of the methodology, as currently specified, is its static nature – it evaluates the cost effectiveness of index-linked issuance at a fixed point in time, i.e. it does not forecast the potential evolution of fixed-coupon or index-linked yields (and thus the evolution of break-even inflation rates). Further, as was noted in Section 2, neither does it consider the contribution of the components of fixed-coupon and index-linked yields to the break-even inflation rate, such as the liquidity premium or inflation risk premium and thus their individual impact on the relative demand for the two types of instrument. Both of these issues could be addressed by incorporating the methodology into a stochastic debt simulation model, which forecasts the future path of conventional and index-linked yields and simulates potential changes in the underlying yield premia. A stochastic debt simulation model could also provide a distribution of inflation outcomes, more readily allowing for an analysis of the impact of different inflation scenarios on index-linked issuance.

Finally, the calculations do not take into account the potential elasticity of supply for fixed-coupon or index-linked bonds, or how the market might react to major shifts in issuance between both types of bond. As such, the methodology can be seen to be more appropriate for considering marginal, rather than wholesale, changes in issuance patterns.

A.6. Conclusion

The approach set out in this paper should allow an issuer to either estimate the cost effectiveness of past index-linked issuance at a set point in time, or to consider the potential cost effectiveness of future issuance. The methodology set out in this paper can also act as a starting point for a more sophisticated approach to evaluating issuance of index-linked bonds, either by undertaking a decomposition of the constituent parts of the break-even inflation rate or by using a stochastic model over a multi-period horizon.

As has been noted earlier, this methodology can provide a useful policy role, on an forward-looking basis, in helping to determine a debt manager's approach to the issuance of index-linked bonds. However, rather than being undertaken in isolation, it should form part of a wider evaluation of the costs and risks of issuing index-linked bonds.

Appendix A.1.: Cost effectiveness calculations

This appendix sets out the calculations that underpin the methodology described in this paper.

A.1.1. Calculating a break-even index (BEI)

A1. The starting point for the calculation is a value for the break-even inflation rate (BEIR). If the BEIR is to be calculated using relative bond yields or yield curve data (as considered in section 3.1) then the Fisher identity[13] can be used:

$$BEIR = \left(\frac{1 + \frac{y}{2}}{1 + \frac{r}{2}} \right)^2 - 1$$

Where:

y = nominal yield on fixed-coupon bond (or nominal yield from yield curve)

r = real yield on index-linked bond (or real yield from yield curve)

A2. The BEIR is used to calculate a "break-even inflation index" (BEI), which continues the inflation series after the point of issuance of the tranche at a constant rate equal to the break-even inflation rate.

A3. The BEI runs for months i=(1,2,...t,t+1,...n), where t is the month of the index relating to the issuance of the tranche and n is the month of the index relating to the redemption payment (both lagged by the correct number of months in line with the indexation lag of the bond), BEIR is the calculated break-even inflation rate (as a decimal) and RPI_i is the price index value for month i:

$$BEI_i = RPI_i \mathrm{I}_{i \le t} + RPI_{i-1}(1+BEIR)^{\frac{1}{12}} \mathrm{I}_{i=t+1} + BEI_{i-1}(1+BEIR)^{\frac{1}{12}} \mathrm{I}_{i>t+1}$$

$$\text{where } \mathrm{I}_A(x) = \begin{cases} 1 \text{ if A is true} \\ 0 \text{ otherwise} \end{cases}$$

A4. The BEI data can be used to calculate Reference BEIs (RefBEI) for any calendar day[14]:

$$\mathrm{RefBEI_d} = \mathrm{RefBEI}_M + \left(\frac{d-1}{D}\right)\left(\mathrm{RefBEI}_{M+1} - \mathrm{RefBEI}_M\right)\mathrm{I}_{d=1}$$

$$\text{where } \mathrm{I}_A(x) = \begin{cases} 0 \text{ if A is true} \\ 1 \text{ otherwise} \end{cases}$$

D =	number of days in the calendar month in which the given date falls
t =	the calendar day corresponding to the given date
$\mathrm{RefBEI_M}$ =	Reference BEI for the first day of the calendar month in which the given date falls
$\mathrm{RefBEI_{M+1}}$ =	Reference BEI for the first day of the calendar month immediately following the given date.

A5. The reference BEI for the first calendar day of any calendar month is the BEI for the calendar month falling three months earlier. The reference BEI for any other day in the month is calculated by linear interpolation.

A6. These RefBEIs are then used to calculate a series of break-even index ratios (BIR), where each BIR is calculated as:

$$\mathrm{BIR_d} = \left[\frac{\mathrm{RefBEI_{date}}}{\mathrm{RefBEI_{first\ issue\ date}}}\right]$$

A7. Where $\mathrm{RefBEI_{first\ issue\ date}}$ for a given bond remains constant over its life.

A.1.2. Calculating the costs or savings from index-linked issuance

For three-month index-linked gilts the cost saving is the sum of the discounted differences between the cash flows on the counterfactual and the index linked gilt from the first divided (d) to maturity (m), d=1...m.

$$\sum_{d=1}^{m}\left(\left(d_d\left\{BIR_d - IR_d\right\}\right)\frac{n}{100}\delta_d\right) + \left(\left\{BIR_m - IR_m\right\} n\delta_m\right)$$

Where:

BIR =	the index-ratio calculated using the BEI
IR =	the index-ratio calculated using the actual inflation index
d_d =	the dividend payment on the relevant date
δ_d =	the discount factor applicable to the cash flow
n =	the nominal amount of the index-linked bond being considered

Notes

1. Such as the potential to diversify a sovereign's investor base, fiscal insurance benefits for the government and the creation of a market-based measure of inflation expectations to assist in the conduct of monetary policy.
2. Treasury Inflation Protected Securities, inflation-linked bonds issued by the US Treasury.
3. Other factors include the differential taxation treatment between fixed-coupon and index-linked bonds, as well as the different duration and convexity properties of the two instruments (in this paper we assume that a debt manager is interested in making relative issuance decisions based on the maturity of the instruments that it issues, rather than their duration characteristics). Also see Christensen et al. (2004) for a discussion on the potential for bias in the break-even rate when the term structure of inflation expectations is not flat.
4. Reflecting their different investor base, which typically includes a greater proportion of buy-and-hold investors, such as pension funds that purchase them for liability matching purposes, as well as a general lack of direct hedging instruments (e.g. index-linked bond futures).
5. See, for example, Christensen and Gillan (2011) for an attempt to estimate the inflation risk premium in the context of as assessment of the cost effectiveness of US TIPS issuance.
6. Based on segmented market theory, we assume that demand for government bonds is segmented, that is different types and maturities of bond are not substitutes for one another.
7. There is a difference between smaller inflation forecasting errors, and major errors resulting from large positive (or negative) inflation shocks. In issuing index-linked bonds, particularly at longer maturities, an issuer will have to consider the additional inflation risk that it is assuming in the context of the rest of its balance sheet.
8. The methodology in this paper, developed at the UK DMO in 2006, is similar to that later developed independently by Roush (2008).
9. However, one of the issues to consider in using a yield curve model is that doing so can smooth out bond-specific distortions (e.g. due to liquidity, off-market coupon) from the analysis that it might be desirable to capture.
10. Allowing for some transition period for inflation from its current level to the target. For example, in the case of the United Kingdom, a path from the rate of inflation today to an inflation target fixed two years in the future.
11. In the case of the United Kingdom, the Bank of England targets the Consumer Prices Index (CPI), whereas the cashflows on index-linked gilts are linked to the Retail Prices Index (RPI). As such, an assumption has to be made about the long-run difference between the two inflation indices.
12. In the case of analysing US TIPS issuance, Dudley et al. (2009) argue that an "ex-post" approach is not appropriate because there is only a small sample of data available, which does not allow for an averaging out of inflation forecast errors (as discussed in section 2).
13. This example assumes semi-annual coupon paying bonds.
14. See also UK DMO (2005:32).

References

Christensen J., et al. (2004). "Real Return Bonds, Inflation Expectations, and the Break-Even Inflation Rate", Bank of Canada Working Paper, No. 43.

Christensen, J. and J. Gillan (2011), "Has the Treasury Benefited from Issuing TIPS?", FRBSF Economic Letter, 2011-12, April 18.

Deacon, M. and J. Knight (2008), "An Historical Perspective on Issuing Index-linked Gilts and Launching Ultra-long Bonds", in B. Benaben and S. Goldberg (eds.), Inflation-Linked Risks and Products, Risk Books.

Dudley, W.C., R. Roush and M.S. Ezer (2009), "The Case for TIPS: An Examination of the Costs and Benefits", Reserve Bank of New York Economic Policy Review, No. 10(1), pp. 47-63.

Fleckstein, M., F.A. Longstaff, and H. Lustig (2010), "Why Does the Treasury Issue Tips? The Tips-Treasury Bond Puzzle", NBER Working Paper, No. 16358.

Knight, J. (2013), "Assessing the cost effectiveness of index-linked bond issuance: a methodological approach, illustrated using UK examples", OECD Working Papers on Sovereign Borrowing and Public Debt Management, No. 7, OECD Publishing.

Roush, J. E. (2008), "The "Growing Pains" of TIPS Issuance", FEDS Working Paper, August 2008.

Sack, B. and R. Elsasser (2004), "Treasury Inflation-Indexed Debt: A Review of the US Experience", Federal Reserve Bank of New York Economic Policy Review, No. 15(1), pp. 47-63.

UK Debt Management Office (2005), "Formulae for Calculating Gilt Prices from Yields", 3rd ed.

Annex B

Methods and sources

B.1. Regional aggregates

- Total OECD denotes in this Outlook the following 34 countries: Australia, Austria, Belgium, Canada, Chile, Czech Republic, Denmark, Estonia, Finland, France, Germany, Greece, Hungary, Iceland, Ireland, Israel Italy, Japan, Korea, Luxembourg, Mexico, Netherlands, New Zealand, Norway, Poland, Portugal, Slovak Republic, Slovenia Spain, Sweden, Switzerland, Turkey, the United Kingdom and the United States.
- The G7 includes seven countries: Canada, France, Germany, Italy, Japan, United Kingdom and the United States.
- The OECD euro area includes 15 countries: Austria, Belgium, Estonia (included after 2010), Finland, France, Germany, Greece, Ireland, Italy, Luxembourg, Netherlands, Portugal, Slovak Republic (included after 2008), Slovenia and Spain.
- The Emerging OECD group includes eight countries: Chile, Czech Republic, Hungary, Mexico, Poland, Slovak Republic, Slovenia and Turkey.
- The Other OECD countries aggregation includes nine countries: Australia, Denmark, Iceland, Israel, Korea, New Zealand, Norway, Sweden and Switzerland.
- The G-20 includes: Argentina, Australia, Brazil, Canada, China, India, Indonesia, Japan, Korea, Mexico, Russia, Saudi Arabia, South Africa, Turkey, United States and selected governments of the European Union.

B.2. Sovereign assets groupings

- The data used for the credit rating country groupings are from the three main credit rating agencies: Moody's, Fitch and Standard and Poor's.
- Safe (AAA) sovereign assets rule #1: The classification of an issuer as AAA is based on two of three best rating grades, that is, if a sovereign issuer has been attributed triple-A by two rating agencies, the country is classified as triple-A. See for details the table B.1 with sovereign ratings by country. The cut-off date for credit ratings is 30 November 2013.
- Safe (AAA+AA+A) sovereign assets rule #2: If a sovereign is rated by one of the major agencies as AAA or AA or A, then the asset is considered as "safe". See for details the table B.1 with sovereign ratings by country. The cut-off date for credit ratings is 30 November 2013.

B.3. Sovereign long-term foreign currency ratings

Table B.1. **Long-term foreign currency ratings by country**

Country	2006			2007			2008			2009		
	S&P	Moody's	Fitch	S&P	Moody's	Fitch	S&P	Moody's	Fitch	S&P	Moody's	Fitch
Australia	AAA	Aaa	AA+	AAA	Aaa	AA+	AAA	Aaa	AA+	AAA	Aaa	AA+
Austria	AAA	Aaa	AAA	AAA	Aaa	AAA	AAA	Aaa	AAA	AAA	Aaa	AAA
Belgium	AA+	Aa1	AA+	AA+	Aa1	AA+	AA+	Aa1	AA+	AA+	Aa1	AA+
Canada	AAA	Aaa	AAA	AAA	Aaa	AAA	AAA	Aaa	AAA	AAA	Aaa	AAA
Chile	A+	A2	A	A+	A2	A	A+	A2	A	A+	A1	A
Czech Republic	AA-	A1	A	AA-	A1	A	AA-	A1	A+	AA-	A1	A+
Denmark	AAA	Aaa	AAA	AAA	Aaa	AAA	AAA	Aaa	AAA	AAA	Aaa	AAA
Estonia	AA-	A1	A	AA-	A1	A	AA-	A1	A-	AA-	A1	BBB+
Finland	AAA	Aaa	AAA	AAA	Aaa	AAA	AAA	Aaa	AAA	AAA	Aaa	AAA
France	AAA	Aaa	AAA	AAA	Aaa	AAA	AAA	Aaa	AAA	AAA	Aaa	AAA
Germany	AAA	Aaa	AAA	AAA	Aaa	AAA	AAA	Aaa	AAA	AAA	Aaa	AAA
Greece	A	A1	A	A	A1	A	A	A1	A	BBB	A2	BBB+
Hungary	BBB	A2	BBB+	BBB	A2	BBB+	BBB	A3	BBB	BBB-	Baa1	BBB
Iceland	A	Aaa	AA-	A	Aaa	A+	BBB-	Baa1	BBB-	BBB-	Baa3	BBB-
Ireland	AAA	Aaa	AAA	AAA	Aaa	AAA	AAA	Aaa	AAA	AA	Aa1	AA-
Israel	A+	A2	A-	A+	A2	A-	A+	A1	A	A+	A1	A
Italy	A	Aa2	AA-	A	Aa2	AA-	A	Aa2	AA-	A	Aa2	AA-
Japan	AA-	Aaa	AA	AA-	Aaa	AA	AA-	Aaa	AA	AA-	Aa2	AA
Korea	A	A3	A+	A	A2	A+	A	A2	A+	A	A2	A+
Luxembourg	AAA	Aaa	AAA	AAA	Aaa	AAA	AAA	Aaa	AAA	AAA	Aaa	AAA
Mexico	BBB	Baa1	BBB	BBB	Baa1	BBB+	BBB	Baa1	BBB+	BBB	Baa1	BBB
Netherlands	AAA	Aaa	AAA	AAA	Aaa	AAA	AAA	Aaa	AAA	AAA	Aaa	AAA
New Zealand	AA	Aaa	AA+	AA	Aaa	AA+	AA	Aaa	AA+	AA	Aaa	AA+
Norway	AAA	Aaa	AAA	AAA	Aaa	AAA	AAA	Aaa	AAA	AAA	Aaa	AAA
Poland	A-	A2	BBB+	A-	A2	A-	A-	A2	A-	A-	A2	A-
Portugal	AA	Aa2	AA	AA	Aa2	AA	AA	Aa2	AA	AA	Aa2	AA
Slovak Republic	A+	A1	A	A+	A1	A	A+	A1	A+	A+	A1	A+
Slovenia	AA	Aa2	AA	AA	Aa2	AA	AA	Aa2	AA	AA	Aa2	AA
Spain	AAA	Aaa	AA+	AAA	Aaa	AA+	AAA	Aaa	AA+	AAA	Aaa	AA+
Sweden	AAA	Aaa	AAA	AAA	Aaa	AAA	AAA	Aaa	AAA	AAA	Aaa	AAA
Switzerland	AAA	Aaa	AAA	AAA	Aaa	AAA	AAA	Aaa	AAA	AAA	Aaa	AAA
Turkey	BB	Ba3	BB-	BB	Ba3	BB-	BB	Ba3	BB-	BB	Ba3	BB-
United Kingdom	AAA	Aaa	AAA	AAA	Aaa	AAA	AAA	Aaa	AAA	AAA	Aaa	AAA
United States	AAA	Aaa	AAA	AAA	Aaa	AAA	AAA	Aaa	AAA	AAA	Aaa	AAA
Supranational												
European Stability Mechanism (ESM)[1]												
European Financial Stability Facility (EFSF)												
European Union	AAA	Aaa	AAA	AAA	Aaa	AAA	AAA	Aaa	AAA	AAA	Aaa	AAA

Notes: Cut-off date is 30 November 2013.

1. Standard & Poor's has not yet assigned its ratings for the ESM.

Source: Credit ratings from Moody's, Fitch and Standard and Poor's.

Table B.1. **Long-term foreign currency ratings by country** *(cont.)*

Country	2010			2011			2012			2013		
	S&P	Moody's	Fitch	S&P	Moody's	Fitch	S&P	Moody's	Fitch	S&P	Moody's	Fitch
Australia	AAA	Aaa	AA+	AAA	Aaa	AAA	AAA	Aaa	AAA	AAA	Aaa	AAA
Austria	AAA	Aaa	AAA	AAA	Aaa	AAA	AA+	Aaa	AAA	AA+	Aaa	AAA
Belgium	AA+	Aa1	AA+	AA	Aa3	AA+	AA	Aa3	AA	AA	Aa3	AA
Canada	AAA	Aaa	AAA	AAA	Aaa	AAA	AAA	Aaa	AAA	AAA	Aaa	AAA
Chile	A+	Aa3	A	A+	Aa3	A+	AA-	Aa3	A+	AA-	Aa3	A+
Czech Republic	AA-	A1	A+	AA-	A1	A+	AA-	A1	A+	AA-	A1	A+
Denmark	AAA	Aaa	AAA	AAA	Aaa	AAA	AAA	Aaa	AAA	AAA	Aaa	AAA
Estonia	AA-	A1	A	AA-	A1	A+	AA-	A1	A+	AA-	A1	A+
Finland	AAA	Aaa	AAA	AAA	Aaa	AAA	AAA	Aaa	AAA	AAA	Aaa	AAA
France	AAA	Aaa	AAA	AAA	Aaa	AAA	AA+	Aa1	AAA	AA	Aa1	AA+
Germany	AAA	Aaa	AAA	AAA	Aaa	AAA	AAA	Aaa	AAA	AAA	Aaa	AAA
Greece	CC	Ba1	BBB-	CC	Ca	CCC	B-	C	CCC	B-	Caa3	B-
Hungary	BBB-	Baa3	BBB-	BB+	Ba1	BBB-	BB	Ba1	BB+	BB	Ba1	BB+
Iceland	BBB-	Baa3	BB+	BBB-	Baa3	BB+	BBB-	Baa3	BBB-	BBB-	Baa3	BBB
Ireland	A	Baa1	BBB+	BBB+	Ba1	BBB+	BBB+	Ba1	BBB+	BBB+	Ba1	BBB+
Israel	A+	A1	A	A+	A1	A	A+	A1	A	A+	A1	A
Italy	A	Aa2	AA-	A	A2	A+	BBB+	Baa2	A-	BBB	Baa2	BBB+
Japan	AA-	Aa2	AA	AA-	Aa3	AA	AA-	Aa3	A+	AA-	Aa3	A+
Korea	A	A1	A+	A	A1	A+	A+	Aa3	A+	A+	Aa3	AA-
Luxembourg	AAA	Aaa	AAA	AAA	Aaa	AAA	AAA	Aaa	AAA	AAA	Aaa	AAA
Mexico	BBB	Baa1	BBB	BBB	Baa1	BBB	BBB	Baa1	BBB	BBB	Baa1	BBB+
Netherlands	AAA	Aaa	AAA	AAA	Aaa	AAA	AAA	Aaa	AAA	AA+	Aaa	AAA
New Zealand	AA	Aaa	AA+	AA	Aaa	AA	AA	Aaa	AA	AA	Aaa	AA
Norway	AAA	Aaa	AAA	AAA	Aaa	AAA	AAA	Aaa	AAA	AAA	Aaa	AAA
Poland	A-	A2	A-	A-	A2	A-	A-	A2	A-	A-	A2	A-
Portugal	A	A1	A+	BBB	Ba2	BB+	BB	Ba3	BB+	BB	Ba3	BB+
Slovak Republic	A+	A1	A+	A+	A1	A+	A	A2	A+	A	A2	A+
Slovenia	AA	Aa2	AA	AA-	A1	AA-	A	Baa2	A-	A-	Ba1	BBB+
Spain	AA	Aa1	AA+	AA-	A1	AA-	BBB-	Baa3	BBB	BBB-	Baa3	BBB
Sweden	AAA	Aaa	AAA	AAA	Aaa	AAA	AAA	Aaa	AAA	AAA	Aaa	AAA
Switzerland	AAA	Aaa	AAA	AAA	Aaa	AAA	AAA	Aaa	AAA	AAA	Aaa	AAA
Turkey	BB	Ba2	BB+	BB	Ba2	BB+	BB	Ba1	BB+	BB+	Baa3	BBB-
United Kingdom	AAA	Aaa	AAA	AAA	Aaa	AAA	AAA	Aaa	AAA	AAA	Aa1	AA+
United States	AAA	Aaa	AAA	AA+	Aaa	AAA	AA+	Aaa	AAA	AA+	Aaa	AAA
Supranational												
European Stability Mechanism (ESM)[1]							—	Aa1	AAA	—	Aa1	AAA
European Financial Stability Facility (EFSF)	AAA	Aaa	AAA	AAA	Aaa	AAA	AA+	Aa1	AAA	AA+	Aa1	AA+
European Union	AAA	Aaa	AAA	AAA	Aaa	AAA	AAA	Aaa	AAA	AAA	Aaa	AAA

Notes: Cut-off date is 30 November 2013.

1. Standard & Poor's has not yet assigned its ratings for the ESM.

Source: Credit ratings from Moody's, Fitch and Standard and Poor's.

Table B.2. – **S&P, Moody's and Fitch rating systems**

	Characterisation of debt and issuer	Rating		
		S&P	Moody's	Fitch
Investment grade	Highest quality	AAA	Aaa	AAA
	High quality	AA+	Aa1	AA+
		AA	Aa2	AA
		AA-	Aa3	AA-
	Strong payment capacity	A+	A1	A+
		A	A2	A
		A-	A3	A-
	Adequate payment capacity	BBB+	Baa1	BBB+
		BBB	Baa2	BBB
		BBB-	Baa3	BBB-
Non-investment grade	Likely to fulfil obligations, ongoing uncertainty	BB+	Ba1	BB+
		BB	Ba2	BB
		BB-	Ba3	BB-
	High credit risk	B+	B1	B+
		B	B2	B
		B-	B3	B-
	Very high credit risk	CCC+	Caa1	CCC+
		CCC	Caa2	CCC
		CCC-	Caa3	CCC-
	Near default with possibility of recovery	CC	Ca	CC
				C
	Default	SD	C	DDD
		D		DD
				D

Source: Credit ratings systems from Moody's, Fitch and Standard and Poor's and ECB (2011), Sovereign credit ratings and financial markets linkages, working paper No. 1347, June 2011.

B.4. Background on OECD Surveys used in the Outlook

- The Secretariat circulated a Borrowing Questionnaire to 34 OECD debt-management offices (DMOs) to obtain information on borrowing activities in 2013 and 2014.

B.5. Calculations, definitions and data sources

- Gross borrowing requirements (GBR) as a percentage of GDP is calculated using nominal GDP data from the OECD Economic Outlook 94/Vol 2, 19 November 2013.
- GDP at 2005 PPP USD from the OECD Economic Outlook 94 database, November 2013, is used to calculate the GDP-weighted average 10-year government bond yield.
- To facilitate comparisons with previous Outlooks, figures are converted into US dollars using exchange rates from 1 December 2009. Source: Datastream.
- All figures refer to calendar years.
- Aggregate figures for gross borrowing requirements (GBR), net borrowing requirements (NBR), central government marketable debt, redemptions, and debt maturing are compiled from the answers to the Borrowing Survey. The Secretariat inserted its own estimates/ projections in cases of missing information for 2013 and/or 2014, using publicly available official information on redemptions and central government budget balances.

- GBR estimates by country (projections) are based on country responses to the OECD Survey and comments by OECD DMOs on preliminary calculations by the Secretariat.
- The Secretariat uses the following general conventions in calculating central government marketable gross borrowing requirements (GBRs): deficit projections (publicly available information from official national sources) plus redemptions (publicly available information from official national sources and Bloomberg). GBRs exclude cash management instruments (i.e., only T-bills and long-term instruments are being used). Short-term (ST) GBRs are calculated using the standardised OECD method: ST debt stock at the end of the previous year plus ST net borrowing over the calendar year.
- Some GBR estimates by country (based on OECD methodology) may differ from those calculated by governments as different concepts are applied (e.g. fiscal year-calendar year conversions and net financing requirement concept) and/or a different basis is used for official projections.
- Cut-off date for information (projections) used in the GBR estimates is 5 December 2013.
- Sources: 2013 OECD (Working Party on Debt Management) Survey on central government marketable gross debt and GBRs; National Debt Management Offices; National authorities' sources; OECD Economic Outlook 94 database; Bloomberg and Datastream.

B.6. A suggested new approach to the measurement and reporting of gross short-term borrowing operations by governments[1]

B.6.1. *Introduction and summary*

Since 2009, the OECD has published a central government borrowing outlook.[2] This gross and net borrowing outlook is based on submissions by debt management offices (DMOs) across the OECD area. The survey includes a question on estimates and projections of the gross short-term marketable borrowing needs for each OECD country (covered by issuing notes and bills with a maturity of up to one year).

The reporting on gross short-term issuance operations has raised questions concerning which method to use to reliably estimate the size of these operations, especially when the objective is to make meaningful cross-country comparisons. This policy issue was discussed at the annual meeting of the OECD Working Party on Public Debt Management (WPDM),[3] held on 20-21 October 2009. To that end, the Swedish and Danish delegates submitted four methods for discussion. They also noted that all methods – except one – provide distorted measures of gross short-term borrowing needs, thereby hampering the calculation of meaningful, cross-county estimates and projections.

These distortions and complications were outlined in some detail in a supporting OECD discussion note on the measurement of gross short-term borrowing needs. More specifically, the note, circulated among WPDM Delegates, explains the various difficulties or complications in measuring the size of short-term borrowing requirements by discussing four different measurement methods. The discussion note concludes that all methods for measuring short-term borrowing needs studied here – except one (referred to as Method 2 below) – provide either significantly underestimated or substantially overestimated measures. At the end of the debate, Delegates of the OECD WPDM agreed to adopt a uniform method[4] defined as follows:

Gross Short-Term[5] Marketable Borrowing Requirements [GBR(ST) t] in calendar year t (CY=t) is equal to Net Short-Term Borrowing Requirements in CY=t [NBR(ST) t] plus the outstanding amount of the stock of T-bills and T-notes at the beginning of CY=t.

This measure yields in principle meaningful estimates and projections that are comparable across different countries.

B.6.2. *Basic terminology on borrowing operations and funding strategy*

In this note we are making a policy distinction between funding strategy and borrowing requirements. Gross borrowing requirements are calculated on the basis of budget deficits and redemptions (Table B.3).

Table B.3. **Definition of total gross borrowing requirement**

Revenues	T
Tax Revenues	
Other Revenues	
Expenditures	G
General Expenditures	
Interest Payments	
Budget Deficit (BD)	T - G < 0
Budget Surplus (BS)	T - G > 0
Total Net Borrowing Requirement (NBR) = BD = [- (T-G)]	
Total Redemptions of:	
Short term debt	TR(ST)
Long term debt	TR(LT)
Total Redemptions (Refinancing Requirement)	TR = TR(ST) + TR(LT)
Total Gross Borrowing Requirement (GBR)	GBR = TR + BD = TR + NBR
	GBR = TR - BS

Source: OECD Staff.

The funding strategy entails decisions about how the borrowing requirements or needs are going to be financed (e.g. by using long-term bonds, short-term securities, nominal or indexed bonds, etc.). Clearly, total gross borrowing requirements (Table B.3) should be the same as total expected or projected funding amounts (Table B.4).

Table B.4. **The funding strategy**

Components of cash inflows	Components of cash outflows
How to finance?	Total Repayments (TR)
Marketable Debt Issuance	Marketable Debt Repayments
– Short Term Securities	– Redemptions
(Money Market Instruments ([1]))	– Interest/ Coupon repayments
– Long Term Securities	Interest repayments of maturing debt
(Capital Market Instruments)	Interest repayments of other coupon paying debt
Domestic bonds	
International bonds	
Non-marketable Debt	Non-marketable Debt Repayments
– Loans	– Redemptions
– Other	– Interest/ Coupon repayments
	Interest repayments of maturing debt
	Interest repayments of unmaturing debt
([1]) Excluding the issuance for monetary policy purposes	

Source: OECD Staff.

B.6.3. How to measure gross short-term borrowing operations

Although applications of the standard definitions of gross and net longer-term borrowing requirements are clear cut, this is not the case for gross short-term borrowing requirements. The simple question on how to estimate gross short-term borrowing requirements on a yearly basis (say CY 2010 or CY 2011) is not straightforward. We will show via a simple example in this section (and more complicated ones in Table B.5) that answers can easily become meaningless. For example, if daily or monthly (re)financing operations are aggregated within a year (or by including every single redemption of short-term paper within the year), then estimates of gross short-term borrowing requirements can become huge and essentially meaningless, especially when making comparisons across countries.

Take the following two simple examples to demonstrate why a mechanical within-year aggregation of issuance and redemption activities can easily lead to a meaningless or inflated calculation or estimate of GBR(ST).

Example 1:

On 1 January 2009, the total stock of debt of government A consists entirely of short-term debt [D(ST)= €100m]. Assume that this outstanding debt will need to be redeemed at the end of August and will be refinanced by issuing a six month T-bill. At the beginning of each month, government A needs to borrow €50m by issuing short-term treasury notes with a maturity of one month (total borrowing in each month: TB=€50m). At the end of each month, government A redeems the short-term stock of debt (total redemptions at the end of each month: TR=€50m, except in August when TR=€150m). The pattern in the chart resembles largely rollover (refinancing) operations during the calendar year 2009.

2009	Jan.	Feb.	Mar.	Apr.	May	June	July	Aug.	Sept.	Oct.	Nov.	Dec.
TB:	50	50	50	50	50	50	50	150	50	50	50	50
TR:		50	50	50	50	50	50	150	50	50	50	50

Example 2:

On 1 January 2009, the total stock of debt of government B consists again entirely of short-term debt [D(ST)= €100m]. This outstanding debt will also need to be redeemed at the end of August. The borrowing needs of government B are the same as those of government A but its credit reputation is better. The funding strategy of government B can therefore be based on the issuance of T-bills with a maturity of up to 12 months. The within-year issuance and redemption patterns of government B are therefore radically different from those of government A.

2009	Jan.	Feb.	Mar.	Apr.	May	June	July	Aug.	Sept.	Oct.	Nov.	Dec.
TB:	50							100				
TR:								100				

Simply aggregating all funding/redemption operations during the calendar year 2009 would result in the following two estimates for total GBR(ST). In the case of example 1, using Method 4 (see Table B.5)[6] results in an estimate for GBR of 2009: 12 * €50m + €100m = €700m, while using Method 2 results in a more meaningful estimate of €150 million.[7] In the case of example 2, this results in an estimate of €150 for both Methods 1 and 2.

Some countries, such as Denmark and Sweden, use the concept of net short-term borrowing requirements for funding horizons of less than one year. This means that the calculation of gross borrowing requirements is not inflated by simply adding all short-term operations within the calendar year. A drawback of this approach, however, is that it clearly underestimates the calculation of GBR(ST) because the refinancing of the stock of T-bills and T-notes at the beginning of the calendar year is completely ignored. A cross-country analysis should not only focus on the financing of budget deficits but also include comparable refinancing operations with corrections for artificially inflated short-term rollover operations within the year. Method 2 constitutes, therefore, a pragmatic and sensible compromise solution by simply adding the net short-term borrowing amount to the stock of T-bills and T-notes at the beginning of the calendar year (as, by definition, they need to be refinanced within the year). This method yields, in principle, meaningful estimates that are comparable across different countries.

B.6.4. Four different methods for measuring gross short-term borrowing operations

To illustrate the differences in outcomes by using different approaches, we have made additional hypothetical calculations in Table B.5 based on four different methods for measuring gross short-term borrowing requirements,[8] including Method 2. Method 1 calculates total gross borrowing requirements by ignoring the complications associated with short-term operations by focusing on (redemptions of) long-term debt (longer than one year) only. Method 3 takes as gross funding estimate all redemptions for bonds, the refinancing of all three-month T-bills and cash. Method 4 calculates total gross borrowing requirements by aggregating all redemptions (as with Method 3) plus daily cash operations during the year.

These examples also show that three out of four methods either significantly underestimate or substantially inflate gross borrowing requirements, while Method 2 yields an economically sensible estimate. Table B.6 provides a slightly more complicated numerical example of the application of the suggested new approach to the measurement and reporting of GBR (ST) (i.e. Method 2).[9]

We conclude that the proposed new measure is both a pragmatic and sensible solution.

Table B.5. **Different methods for calculating gross borrowing requirement (GBR)**

Method 1: Initial stock of debt is not taken into account [D(.)=0], while all long-term redemptions are being refinanced.[1] GBR = TR(LT).

	NBR	Bonds	T-bills	Cash	Total
Stock of Debt 2009-01-01		150	47	3	200
Net borrowing requirement (**NBR**)	0				
Redemptions (refinancing) (**TR**)		30	0	0	
Gross borrowing requirement (**GBR**)	0	30	0	0	30
Stock of debt 2010-01-01		150	47	3	200
Gross borrowing requirement = EUR 30 bn					
Method 2: Refinancing of the stock of T-bills plus cash at the beginning of year plus NBR. GBR = D(ST) + NBR(ST).					
Stock of debt 2009-01-01		150	47	3	200
NBR	0				
Redemptions		30	47	3	
GBR	0	30	47	3	80
Stock of debt 2010-01-01		150	47	3	200
Gross borrowing requirement EUR 80 bn					
Method 3: Initial stock of debt is not taken into account, while all redemptions (including all three-month T-bills) and cash balance are being refinanced. GBR = TR=TR(ST)+TR(LT) + Cash.[2]					
Stock of debt 2009-01-01		150	47	3	200
NBR	0				
Redemptions		30	188	3	
GBR	0	30	188	3	221
Stock of debt 2010-01-01		150	47	3	200
Gross borrowing requirement EUR 221 bn					
Method 4: Initial stock of debt is not taken into account, while all redemptions (including all three- month T-bills) plus daily cash positions are being refinanced. GBR = TR=TR(ST)+TR(LT) +Cash.					
Stock of debt 2009-01-01		150	47	3	200
NBR	0				
Redemptions		30	188	750	
GBR	0	30	188	750	968
Stock of debt 2010-01-01		150	47	3	200
Gross borrowing requirement EUR 968 bn					

1. Assume net borrowing requirement (NBR) is zero. In other words: NBR=0 together with D(.)=0 → issuance equals total long-term redemptions → GBR = TR(LT).
2. Assume NBR is zero. T-bills have three month original duration. NBR=0 together with D(.)=0 → issuance equals total short-term and long-term redemptions → GBR = TR=TR(ST)+TR(LT) +Cash.

Table B.6. **Application of Method 2 to calculate GBR**

The basic procedure is to add redemptions of all debt maturing within the year + outstanding stock of T-bills (at the beginning of the year) to the net borrowing requirement.

	Total debt	T-bond	T-bills	Cash
Government debt 31-12-2008[1] (in Bn EUR)	200	150	45	5
Net cash borrowing requirement (should at least approx. approx. equal the cash budget deficit)	20			
Redemptions (debt beginning of year maturing within 12 months)	80	30	45	5
Bonds maturing during 2009		25		
T-bills on 31-12-2009 shorter than 12 months[2]			45	
Cash position on 31-12-2009				5
Buy back of bonds during 2009		5		
Gross borrowing requirement (GBR)	100	45	50	5
Net funding in bonds		15		
Net funding in T-bills[3]			5	
Net funding in cash[4]				0
Government debt 31-12-2009	220	165	50	5
In Bn EUR during 2009				
Financing plan on a yearly basis in this example:		45	50	5

1) Initial stock of debt at the beginning of 2009.

2) i.e. maturing during 2009.

3) Equals the increase in T-bill stock on yearly basis (i.e. refinancing during the year is netted out) but the excess of all issuance over all maturing T-bills is included in the net figure. Gross funding of T-bills is initial stock + net funding.

4) Equals the change in cash position between the last day of 2008 and the last day of 2009 (i.e. the same treatment as for T-bills).

Note 1: **Actual total issuance operations** of T-bills and deposits (cash) will be much larger due to refinancing of short debt during the year.

Note 2: **Net funding per instrument** is by definition equal to gross borrowing minus redemptions per instrument.

Note 3: **Gross funding per instrument** calculated by summing redemptions per instrument with issuance per instrument from the government's funding or financing plan.

Table B.7. **Comparison on non-standardised method and standardised methods Fiscal and borrowing outlook in OECD countries for the period 2007-14**

Trillion USD

Methods 3 and 4, Non-standardised methods	2007	2008	2009	2010	2011	2012	2013	2014
Central government marketable GBR (with cash)	24.4	24.9	29.3	29.1	29.4	29.8	29.6	29.3
Central government marketable GBR (w/o cash)	13.7	16.7	21.2	20.5	21.0	21.6	21.4	21.2
Central government marketable debt (w/o cash)	22.9	25.2	28.4	31.7	34.3	36.4	38.4	39.8
Central government marketable NBR (w/o cash)	0.6	2.2	3.3	3.2	2.3	2.4	2.0	1.5
General government deficit	0.6	1.5	3.7	3.6	3.0	2.8	2.3	2.1
Methods 2, Standardised method								
Central government marketable GBR (with cash)	7.1	8.7	11.2	11.3	10.8	11.5	11.2	11.1
Central government marketable GBR (w/o cash)	6.7	8.2	10.7	10.9	10.4	11.0	10.8	10.6
Central government marketable debt (w/o cash)	22.9	25.2	28.4	31.7	34.3	36.4	38.4	39.8
Central government marketable NBR (w/o cash)	0.6	2.2	3.3	3.2	2.3	2.4	2.0	1.5
General government deficit	0.6	1.5	3.7	3.6	3.0	2.8	2.3	2.1

Notes: GBR=gross borrowing requirement, NBR=net borrowing requirement
Figures are calculated using the exchange rates as of 1st December 2009.
Source: 2013 Survey on central government marketable debt and borrowing by OECD Working Party on Debt Management, OECD Economic Outlook 94 database, and OECD staff estimates.

Notes

1. This section is based on an article by Hans J. Blommestein, Ove Sten Jensen and Thomas Olofsson, (2010), "A New Method for Measuring Short-term Gross Borrowing Needs,", OECD Journal: Financial Market Trends, Vol. 2010/1.
2. For details see Blommestein and Gok (2009).
3. The WPDM consists of senior debt managers from OECD countries.
4. Referred to as Method 2 in the discussion below.
5. All short-term estimates and projections concern borrowing operations for a borrowing horizon of less than one year.
6. Method 4 calculates total GBR by aggregating all issuance and redemption operations for both long-term and short-term debt within a certain year, while also including daily cash operations, and correcting for rollover or refinancing activities. When total borrowing (TB) and total redemptions (TR) are corrected by excluding rollover refinancing operations within the year, they are referred to as follows: TB* and TR*. In both examples 1 and 2, TB*=€50m and TR*=0.
7. Method 2 calculates GBR by taking short-term debt stock at the beginning of the year [D(ST)] and adding the total short-term net borrowing requirement [NBR(ST)]. In other words: GBR = D(ST) + NBR(ST) = D(ST) + TB*= €100m + €50m= €150 million.
8. For the sake of simplicity, the deficit (net borrowing requirement) is assumed to be zero in the calculations in appendix B.1.
9. There are additional complications that we ignore in this note such as the statistical treatment of foreign currency borrowing (in some countries forex borrowing cannot be used to finance the budget so it needs to be matched with a change at the asset side – government account/forex reserves); on-lending activities (changes at both the liability side and asset side via income in the form of interest payments); discussions in some countries about the treatment of the provision of T-bills by the government to the central banks (for use in special liquidity schemes); the statistical treatment of capital injections (again, there are changes at the liability and asset side of the government balance sheet) etc.

Glossary

Term	Definition
Central government	Defined as comprising all departments, offices, establishments and other bodies classified under general government, which are agencies or instrument of the central authority of a country, except separately organised social security funds irrespective of whether they are covered in, or financed through, ordinary or extraordinary budgets, or extra-budgetary funds. (Source: OECD Economics Department Glossary)
Central government gross borrowing	The gross financing requirement is compiled as the net financing requirement with the addition of redemptions on the domestic and foreign debt. (Source: Denmark National Bank Glossary)
Central government net borrowing	Defined as central government gross borrowing minus central government redemptions.
General government	The general government sector consists mainly of central, state, and local government units together with social security funds imposed and controlled by those units. In addition, it includes non-profit institutions engaged in non-market production that are controlled and mainly financed by governments units or social security funds. (Source: OECD, Statistics Department, System of National Accounts, 1993, par. 4.9)
General government financial balance	The general government financial balance corresponds to what is commonly referred to as the public surplus or deficit. In the national Accounts (SNA basis), it refers to the "net lending/net borrowing of general government". Government net lending is general government current tax and non-tax receipts less general government total outlays. (Source: OECD Economic Outlook sources and methods, OECD Statistics Department, National Accounts)
General government gross financial liabilities	Debt is a commonly used concept, defined as a specific subset of liabilities identified according to the types of financial instruments included or excluded. Generally, debt is defined as all liabilities that require payment or payments of interest or principal by the debtor to the creditor at a date or dates in the future. Consequently, all debt instruments are liabilities, but some liabilities such as shares, equity, and financial derivatives are not debt. (Source: OECD, Statistics Department, System of National Accounts, 2008, par. 22.104)
General government net financial liabilities	Net financial liabilities are defined as the gross financial liabilities of the general government sector less the financial assets of the general government sector. Such assets may be cash, bank deposits, loans to the private sector, participation in private sector companies, holdings in public corporations or foreign exchange reserves, depending on the institutional structure of the country concerned and data availability. The status and treatment of government liabilities in respect of their employee pension plans in the national accounts have been diverse across countries, making international comparability of government debts difficult. The current interpretation of the 1993 SNA is that: i) "autonomous" funded pension plans should be classified outside the general government sector, which entails that their assets and liabilities are not reflected in the general government debt data; ii) non-autonomous pension plans should be classified inside the general government sector and only the funded component should be reflected in the general government liabilities. Furthermore, the 1993 SNA recommends that the liability inherent in unfunded schemes be recorded as a memorandum item for the government sector. However, while some countries have produced some estimates of these implicit liabilities, few follow the 1993 SNA recommendation. (Source: OECD Economic Outlook sources and methods, OECD Statistics Department, National Accounts)
General government net debt interest payments	Interest paid for general government debt net of interest received for general government assets. (Source: OECD Economic Outlook sources and methods, OECD Statistics Department, National Accounts)
Index-linked securities	Index-linked securities are instruments with coupon and/or principal payments which are linked to commodity prices, interest rates, stock exchange or other price indices (also known as inflation-indexed bonds or colloquially as linkers). The benefits to the issuer include a reduction in interest costs if the deal is targeted at a particular group of investors' requirements, and/or an ability to hedge an exposed position in a particular market. Issues linked to the Retail Price Index also provide investors with protection against inflation. (Source: Bank of England)
Index-linked gilts (IGs)	IGs are gilts whose coupons and final redemption payment are related to movements in the Retail Prices Index. There are two fundamental designs of index-linked gilts - those with an 8-month indexation lag launched in 1981 and those with a 3-month lag launched in 2005. (Source: UK Debt Management Office)

Term	Definition
Marketable debt	Securities that can be bought and sold in the secondary market.
Redemption	Principal payment (exclude interest payments)
Refinancing risk	The risk that a borrower has to finance repayments on its debt in a period with a temporary general high interest level or in a period, where the loan terms of the specific borrower are particularly unfavourable. (Source: Denmark National Bank Glossary)
Rollover risk	The risk of not being able to refinance debt obligations.
Variable rate note	Variable rate notes have a floating or variable interest rate, or coupon rate. It is a long-dated debt security whose coupon is refixed periodically on a "refix date" by reference to an independent interest rate index such as LIBOR or Euribor. (Source: Bank of England)

ORGANISATION FOR ECONOMIC CO-OPERATION AND DEVELOPMENT

The OECD is a unique forum where governments work together to address the economic, social and environmental challenges of globalisation. The OECD is also at the forefront of efforts to understand and to help governments respond to new developments and concerns, such as corporate governance, the information economy and the challenges of an ageing population. The Organisation provides a setting where governments can compare policy experiences, seek answers to common problems, identify good practice and work to co-ordinate domestic and international policies.

The OECD member countries are: Australia, Austria, Belgium, Canada, Chile, the Czech Republic, Denmark, Estonia, Finland, France, Germany, Greece, Hungary, Iceland, Ireland, Israel, Italy, Japan, Korea, Luxembourg, Mexico, the Netherlands, New Zealand, Norway, Poland, Portugal, the Slovak Republic, Slovenia, Spain, Sweden, Switzerland, Turkey, the United Kingdom and the United States. The European Union takes part in the work of the OECD.

OECD Publishing disseminates widely the results of the Organisation's statistics gathering and research on economic, social and environmental issues, as well as the conventions, guidelines and standards agreed by its members.

OECD PUBLISHING, 2, rue André-Pascal, 75775 PARIS CEDEX 16
(20 2014 01 1 P) ISBN 978-92-64-20416-4 – 2014-02